YANNIS PALAIOLOGOS is a features reporter for *Kathimerini* newspaper in Greece. He was born and raised in Greece, and studied PPE and post-graduate philosophy at Oxford. He lives in Athens.

The 13th Labour of Hercules

of Hercules

Inside the Greek Crisis

Updated with a new epilogue

YANNIS PALAIOLOGOS

Portobello
BOOKS

First published by Portobello Books 2014
Paperback edition published 2015
This edition with new epilogue published 2016

Portobello Books
12 Addison Avenue
London
W11 4QR

A CIP catalogue record for this book is available from the British Library

9 8 7 6 5 4 3 2 1

ISBN 978 1 84627 624 8
eISBN 978 1 84627 574 6

Typeset by Avon DataSet Ltd, Bidford on Avon, Warwickshire
Printed and bound by CPI Group (UK) Ltd, Croydon, CR0 4YY

MIX
Paper from
responsible sources
FSC® C020471
www.fsc.org

TO GREECE'S YOUNG

Who will have to pick up the pieces

'Too late, the surviving inhabitants of such a nation would crawl from ruins of their own creation and realize that, throughout all their self-imposed agony, there had been absolutely nobody at the top who had understood how things really worked, what it was all about, what was really going on.'

Kurt Vonnegut, *Galapagos*

Contents

	Prologue	ix
1	The Keratea Troubles	1
2	A Taxing Issue	27
3	The Torn Safety Net	51
4	Pensions, Retired	74
5	The Return of Class War	94
6	Investment and the Deep Blue Sea	119
7	Power Struggle	142
8	Big Ships in a Perfect Storm	169
9	Nightmares from Weimar	190
10	Out with the Old	219
	Epilogue	241
	Acknowledgements	275
	Notes	277
	Index	296

Prologue

On Monday 9 January 2012, a Greek nation already battered by years of recession and a punishing austerity regime, and anxious about delicate negotiations on the reduction of the country's gargantuan public debt, woke up to some depressing news of a different kind. Before dawn an audacious heist had taken place at the National Gallery in downtown Athens, a few blocks from the prime minister's office and parliament. The thieves had spent the previous evening setting off alarms to confuse the sole guard on duty. Then, at around 4.30 a.m., they disabled the alarm on the balcony and entered the premises. Within seven minutes they made off with Pablo Picasso's 'Woman's Head', the only Picasso oil painting in any Greek museum, which the artist had donated to the country in recognition of its resistance against the Nazi occupation of Greece. They also stole a painting by Mondrian and a seventeenth-century sketch by Italian artist Guglielmo Caccia. Had the motion detectors in the exhibition hall, miraculously still in working order, not alerted the guard that something was up, they would have got away with another Mondrian as well.

The theft made headlines around the world and caused much hand-wringing in the Greek press. It prompted the Minister for Citizen Protection, Christos Papoutsis, a man whose keen sense of the faults of others is matched by his total blindness to his own, to pronounce the security measures at the gallery 'non-existent'. Amidst the sound and fury, the Office of the Inspector General of Public Administration decided to look into the matter, to see if Papoutsis had a point.

Two-and-a-half months later, the Office of the Inspector

General released the findings of its inquiry. The report was predictably scathing. It found that neither the National Gallery nor the General Directorate for the Restoration of Museums and for Technical Works had set any standards for security in places holding Greece's most treasured cultural possessions. The privately installed and maintained security and surveillance system at the gallery had not been upgraded in over ten years and the guards had received no training in how to react in the event of an attempted robbery. There was no instruction manual or functioning intercom system, so the guards communicated with their mobile phones, and they had no online connection either to the Ministry of Culture, the police or the private security contractor. In the last two years, the report continued, there had been no more than two or three demonstrations of how the system works, and these were essentially glorified fire drills. It also noted – its authors probably suppressing pangs of mirthless laughter – that the alarm tended to go off randomly because its batteries had run out and had not been replaced. Crucially, the CCTV camera tapes had not been properly maintained. Because of this, many of the images captured by the cameras were not recorded, or could only be stored at low resolution. Finally, beyond being ill-trained and under-equipped, the guards were far too few in number, as was the case on the night of the break-in.

After the findings were published, it was time for the latest round of a traditional Greek game of *ballaki euthinon*, which can be loosely translated as the 'little ball of blame' and is extremely popular among the ranks of public officials potentially implicated in a major debacle. The rules are simple: when responsibility for a disaster in question heads your way, you do your best to flick it as far away as possible, preferably by directing it towards some other murkily involved party.

So it was that the management of the National Gallery reacted vehemently to the report's findings, blaming the Ministry of Culture. The Minister of Culture in turn blamed the General

Directorate for the Restoration of Museums and for Technical Works, and there were calls from the General Directorate for a second inquiry, which they themselves would oversee. The accused, in other words, would examine – no doubt with strict impartiality – their own guilt.

Thus a priceless work of art donated to the Greek people for their heroism in days past became another victim of the boundless fecklessness of those who manage the country's affairs today. The heist highlights many of the central aspects of the breakdown of the Greek state: the complex and vague legal language that blurs accountability; the absence of monitoring and quality control of private contractors; services with too few employees, partly as a result of panicked cuts to meet targets set by the country's international creditors; men and women left without training or resources, essentially to fend for themselves. Underlying it all, there is a pervasive irresponsibility, a sense that no one is in charge, no one is willing or able to act as a custodian of the common good that government is meant to represent.

The rot of state institutions in Greece had taken hold long before the Great Crisis of 2009. From its first steps as a modern nation-state, after the successful War of Independence against Ottoman Turkey in the 1820s, efforts to build a strong, centralized administration were stymied. Ioannis Capodistrias, the first governor of modern Greece, was assassinated in 1831 by members of a powerful Peloponnesian clan whose local clout was threatened by his attempt to create an effective central government modelled on the advanced states of Western Europe. Since then, despite considerable progress, family and local affiliations in Greece have remained unusually strong by European standards, giving rise to client-based politics which are still today at the heart of the country's political and administrative malaise. Voters continue to behave and to be treated by politicians as clients – to be kept loyal with public sector jobs, government contracts or targeted tax breaks – rather than citizens. Meanwhile, allegiance to the state remains weak to non-existent.

The age-old resistance to the impersonal, rules-based, centralizing state has been combined throughout modern Greek history with a fierce factionalism, often breaking out into open civil conflict, even at times of great peril for the country, when it can least afford it. The War of Independence against the Ottomans had barely notched its first victories when hostilities broke out between different leaders of the national revolution. During the First World War, the opposition between the prime minister, Eleutherios Venizelos, Greece's greatest modern politician, and its constitutional monarch, Constantine I, about the country's stance led to the National Division (*Ethnikos Dichasmos*), with two governments vying for control of Greek territory and deep wounds opening in the fabric of society which took decades to heal.

Then, in the aftermath of the Greeks' glorious exploits against the Axis Powers (the successful repulsion of Mussolini's invasion, an honourable struggle against Hitler's hordes and the indefatigable, mass resistance against the three-and-a-half-year occupation), came the civil war between nationalists and communists. It lasted between 1944 and 1949, with an uneasy interlude of peace in 1945–6, and ended in victory for the nationalists, with the indispensable aid of the US. Greece was the first flare-up of the Cold War, inspiring the declaration of the Truman Doctrine (the policy of containing Soviet expansionism, which became the core of US foreign policy for the next forty years). KKE, the Greek Communist Party, which had led the resistance to the Nazis, was outlawed, its leaders and followers imprisoned or escaping to the Soviet bloc countries. For the next eighteen years of 'managed' democracy, during which power resided as much with the King and the US embassy as with parliament and the elected government, men and women with left-wing sympathies were relegated to various shades of second-class citizenship: they were blocked from employment in the public sector, while the more militant among them were persecuted and kept in re-education camps on desert islands in the Aegean.

In 1967 this suppressed oppression came out into the open, as anti-communist hysteria, endless political bickering and public agitation led to the *coup d'état* of the colonels, narrowly beating to the punch a similar violation planned by royalist generals. The military junta lasted seven years. During its dark and occasionally absurd rule, Greece was cut off from the process of European integration, into which it had been placed before the coup by the long-serving conservative prime minister, Constantine Karamanlis. Inside the country, in the early days at least, some welcomed the return to order and the anti-communist thrust of the regime. But its abuses soon depleted any public support it might initially have commanded, further deepening Greeks' suspicion of state power and turning them away from the authoritarian conservatism that had dominated Greek politics since the end of the civil war.

The fall of the junta in 1974, after a disastrous attempt to enforce the union (*Enosi*) of Greece with Cyprus which led to the Turkish invasion of the island, ushered in the longest period of political stability and growing prosperity in Greece's modern history. Constantine Karamanlis returned home from Paris to lead the process of normalization. As head of the centre-right New Democracy and prime minister from 1974–80, he presided over the ratification of a new constitution, a referendum which finally laid to rest the question of the form of government (69 per cent voted in favour of a republic) and the legalization of the Greek Communist Party. All political prisoners were released, while the ringleaders of the coup were given life sentences. Above all, and despite fierce resistance, not least from PASOK, the fast-rising socialist party which in 1977 assumed the role of official opposition, he led Greece into the European Economic Community, signing the accession treaty in 1979.

But by that point the political tide was already turning. PASOK, and its charismatic leader Andreas Papandreou, a former head of the Economics department at the University of California in Berkeley, the son of a prime minister turned anti-imperialist firebrand upon his return to Greece in the mid-1960s, was riding the surge of long-suppressed left-wing sentiment all the way to the top. In the 1981 elections, PASOK won 48 per cent of the vote and an absolute parliamentary majority. In a triumph of democratic politics, for the first time in Greece's history the left was in power. That same year, Greece officially became the tenth member of the EEC.

It was a moment pregnant with opportunity. With European money about to flow in, with a left-wing government led by a brilliant economist adored by large swathes of the population, it could have been the beginning of an age of greater equality, spreading meritocracy and sustainable growth.

Sadly, the chance was wasted. Papandreou – Andreas, as he was universally known – chose populist acclaim over good economics. Instead of transforming the client-based structure of Greek politics, the left was transformed by it. The result was clientelism on steroids: PASOK went on a public sector recruitment spree, offering wages rises entirely divorced from productivity growth and pensions irrespective of contributions. It also directed the new-found manna of EEC funds towards cronies and party insiders, without even a semblance of an integrated strategy for the country's further development or its adjustment to globalization and the European single market.

Other than by European money, Greek-style socialism was funded by unrestrained government borrowing, needed to cover both the inexorably expanding state and the revenue shortfalls caused by persistent tax evasion. Greece's public debt exploded, from 23 per cent of GDP at the beginning of the 1980s to 60 per cent at the end of the decade, when Papandreou was voted out, and 100 per cent four years later. It would remain around that level for another fifteen years, until the Great Crisis would impel it further upward, into the airless strata of national bankruptcy.

The reason for the persistence of a model that was so evidently economically unsustainable was its remarkable political success. Under its influence, New Democracy became a mirror image of PASOK, offering its clients the same seductive diet of lifetime government jobs, immunity from the taxman, a steady stream of public contracts and fat pensions just as their hair began to turn grey. Mismanagement of European funds became endemic, and reached epidemic proportions.

Greeks in the post-junta republic learned that one thing in life was paramount, above merit, effort or originality: their connection to the party. Following well-worn tradition, supporters of the two parties fanatically opposed each other, but as time passed it became clear that their clash was not ideological. It was a naked conflict for the spoils of the state.

Party politics seeped into and poisoned everything: student groups, unions, professional associations, newspapers, the justice system. To paraphrase a notorious dictum, there was no such thing as civil society; there were only individual men and women and their families, and the party they identified with. Reformists in both parties, especially during the 1990s, made valiant bids to alter Greece's doomed trajectory. But the headwinds they faced – from entrenched interests but also due to the dulling effect of growing material comfort – were too strong.

By the autumn of 2009, a year after the collapse of Lehman Brothers and five-and-a-half years into the lethargic leadership of Costas Karamanlis, nephew and pale shadow of Constantine, Greece's institutions had become hollow shells, ravaged by decades of maladministration and the insidious influence of party politics. All that was needed was a light breeze for them to come crumbling down. What had begun on Wall Street was a global economic hurricane, against which Greece was singularly ill-equipped to defend itself.

★

The Great Crisis accelerated the rot, until it became common parlance to speak of Greece as a semi-failed state. The IMF reported on missed reform targets. High-flying investment bankers, fresh from annihilating the global economy, were once again busy pulling in mountains of money in bonuses and lecturing small countries about their fiscal responsibilities. Self-serving speeches by German politicians decried the Greeks' innate penchant for corruption and sloth while skipping over the recklessness of their own financial institutions and the crooked practices of their big exporters in fuelling the crisis.

A different approach to Greece's collapse viewed the breakdown of government institutions as the outcome rather than the cause of the harsh austerity imposed by the troika (the European Union, the International Monetary Fund and the European Central Bank). Proponents of this view emphasized the statistics about cuts to wages and pensions, the shrinking coverage offered by the public health care system, the swelling armies of the unemployed and the poor.

But it was rare indeed for a report or a news story in the international press to grasp the nuances of what it *has been like* to live and work – or, more likely, not work and try to survive – since 2010 in Greece. Few reporters and commentators have gone beyond the policy mechanics leading from the inertia of prosperity to the economic and administrative disarray of the Great Crisis. The deeper explanation can be summarized thus: a state shorn of its guardians, laid waste by plunderers great and small in the good times, had lost too much legitimacy to be able to impose the heavy burdens of adjustment when it could no longer be put off.

The experience of social, economic and administrative implosion since 2010 and the years of myopia, corrupted ideals and sheer, breathtaking incompetence that laid the groundwork for it, is the topic of this book. Many of the things that Greeks thought of as unthinkable were rapidly turned by the crisis into the order of the day, resulting in a profoundly disorienting effect. Pension cuts and increases in the retirement age; employers delaying salary payments for weeks or months at a time; middle-class, middle-aged people suddenly left without health insurance; the rise of an extremist racist party and its entry into parliament; foreign technocrats with veto powers over the state budget: this dramatic change of scenery has left people much poorer and considerably angrier, and old-style politicians are struggling to keep up.

As a Greek who grew up and lives in Athens but who attended university abroad and spent seven years away from home, as someone still young enough to hope for recovery but also to escape, I have not been immune from all this. I have had my wages cut, and have received telephone calls from dismissed colleagues enquiring after jobs – any jobs – because they did not know how to pay next month's bills. I have been in countless discussions about who is to blame for what's happened, about why a party with barely concealed Nazi sympathies has come to command the support of more than one in ten Greeks, about the prospects for innovative young entrepreneurs and the desperate need for a new political culture, which will treat us as citizens instead of clients. My wedding day, on 15 June 2011, coincided with one of the more violent general strikes of the Great Crisis, and was nearly called off. My mother, who already has two daughters living abroad, and whose professions of deep affection for me seem sincere, has repeatedly exhorted me to follow the lead of so many others and leave the country.

If the Great Crisis does not bring about meaningful political and economic change to Greece, I may yet be forced to do so. But writing this book, despite the wealth of evidence for pessimism that it has provided me, has also reinforced my belief in Greece's ability to recover. This rich, spoilt, talent-filled, violence-prone, proud, conspiracy-minded, dangerously atomized, stunningly beautiful country on the edge of the European continent was a perfect candidate for a sovereign debt crisis, yet it remains a place of boundless possibilities.

The chapters that follow will give a notion of both the pitfalls and the potential, beyond the headlines and the truisms about the vices of over-borrowing, the bane of tax evasion and the horrors of self-defeating austerity. Modern Greeks have always had a complicated relationship with their ancient past. Pride in being the descendants of the founders of Western civilization is mixed with shame at our own comparative failings, as well as a sense of insecurity about the true nature of the relationship across the centuries. Rebuilding Greece – its politics, its economy, the bonds of trust indispensable to well-ordered society – is a truly Herculean task, worthy of our illustrious ancestors. Our ability to carry it out is still an open question.

1

The Keratea Troubles

It was a freezing, windy December night. Under driving sleet, flanked by heavy police protection, a convoy of bulldozers and lorries moved towards a hill near the small town of Keratea (population 10,642), a few dozen kilometres south-east of Athens. They belonged to Mesogeos, a company specializing in the construction of sanitary landfill sites, which had won the competitive tender to dig a new landfill in the area.

The reason for the stealthy, night-time operation was that the people of Keratea were overwhelmingly opposed to the construction of the site. On the previous day, Friday 10 December 2010, town officials had issued warnings against any move to begin work on the project. The authorities hoped to get the equipment in place overnight and present the local population with a fait accompli, thus breaking their will to resist.

It was a colossal miscalculation. The town's outgoing mayor, Stavros Iatrou, obsessively opposed to the construction of the landfill, had been tipped off that some kind of operation was imminent. His sources had mistakenly told him that it would take place at around seven or eight o'clock the next morning. Just to be on the safe side though, on Friday night he took his brother and a couple of his deputy mayors up to the 'mayoral mansion of the mountain', as he called it. It was an illegal shack on the dirt road to the landfill site that he had had built to serve as a last line of defence against the bulldozers. When the convoy and the police arrived around 4 a.m., he attempted to block their way with his four-wheel-drive and was arrested – but not before he had given the signal for the church bells and sirens to sound in Keratea.

The first townspeople converged on the road leading towards the landfill site before dawn. By morning, when Iatrou was released to join the protesters, the crowd had grown to three hundred people. Local officials and parliamentarians representing the district which includes Keratea had gathered at the scene and negotiations were under way with the riot police.

As morning gave way to early afternoon, an agreement was reached for the crowd to disperse, so long as riot police did the same. According local officials, after most of the townspeople had left, the police reneged on their promise. Scuffles broke out between the officers and the rearguard of the protesters. Realizing what was happening, the people of Keratea returned en masse and charged the lines of the officers, led by a feisty female deputy mayor in high heels. After that, all hell broke loose.

It was the opening salvo of what became known as the 'Keratea insurgency'. For the next few days, crowds used Molotov cocktails, sticks, stones, flares and anything else to attack the police. They torched two fire engines, smashed a power panel, sinking the area into darkness, and tried repeatedly to break through the police cordon protecting the contractor's equipment. People fired their hunting rifles into the air, set fire to reed-thickets and sparred with the police in the fields by the roadside. In response, the cops made copious use of teargas, and of their clubs. By the time it was over, several people had been arrested, including four brothers, and among those injured was Iatrou himself and a TV journalist who was taken to hospital with severe injuries from clubbing by riot police officers.

The 'Keratea insurgency' lasted 128 days. It laid bare the break-down in the relations between the state and the people in Greece in the era of national bankruptcy and externally imposed austerity. After months of increasingly fierce conflict between citizens and police on the streets near and even inside Keratea, with priests making Molotov cocktails in churches, retired army officers turning into street-fighters and protesters storming the local police station to release prisoners, after endless rounds of political buck-passing and repeated showdowns in court, it took a threatened lawsuit by the Police Officers' Union of Attica against their superior officers and the coming of Easter for a truce to be reached.

The Keratea Troubles reveal much about the malaise that prevents Greece from standing on its feet again. But how did this small town become a symbol of Greece's disease? What past was prologue to the four-month 'insurgency' that shook the country and inspired many other Greeks to resist the authority of the state in any way they could?

At some point in Don De Lillo's *Underworld*, during a philosophical conversation about raw sewage treatment, one of the novel's main characters quips: 'All waste aspires to the condition of shit.'[1] There is no place in Europe where waste falls as short of its aspirations as in Greece.

In August 2012 the European Commission published a report grading the twenty-seven member states on the quality of their waste management policies.[2] The grades were based on eighteen criteria, in accordance with which green, yellow and red flags were handed out. At the bottom of the rankings, below the other countries of Southern Europe, below the formerly Communist countries of Eastern Europe, who only joined the EU in 2004, and even below its Balkan neighbours, the dirt-poor states of Romania and Bulgaria, stood Greece.

There were only two out of eighteen categories in which Greece avoided a red flag. Among others, it received a failing grade in the amount of waste recycled, the amount recovered for energy production, the absence of pay-as-you-throw systems for waste, the absence of restrictions on the types of waste that can be landfilled and, as a result of most of the above, the extraordinary amount of waste that still ends up buried in the ground. Only one of the country's seventy-one landfills for non-hazardous waste was found to be in compliance with the EU landfill directive. In the depths of Greece's soil, it seems, the glories of its ancient past cohabit awkwardly with the sins of its debauched present.

As in many other areas of public policy where it lags behind its neighbours, it's not that the Greek government does not (eventually) pass the laws that Brussels mandates. Instead, as Konstantinos Aravossis, an Industrial Management professor at the National Technical University of Athens puts it: 'The problem is the actual adoption and implementation of these measures in practice.'

For nearly two decades, the trend in the European Union has been to move away from burying garbage and towards prevention and various forms of re-use, from recycling and composting to the utilization of processed waste for energy production. According to the latest Eurostat figures (through 2010),[3] there has been uneven progress in efforts by member states to switch from landfilling to more technologically advanced, economically fruitful and environmentally safe methods of waste management. The EU average is 38 per cent (i.e. 38 out of every 100 kilograms of waste produced is sent to landfills). The northern countries are the ones leading the way, with Germany and the Netherlands burying less than 1 per cent of the total municipal waste they generate. Greece, at 82 per cent, is sixth from the bottom. The only countries performing worse are Latvia, Lithuania and Malta, all of whom joined the EU in 2004, and Romania and Bulgaria, which joined in 2008 and still rely almost exclusively on landfilling to manage their waste. Greece has been a member of the EU since 1981.

For many years after they joined the European community of nations, the Greeks did their best to put the 'waste' in waste management. The area most dramatically affected was Attica, the province that includes metropolitan Athens. Attica covers less than 3 per cent of the total surface area of Greece, yet for the last thirty years it has been home to about 35 per cent of the population of the country. It is appallingly overcrowded, and one of the main consequences has been that, in the whole period since the end of military rule in 1974, it generated far more garbage than it knew what to do with.

From the early years after the restoration of democracy, a system of managed chaos emerged which allowed the association of the municipalities of Attica, its powerful, initially Communist-controlled union and local business interests with the right political connections to deal with waste management for their own benefit, if not necessarily that of the public. As a rule, projects were awarded directly to the preferred insiders. The law disallowing this was bypassed through the tried and tested method of the 'garbage crisis': a mountain of waste would conveniently collapse, or a fire would catch in a rubbish dump, 'forcing' local authorities to circumvent competitive tender procedures and seek the aid of their favourite contractors. According to the ill-informed but unquestioned dogmas of the time, the companies dominating the sector constructed a plethora of unregulated landfills, hazardous both to the environment and to human health, where the wider problem kept being buried whenever it raised its ugly, foul-smelling head.

As European legislation evolved, these landfills – of which there were more than 3,000 as recently as 2006[4] – fell further and further behind accepted standards. But the lack of strategic planning, the prevailing left-wing 'scientific' consensus in favour of landfilling and against more technologically advanced methods (which were falsely attacked as causing pollution, or, more deliciously, as forms of privatization and selling out to foreign capital) and the business interests which this consensus served, all conspired to prevent the modernization of the system. Successive governments were unable to end the national disgrace of illegal rubbish dumps. As Professor Aravossis points out, 'it is the easiest thing for a municipal council to decide that x landfill will be shut down. The problem is that the garbage still has to be sent somewhere. So if there is no facility to take it in, by necessity either the landfill that was "shut down" is unofficially reopened, or another one is dug up to replace it.' Aside from the environmental degradation and the public health concerns raised by the (officially or otherwise) active illegal land-fills, this dramatic policy failure means that the bankrupt Greek state is threatened with crippling EU fines. In February 2013 the European Commission declared it would take Athens back to court for the 78 illegal landfills still active and the 318 still not rehabilitated. The Commission would propose a daily penalty of €71,193 per day for each one.[5]

After many delays, false starts, contradictory decisions at different levels of public administration, squandered European funds and intense local opposition to every new proposed site, the socialist PASOK government finally passed a Regional Plan for waste management in Attica in 2003. The law divided Attica into three sub-regions – western, north-eastern and south-eastern – and designated in each a preferred site for the construction of a sanitary landfill. The largest of the three sites would be in Fyli, in western Attica, a few hundred metres from the Ano Liosia landfill, the largest in the region and the successor of the unregulated dump that had been a major source of contamination. The other two were set to be constructed in Keratea and in Grammatiko, in south-eastern and north-eastern Attica respectively.

In the next few years, the EU agreed to help fund the three projects and the contracts were awarded. By late 2007, the Council of State, Greece's highest administrative court, with a venerable track record of environmentally friendly jurisprudence, had rejected appeals against all three of them. The last petition to be rejected was that of the municipality of Keratea, in October. The Fyli site, already receiving garbage in a transitional cell from 2004, commenced official operation in June 2006. In most European countries, these developments would probably signal the beginning of the end of local resistance. In Keratea, the failed petition was the point when the real fun began.

For the next three years until the fateful morning of 11 December 2010, the people of Keratea would intensify their campaign, both in the courts and in the streets, to block the construction of the landfill (there was a similar movement in Grammatiko, but it petered out after construction began in 2009). Led by Iatrou, who had been elected mayor in 2006, they tried everything: they published books and appeared on TV to highlight the archaeological significance of Ovriokastro, where the landfill was to be dug; they held press conferences and took part in demonstrations in Athens in front of government offices; they organized concerts near the town featuring many of the biggest names in Greek popular music; they boycotted the 2009 elections for the European Parliament (62 per cent of eligible Keratea voters stayed away from the polls). Presaging things to come, they also engaged in more aggressive forms of 'struggle', like raising banners and chanting slogans at waste management conferences, or violently blocking the access of employees of the central government or the contractor to the landfill site.

During the winter of 2009–10, Greece's fiscal problems became the focus of international attention. In May 2010 Prime Minister George Papandreou signed the fateful memorandum of understanding with the European Commission (the executive arm of the European Union), the European Central Bank and the International Monetary Fund setting out the draconian terms of Greece's €110 billion bailout. The bailout agreement would from that time on be known simply as the Memorandum (*Mnimonio*), with capital 'M', and would become the most abused term in the vocabulary of Greek politics.

As the year went on, the first waves of tax hikes and cuts in wages, benefits and pensions started hitting people. By December, with the economy in steep recession and unemployment on its long upward climb, anger about the landfill in Keratea had mixed with growing frustration about collapsing incomes to create one of the most virulent strains of the NIMBY disease in the modern history of the country. When the Papandreou government decided to push ahead with the construction of the landfill, and tried to get the equipment in place at night with the escort of 600 riot policemen, it was the spark that lit the fuse.

Stavros Iatrou should have his picture next to the word 'mercurial' in the dictionary. A small man with a large forehead crowned by a shock of silver hair, in conversation he digresses from one subject to the next with the speed of his darting eyes. He previews very important things he is going to tell you by saying 'this is very important' – just in case you are not paying attention. He presents himself as a contrarian truth-teller, who reveals all the secrets the System does not want you to know, and highlights the scars he has borne from his decades of activism. In his mid-fifties, an environmental engineer by training and an insurgent by conviction, he has been involved in the local politics of his area since he was first elected municipal councillor of Keratea in 1978, at the tender age of twenty-two.

Before that, as a student, he had been a member of KNE, the youth wing of the Greek Communist Party. He had been swept along by the flood of left-wing radicalism that had overtaken the universities after the fall of the junta in 1974. In his more mature years, he joined Synaspismos, the main constituent group of the hard-left SYRIZA coalition whose popularity has soared in the Age of the Memorandum.

Iatrou, then, is a man of the left – but his is a leftism of lived experience, not rigid, theoretical ideology. His heroes are Themistocles, the ancient Athenian politician and general who is believed to have hailed from the area around Keratea, and Aris Velouchiotis, the Communist guerrilla who was among the leaders of Greek resistance to the Nazi occupiers during the Second World War.

He is particularly drawn to their penchant for deception and misdirection. 'Themistocles knew he had to get the Athenians to build a fleet and, to finance this, he knew that they needed the silver from the mines of Lavrio,' he tells me. 'So he did what he had to do. He went to the oracle in Delphi and paid her off, to get the divination he required. My goals were more modest, but I see myself as continuing in his tradition.' He is proud of the fact that, in the interests of keeping the landfill away from Keratea, he often deceived ministers and other officials seeking to get the wheels rolling on the project.

Like most people from Keratea, Iatrou is an Arvanite by origin. The Arvanites are a population group descended from migrants from Albania who settled in Greece several centuries ago and who are famous for their stubbornness and unruly spirit. A local saying encapsulates their mentality: there was a fight between an Arvanite and a wall, it goes, and the wall went away.

As the campaign against the landfill intensified after 2007, Iatrou claims he made use of loyalties deriving from common Arvanite roots to develop a network of informants in the state apparatus which gave him early warning of any move that the municipalities' association or the ministries were about to make on Keratea. To maintain secrecy, a covert system of information exchange was set up through a *bougatsa* shop in Keratea (*bougatsa* is a cream-filled pastry that, in the north of Greece in particular, is considered a basic necessity of existence).

The then mayor was taking advantage of a phenomenon still rife in modern Greek life which one would be hard-pressed to find to such an extent in Western Europe: the enduring allegiance to one's 'own people', be they family, clan or local community, trumping any devotion to the state and its dictates, even among the state's own servants. In the choice between betraying one's government and betraying one's friends, it is vanishingly rare in Greece for the state to stand a chance.

Slights, real or imagined, against the people of Keratea because of their Arvanite origins mixed with the widespread feeling that the government in Athens used them as a dumping-ground to fan the flames of resistance against the landfill. In Iatrou's mind, the process for the selection of the new landfill sites was rigged from the start. As he explains, the prefectures of Athens and the port of Piraeus, which together make up nearly nine-tenths of the population of Attica, were excluded a priori so that the burden could be placed squarely on the shoulders of 'the Arvanites, the peasants'. 'They never held a dialogue with us, they thought it was beneath them,' he adds. 'That's what drove us up the wall. I still hold a grudge about it. I don't always behave rationally in politics. Emotion and a sense of dignity play a crucial role.'

The view of the people of Keratea that they are the dumpsite of Attica is hardly borne out by the evidence. It is western Attica, instead, that has taken on more than its fair share of the burdens of development. Apart from the Fyli landfill and of its predecessor at Ano Liosia, the area is home to pretty much the whole of (what's left of) heavy industry in Attica, including one of Greece's two main refineries, two major shipyards, two steel plants and two cement factories.

Even if they exaggerated their sense of victimhood, however, the people of Keratea could certainly point to irregularities in the process through which the new landfill sites were selected for the 2003 Regional Plan. Officials and activists from Keratea, for example, have long held that Mandra, a town in western Attica, escaped selection in part because of the intervention of Theodoros Pangalos, a native of Mandra and one of the heavy hitters of PASOK, whose electoral district included Mandra as well as Keratea (his detractors in Keratea at the time argued that he should have fought for their exclusion from the planning as well). Another site was set aside after pressure was put on the government by the Greek Orthodox Church.

'The process has no scientific credibility,' Iatrou asserts. 'The whole of the establishment – the political system, the Church, the businessmen – have no interest in setting a rational, scientifically sound system of waste management, either in terms of the locations chosen or in the methods used. They just choose whatever serves the established interests, big and small.'

In this assessment, he is seconded by his predecessor and successor, Kostas Levantis. Levantis, a member of PASOK who was mayor of Keratea between 1999 and 2006 and has been, since 1 January 2011, mayor of the expanded municipality of Lavreotiki, is adamant that government claims that they were planning an environmentally light-footed site to bury a small volume of residues of processed waste do not stand up to scrutiny. 'The size of the site, and also the fact that it included a deep ravine, makes it clear that they were preparing to build an old-style landfill,' he tells me. This is hard to argue with: the site chosen by the government extended over 54 hectares. By comparison, the Fyli landfill, where despite the operation of the mechanical recycling plant, about nine-tenths of all garbage generated in Attica gets buried today, is only 37 hectares.

This sense that decisions are being dictated not by strategic assessments of the common good but by the interests of the economically powerful and the politically well connected, was the single most important factor in the refusal of the people of Keratea to back down. The wider significance of their stand stems from the fact that most Greeks, especially since the bailout and the pain of austerity that came with it, feel similarly put upon. Rightly or wrongly, they feel they are being asked to shoulder the burden of adjustment so that those who are truly responsible for the catastrophe can get away unscathed. And more and more with every passing day, they are looking to 'resist', in any way possible. It is a climate that makes it very difficult for the state to function and for society to remain at peace.

When the bulldozers and the riot police came to Keratea, Iatrou, who weeks before had been voted out but was still in office, had a clear strategy. 'We had to hold out for at least four to five days,' he remembers. 'We were mindful that in Grammatiko, once they got the equipment in place, the protests quickly died away and work on the landfill began.'

To keep the temperature of the public scorching, he decided to put his physical integrity on the line. On the second day of the events, as he recounts, he summoned various other local mayors, a couple of MPs and some union chiefs to stand with him on the street and told them not to intervene unless the police attempted to arrest him. Then, speaking far from softly, he attacked the police with a big stick. He was beaten to the point of fainting, but escaped arrest. The news of his clubbing spread through the crowd like electricity, and any hopes for a peaceful resolution evaporated.

The next day, Monday the 13th, opponents of the landfill won a rare legal victory when the local Magistrate's Court in Lavrio granted an injunction against work commencing on the project, because the necessary expropriations had not been completed. Meanwhile, as the Keratea Troubles gained the attention of the media, and in particular the TV stations, which finally had the requisite imagery – petrol bombs, teargas, a spot of blood – to justify extended coverage, people began to flock to the area to support the locals. Everybody came, from anarchist professional revolutionaries who brought with them know-how in urban guerrilla warfare, to far-right groups of retired military officers and modern-day pagans who worship the Olympian gods. Keratea was suddenly more than just another garbage war between a local community and the government; it was about resistance – to the corrupt and bankrupt state and to the Memorandum imposing austerity on the many to wash away the sins of the few.

'Keratea became a symbol because of the way the people fought day in day out, down in the roadblocks, for a whole winter,' Mayor Levantis recalls. Iatrou observes that when outside groups started flowing into the town after 11 December, the link between the anti-landfill campaign and the national problem emerged on its own. 'People began talking about the "Can't Pay Won't Pay" movement, the Memorandum and so on. Soon, down there on the roadblocks, there were rallies and all these activists got to present their positions – they gave long speeches, and talked for one minute about Keratea at the beginning and at the end, and for an hour in-between about not paying tolls on national highways and all these other issues. The anarchists and other leftists in particular told us that in no other part of Greece where they had joined various campaigns did the local community allow them such free rein in discussing their ideas.' The rapport was good even with the far-right elements, according to the former mayor: 'They showed a lot of respect for our fight. Our attitude was: "Do you support our cause? Then welcome, whoever you are."'

The 'Can't Pay Won't Pay' movement in particular was on the rise at that time. Its first appearance dates from 2008, when drivers refused to pay tolls on the ill-maintained death trap of a national highway between Corinth and Patras. In the two years that followed, continuous increases in highway tolls across the country acted as kindling for the initiative, but its focus remained narrowly on the issue of toll payments.

This changed after the signing of the Memorandum. Policies passed by the Papandreou government in order to meet targets for fiscal adjustment provided new targets for the movement. Increases in ticket prices for public transport in Athens of up to 40 per cent, which were due to come into effect on 1 February 2011, had caused a particularly vehement reaction. Activists were exhorting people to oppose the ticket hikes by free-riding.[6] Large numbers of Greeks already avoided paying for their bus and inner city train tickets before the crisis, contributing critically to the catastrophic deficits of the public transport companies. Now, the crisis imbued their free-riding with not-so-subtle tones of moral outrage.

'Can't Pay Won't Pay' took on a new meaning and became a rallying cry for the Age of the Memorandum. Its call for mass non-compliance, later extended to extraordinary property taxes and new measures instituting payments by patients in public hospitals, stemmed from a core tenet according to which 'the people' should not be forced to pay for the crisis caused by the ruling elites. It proved particularly effective, both among the indigent and among the merely indignant, because it cloaked what for the former was a survival strategy and for the latter a means to stick it to the Man, in the sublime garbs of civil disobedience. The supporters of 'Can't Pay Won't Pay' saw the struggle of Keratea in similar terms: a refusal to obey unjust laws in the name of higher principles of justice.

Iatrou has no illusions about this. 'Keratea was not a case of civil disobedience. I have no time for "Can't Pay Won't Pay". When I was still in the Communist Party, I hated the idea that "the law is what is right for the worker" [a prominent slogan of the Party through the years, used to justify disobedience to laws it deems unjust]. What about the rights of the bourgeois? The rights of women?' But was the significance of Keratea not that it legitimized the tendency of Greeks to take the law into their own hands and to reject the dictates of the state if these undermined their own interests? 'Unfortunately, yes,' he admits. 'When people think of the events, mostly they tend to think about the street-fighting and the Molotov cocktails.' Was he not partly to blame for that? Did he not make a deal with the devil in order to maximize support for the campaign? He accepts this, mentioning that the price paid included some local youths who 'sadly, went to extremes'. But overall, he does not seem to regret it.

The people of Keratea attracted support from all across the country and from all political backgrounds during and after their days of rage. Even Dimitris Koufodinas, the chief hitman of the left-wing terrorist group '17 November', in a talk given by telephone from prison to a group at Panteion University in May 2012, seemed to be hinting at Keratea-style local insurgencies as a means to quicken the class consciousness of the people and build a revolutionary mass movement.[7]

But no supporter of the campaign was as significant as Bishop Nikolaos of Mesogaia and Lavreotiki, the top church leader of south-eastern Attica. Bishop Nikolaos is one of the most remarkable figures in the upper echelons of the Greek Orthodox Church.

Born Nikolaos Chatzinikolaou in 1954, he studied Physics in his hometown at the University of Salonica. From there, he went on to Harvard, where he received a postgraduate degree in astrophysics, followed by a second one, an MSc in mechanical engineering from MIT. He got his PhD, which was in the field of Biomedical Technology, from HST (Health Sciences and Technology), a joint programme run by Harvard and MIT.

The bishop, who commands great respect both among his flock in the Lavreotiki region and among politicians and the Church hierarchy, played a crucial role in the early days of the Troubles. On Sunday 19 December, eight days after the violence began, he spoke to a large crowd on the junction of the Keratea small business park, an intersection that had been occupied two days earlier by the riot police. Bishop Nikolaos referred to the struggle of the Keratiotes as 'holy' and 'righteous', bringing tears to many eyes. 'The issue is not that they want to bring you the garbage; it's that they treat you like garbage,' he asserted, a stern rebuke uttered in his mild, mellifluous voice. He warned the government that they cannot ignore the will of the people.

According to former mayor Iatrou, the speech was a catalyst: 'After it, supporters from outside Keratea started flooding in, first from the surrounding areas and then from the whole of Attica.' Mayor Levantis is also generous in his praise of Nikolaos, mentioning that he planned to appear as a defence witness for various Keratea youths arrested in the Troubles, in trials that began in September 2012. Even the anti-clerical Alexis Tsipras of SYRIZA, during one of his visits to Keratea, extolled the part that the bishop was playing in the showdown.

This was not to be the last of Nikolaos's interventions in politics in the Age of the Memorandum. In mid-April 2011 he played a crucial role as a mediator, bringing together Mayor Levantis and the Minister for Citizen Protection in a meeting that would result in the removal of the riot police from Keratea. Then a few months after things had returned to normal there, the government, in a mad scramble to find cash to appease the representatives of the troika, instituted an extraordinary tax to be levied on all property connected to the power grid, the non-payment of which would lead to power being cut. In response, the bishop sent an encyclical to his flock more or less urging those without means to refuse to pay the tax.

The Church's position since Greece went into financial life-support has been a controversial one. In many ways, it has been part of the problem. Traditionally an enemy of modernization (especially if it meant a relegation of its role in education and social life or its separation from the state and the generous funding it receives from it) and deeply suspicious of Western influence, it had little cause to celebrate the Memorandum. Some Church leaders have even come out openly against it, making common cause with populists on the right. On the other hand the charity work undertaken by the Church has been increasingly vital in protecting Greek families from poverty since 2010, as the welfare state has essentially closed up shop.

The growing secularization of Greek life and some prominent scandals, financial and other, involving members of the priesthood, have meant that the influence of the Greek Orthodox Church has waned in recent years, especially in urban centres. But cases like that of Bishop Nikolaos in Keratea show that the influence is still strong. In a country where the state has lost all credibility, the Church continues to play a crucial political role, not always in the service of stability and almost never in the cause of social progress.

By March, tensions were reaching fever pitch in Keratea. The 'insurgency' was four months old, the animosity between the townspeople and the police was growing by the day and there seemed no end in sight. On 16 March the deputy prime minister, Theodoros Pangalos, went to a taverna in Kalyvia, a few kilometres from Keratea, to dine with his wife and a few fellow PASOK parliamentarians. Word got around in the permanently manned roadblocks on Lavriou Avenue and soon more than fifty people took off for Kalyvia to offer their heartfelt greetings to their favourite politician. They pelted him with yoghurt and showered him with abuse. Four platoons of riot police were sent from Keratea to Kalyvia to protect him from harm.

The people of Keratea were already peeved with Pangalos long before the Memorandum came along. His full-throated support for his native Mandra in its attempts to be exempted from landfill planning, combined with his insistence that the rest of the Regional Plan be implemented as it stood – even with the assistance of tanks, as he had colourfully put it – had irked them considerably.[8]

But what, added on to everything else, made him into a kind of super-villain in their eyes was a speech he had given a few months earlier that would live in infamy. The date was 21 September 2010. It was a sleepy session of parliament discussing a bill for the merger and abolition of agencies of the public sector that had outlived their usefulness. No fireworks were expected. At some point, the portly Pangalos, a brilliant but verbally incontinent grandson of a military dictator, a Communist in his youth and a proud Arvanite himself, whom Papandreou had put in charge of downsizing a state which was as bloated as he was, requested the floor. It was a few months after the first bailout had been signed, and the first round of cuts and tax hikes were already producing spontaneous and not-so-spontaneous eruptions of anger by members of the public against politicians, in particular of PASOK, then the sole governing party. The words spoken by Pangalos, ensconced deep in the plush, red-cushioned benches of parliament, came to define the Age of the Memorandum. This is what he said:

> The answer to the outcry that exists against the political personnel of the country, 'how did you eat up all that money?', as people ask, is this: We appointed you. We ate it all up together, in the context of relations of political

clientelism, corruption, bribery and the abasement of the very concept of politics.

The uproar was immediate, and has yet to fade away. Pangalos became the most polarizing political figure of the post-Memorandum era. He was attacked mercilessly, by populists of the left and the right, on blogs and anti-Memorandum media. But there were also those who agreed with the main point, even if they took issue with his right to make it, as a parliamentarian of thirty years' standing who had served multiple terms as minister and therefore whose responsibility for the fall far exceeded that of the ordinary citizen. His short speech became the focal point of conversations up and down the country about who was to blame for Greece's bankruptcy. The core point of contention in countless heated exchanges boiled down to this: Did the politicians 'eat it all up' on their own, or had we, the people, participated willingly, each to the extent of his or her capacities, in the glorious feast that had come to such an inglorious end?

Unsurprisingly, Pangalos has a different interpretation of the meaning of the events in Keratea than that of the locals. The famously undiplomatic politician gives short shrift to the idea that the people of Keratea were worried about the archaeological significance of the landfill, or to their sense of grievance about not being consulted. 'Their fundamental problem,' he tells me, 'was that a landfill would cause the value of their plots to fall. Keratea is the most expansionary settlement in all of Attica, possibly in all of Greece.'

In a country where official land and forest registries remain a halting work in progress, real-estate development has for decades evolved in a totally anarchic manner. Individuals and organized settlements would build wherever they pleased and then apply political pressure for homes to be retrospectively legalized. This was the process that Pangalos was saying Keratea excelled in: 'They were infringing on government property and forested land all over the place, and they continue to do so today. If you travel from Keratea to Lavrio, you will see the various infringements, on the hills left and right, including on the ridgeline.'

Pangalos also has his own view about the make-up of the anti-landfill forces. 'The ranks of the protesters were divided into three elements,' he says. 'One third were the indignant townspeople; another third were anarchists and similar elements from Exarcheia [a neighbourhood of Athens], who had come to face off with the police; and the rest were Albanian immigrants, who were being paid to take part. At night in particular, the roadblocks were manned only by the Albanians.' (This is disputed by the locals, including Mayor Levantis.)

Pangalos seems to revel in his role as a politician unafraid to tell the people home truths. In another widely reproduced speech, he said that the Memorandum was 'bliss' for Greece, and speaking to the French TV station France 5, he said those who believe that the Greek government should refuse to pay its debts and leave the EU are either 'communists, fascists or wankers'. He recently published an e-book entitled *We Ate it Up Together*, along with an accompanying website of the same name where he invites citizens to offer their own testimonies of 'small-time' corruption.

But his abiding passion these days seems to be the long, twilight struggle against SYRIZA. He blames Iatrou and SYRIZA for orchestrating the attack against him in Kalyvia – Iatrou has a case pending against him in court for libel. For Pangalos, the showdown in Keratea was not only exploited, but initiated by SYRIZA. He has referred to Alexis Tsipras, its young leader, as a 'living-room revolutionary' and accused him of creating a climate reminiscent of the civil war with his support for attacks on politicians who voted for the Memorandum. Tsipras's party, in his eyes, represents everything that has gone wrong with the Greek left, and with the country itself.

Yet the central political story of the Age of the Memorandum is how the Greek people fell for Tsipras's beguiling populist mantra and turned their backs on Pangalos and his hard–nosed truth-telling. In the 2009 parliamentary elections, before the crisis erupted, SYRIZA got less than 5 per cent of the national vote. In the election on 6 May 2012, they got nearly 17 per cent and came in second. In the repeat election on 17 June, they increased their share to 26.9 per cent, a mere 2 percentage points behind victors New Democracy. The former deputy prime minister, for his part, decided at age seventy-four that it was time to retire from parliament. The visceral repulsion he inspired in south-eastern Attica and the electoral collapse of PASOK, which dropped from 160 MPs in 2009 to only 33, no doubt contributed to his decision not to run.

Tsipras's support for the campaigners in Keratea and for the 'Can't Pay Won't Pay' movement contributed significantly to his electoral takeoff. He visited Keratea repeatedly during the Troubles and adopted its cause as part of the wider struggle against the Memorandum and the big business interests that he viewed as seeking to profit from the reorganization of waste management in Attica.

In a speech in Keratea on 30 May 2012, between the two electoral contests, he made the connection explicit. He called the town a 'symbol' for the country because it defeated the forces of *diaploki* (an untranslatable Greek word meaning business–government collusion), which tried to impose their will 'like Latin American juntas dealing with Indians'. He told the crowd that the Greek people should follow the example of the people of Keratea, abandon the parties of austerity (New Democracy and PASOK) and give power to SYRIZA. In the May election, the voters of Keratea, egged on by posters and flyers illegally distributed in polling stations by a group of local hotheads, calling a vote for New Democracy and PASOK a 'betrayal of Keratea', had given SYRIZA 28 per cent of the vote. On 17 June that percentage would climb further, to an astonishing 37 per cent.

'Keratea and other small towns of this kind are microcosms of

Greece's debauchery,' Pangalos notes. 'Its citizens were used to a certain way of making a living through the illegal development of the surrounding areas, and they cannot get it into their heads that the old way of making a living is now over. This is true of most Greeks.' Asked if he sees this trend of denial abating and giving way to a more realistic assessment of the country's predicament, he offers a dark prediction: 'I am much afraid that the next parliament will be more nationalist-populist than the present one, i.e. that fascist mentalities and behaviour will be even stronger. There is a cultural crisis in Greece. The progressive-reformist pro-European forces have been reduced to minority status and this is because our standard of living had nothing to do with our technological effectiveness and our cultural maturity.'

On 18 April 2011, Holy Monday, an extraordinary meeting took place in the office of the Minister for Citizen Protection, Christos Papoutsis. Papoutsis hosted Mayor Levantis and Bishop Nikolaos of Mesogaia and Lavreotiki, who had played a critical part in setting up the sit-down. Its purpose was to find a compromise solution that would allow the central government to withdraw the riot police from Keratea without a too-obvious loss of face. The two PASOK politicians came to an understanding, paving the way for the end of the four-month showdown.

It came in the nick of time. By then, the level of hostility among ordinary citizens towards the police and the disregard of the law among the more belligerent elements was spiking dangerously. On the morning of 14 April, bemused motorists discovered that some local commandos had dug a trench, six feet deep, across Lavriou Avenue, the main thoroughfare connecting Athens to the port of Lavrio and the archaeological site of Sounio. The aim of the operation was to prevent the contractor from sending in new equipment to Ovriokastro, to replace the machinery that had been not-so-mysteriously torched a few weeks earlier. The trench was surrounded by ten-inch-tall iron rods drilled into the road, in order to slash the tyres of any bulldozer that might attempt to repair the damage. On that same day, ten protesters and two officers were taken to hospital for injuries sustained in the latest clashes. That night, before dawn, the home of two local policemen, husband and wife, and their four underage children, was attacked with Molotov cocktails. Three cars parked outside were burned to a crisp.

When I had visited the town a few days earlier, one kindly lady in her sixties, watering the plants in her backyard, told me that when she had gone down to the roadblock, the behaviour of the police had nearly turned her into an anarchist. 'I'd make a Molotov cocktail if I knew how,' she said, matter-of-factly. Residents complained that the police swore at them, smashed their vehicles and prevented them from going to work in their fields.

Mayor Levantis blames the aggressive behaviour of the police for the explosive situation: 'They would make incursions into town, fifteen to twenty platoons strong, go into people's backyards, hit old folks.' As he told me, he later found out that the more extreme elements in Keratea were planning an all-out attack on the police on Holy Saturday. It was fortunate that he had come to an understanding with Minister Papoutsis a few days earlier, he said, 'otherwise we would have mourned fatalities'.

The police, for their part, were feeling the heat, and turning it up on their superiors. On 12 April the Police Officers' Union of Attica filed a lawsuit against the Greek Police, for forcing them to work sixteen-hour days in conditions that directly threatened their safety. The head of the union told me at the time that the government had 'disappeared' and had 'let the police become a means for the residents to blow off steam'.

Since then, even though the problem of waste management in Attica is more urgent than ever, things have moved in their traditional, hobbled snail's pace. On 27 August 2012, fully sixteen months after the end of hostilities in Keratea, EDSNA, the newly formed regional association responsible for waste management, issued a decision approving the construction of four integrated waste management facilities in Attica, through the vehicle of private–public partnerships. The total cost of all four projects is budgeted to exceed €430 million and the Greek government, along with EU structural funds, will cover 200 million of it.[9] One of these integrated facilities, each of which includes a solid-waste processing plant, a recycling sorting unit, a composting unit for organic materials as well as a landfill site for the residues, is set to be built in Keratea.

Mayor Levantis told me a couple of weeks after the decision was made public that he was 'satisfied' with it because it was agreed in the meeting (though this is not included in the minutes) to consider the proposal put forward by the municipality of Lavreotiki for integrated facilities for its own waste and that of the neighbouring municipality of Saronikos. The proposed plant would process about two-thirds of the amount of waste anticipated by the Regional Plan, in a 5-hectare site (instead of the 54 hectares originally earmarked).

An amendment passed in parliament in January 2013 approved the site change, though it remained unclear if the rest of the municipality's proposal (regarding volume of waste, methods of management and so on) would also be accepted by the central government. Former mayor Iatrou, who these days serves as municipal councillor of Lavreotiki, calls the EDSNA decision 'a joke driven by the same old construction business interests' and has filed suit against it, but he acknowledges that January's parliamentary amendment may be a game-changer. Regional authorities expect the competitive tender for Keratea and the other facilities in Attica to be completed by the end of 2014 (the initial target was the end of 2013). If this goal is not met, EU funds will be withdrawn and the whole project will grind to a halt for lack of funding.

Meanwhile, the 'sanitary' landfill in Fyli, which is handling the totality of garbage generated daily in Attica, plus extra waste brought (some illegally) from outside the region, is buckling under the weight. Experts claimed in the summer of 2012 that it had two more years until it would have to be shut down. Of course, they had said the same thing two years before that: the area of the dumpsite keeps expanding, eating up the surrounding hills.

Yannis Sgouros, the elected head of the region of Attica, has described the situation in Fyli as 'a Wild West type of environment'. He was referring to the droves of roaming Roma and Pakistani ragmen in the dump site, competing for spoils 'with shotguns and pistols'.[10] Of the 6,000 tonnes of trash sent to Fyli every day, close to 90 per cent ends up buried in the landfill, either directly or as residues from processing and recycling. In theory, this is done in a 'sanitary' manner, with a protective membrane preventing seepage of liquid waste into the ground and soil covering the garbage to minimize atmospheric pollution. But aside from the strain created by the sheer volume of waste, before the bulldozers have time to bury all the garbage, large numbers of Roma and Pakistanis have time to scavenge for anything valuable. They particularly prize copper and iron, which they extract by burning cables and other discarded items, releasing dioxins and other harmful particles into the atmosphere.

In the months when Keratea was in flames, things in Fyli were also coming to the boil. According to landfill workers, in those days hordes of Albanian Roma, up to four hundred at a time, would enter the massive landfill site – never guarded by more than twenty people at any one time – at all hours. Occasionally, they would appear in convoys of twenty or thirty specially modified motorbikes, which included an attached platform for carrying off valuable rubbish. Some of those who did not own such a handy contraption resorted to getting the garbage-truck drivers to carry the 'goods' down from the landfill to the fence next to the road, where they could be offloaded onto their own vehicles. Some drivers who refused suffered serious consequences. One had his jaw broken. Another had his truck smashed as well as his face.

On 19 March 2011, at the height of the Keratea Troubles, a Roma rag-collector was killed inside the Fyli landfill, run over by a waste-compacting vehicle which he did not hear coming because he was listening to music on earphones. Soon, workers at the site were besieged by his angry cohorts, who clashed with the police and set fire to equipment and to the garbage. One worker narrowly escaped with his life when a driver hoisted him onto his truck and whisked him to safety just before the mob got to him.

The war between different tribes of ragmen has also been intensifying. At first, it was mostly between Roma from different parts of the Balkans. Now, Pakistani immigrants, who live in the surrounding areas, and who used to work for the Roma, have got in on the game, leading to frequent and violent confrontations. On 8 April 2011 Albanian Roma killed a Pakistani father and son in clashes at the landfill site. Payback came swiftly, as large numbers of Pakistanis attacked the Roma camp and burned it to the ground.

The site is a shock to the senses. Arriving at the gates, manoeuvring between garbage trucks arriving from all over Attica, one is greeted, first of all, by an overpowering stench. Flags of Greece and the European Union, both badly shredded, hang limply, like haggard criminals strung up for public view. A message on the wall leading up to the entrance says: 'JEFRY [*sic*] GO HOME'. ('Geoffrey' was the middle name of George Papandreou. It was used widely by those who wanted to deride him for his American mother and his foreign ways.)

Driving up to the main site itself, amid swarms of seagulls searching for nourishment in the towers of Athenian trash, mangy dogs lying on the stinking slopes and bulldozers doing their best to put the oceans of waste out of sight, I notice that there are no ragmen around. George, my tour guide and one of the overseers at the site, tells me that since the bloody events of March and April 2011 an informal agreement has been reached between the municipal workers, the police and the peculiar brand of treasure hunters that plague Fyli. 'Before, when too many appeared, we stopped working,' he says. 'We were afraid for our safety. Now, the landfill only operates from seven in the morning to seven in the evening, instead of twenty-four hours. The deal is that they come in after closing hours.' Thus, with the blessing of the local police, both the official and the shadow landfill workers are able to do their work undisturbed.

So life goes on: instead of being exploited as a valuable resource, waste keeps getting wasted at a time when the country can least afford it; the latest attempt to move the Regional Plan forward is plodding along, having survived dozens of court appeals but still falling way behind schedule; and the authority of the state continues to sink in a quicksand of illiquidity, incompetence and unreliability.

2

A Taxing Issue

The origins of Greeks' view of themselves as victims of free-riding by all others Greeks, which lay at the root of the Keratea Troubles, comes from the country's unorthodox approach to taxation. It is the essential function that makes government possible, and the one that the modern Greek state has never quite mastered in almost two centuries of existence.

In late October 2012 *Hot Doc*, a Greek investigative journalism magazine, published a list of 2,059 Greek depositors – investment vehicles as well as individuals – in the Geneva branch of HSBC bank. It included names of famous businessmen and shipping magnates, who had transferred money out of the country. The magazine claimed that the names revealed constituted the infamous 'Lagarde list', handed over in 2010 by then French Finance Minister Christine Lagarde to her Greek opposite number, George Papaconstantinou, to examine for possible cases of tax evasion. In the weeks prior to the revelations of the magazine, Papaconstantinou and his successor as Finance Minister, Evangelos Venizelos, who by that time had become president of PASOK, had been pilloried in the press and in parliament for doing nothing concrete about the depositors on the list. Papaconstantinou would end up indicted for his handling of the affair.

Greek authorities, notoriously slow and ineffective in tackling tax evasion, were very quick on their feet against the publisher of the magazine, Kostas Vaxevanis: a warrant for his arrest was issued on the date of publication. The next day, he was charged with violating the privacy of the individuals on the list (which, of course, he had; none of them was a proven tax evader, after all).

Though his acquittal soon followed and though his decision to publish was controversial, the case demonstrated to the world the depth of the country's disease. It revealed a system incapable of self-catharsis, but still capable of lashing out at those who seek to reveal its misdeeds.

Tax evasion epitomizes the Greek Disease. It is misleading to call it a deviant practice. It is a social phenomenon – historically rooted, rampant, and widely accepted as the way of doing business. The causes are many: a negative view of the state and of the transparency of government spending; the spread of antisocial atomism as the values of social solidarity were turned, post-'74, into tools for the extraction of special privileges by various interest groups; the large number of very small, family-owned businesses with minimalist accounting data; the cosy relationships between certain sectors of the economy and the political class.

For all these reasons, it became routine practice in Greece for highly paid doctors not to give out receipts. Neither did well-paid private tutors, moderately paid plumbers or underpaid gardeners. When buying a home, it used to be standard procedure for the transacting parties, in the presence of lawyers and a notary public, to sign documents massively understating the value of the sale in order to pay fewer taxes on it (the reason this no longer happens is that commercial values have fallen below 'objective values' set by the Ministry of Finance). Many restaurants still bring you the bill jotted down manually on the order sheet. It was only at some point in 2011 that I got my first ever receipt from a Greek taxi driver. Whenever I take my own car for service, I am still offered two choices for the cost: one higher, with VAT, one lower, without it. In the higher echelons of economic activity, shipowners owning small settlements of real estate engaged in (at best) aggressive tax avoidance, construction firms serially under-reported earnings and multinationals engaged in unrestrained transfer pricing practices to shift profits to low-tax jurisdictions (especially Cyprus).

According to a study by the National Bank of Greece, government revenue from personal income tax in Greece came to 4.6 per cent of GDP in the first decade of the twenty-first century, as against an average of 8.7 per cent of GDP in the euro area.[1] A 2012 paper used a Greek bank's extrapolation of customers' real earnings from their declared income, as reflected in the loans it provided them, to estimate a lower bound (a floor) of €28 billion of unreported income in Greece.[2] This translates into €11.2 billion of foregone government revenue (on a 40 per cent tax rate), equal to 31 per cent of the monster budget deficit of 2009 which sent Greece straight into the suffocating embrace of the troika. The paper found that the worst offending professions were doctors, engineers, private tutors, accountants, financial service agents and lawyers. But taxes are evaded by everyone, be it provocatively or passively, at every opportunity or only as the inevitable cost of doing business.

In countries with well-functioning mechanisms of tax enforcement, questions of distributive justice centre on how progressive the tax and pension system should be, whether social benefits and services should be means-tested and other such important questions of political economy. In Greece, such discussions are woefully premature, and can lead to policies that are as unfair as they are economically destructive. The fundamental requirement of distributive justice in Greece is a much more basic one: getting everyone to pay their taxes. So long as this requirement is not met, those who cannot evade will pay an ever-growing share, and those who cheat will continue to thrive at the expense of the rest, even in some cases receiving income support from the government for their meagre declared income.

In the Age of the Memorandum, as salary-earners and pensioners – those who could not hide their income – took one hit after another and as the troika pushed hard for deficit targets to be met, the need to tackle tax evasion took on a new urgency. Two targets were particularly prominent in public debate: the self-employed, long-established champions of cheating, and corrupt public officials, thought to be hiding millions in bribery proceeds in secret bank accounts outside the country. As complaints to the tax police, both anonymous and eponymous, multiplied, lists of various enemies of the people appeared in newspapers – doctors with offices in the upper-class Athenian district of Kolonaki, pop stars, swimming pool owners who had not declared their pools to the taxman (or had wittily renamed them 'irrigation tanks'). Since these were officially approved leaks, no journalist was arrested – but neither were any tax cheats, and many of the doctors named turned out to have committed minor infractions. Minister Papaconstantinou kept referring to tax evasion as a great crime, but it was one of a novel kind: not victimless so much as villain-less.

As austerity deepened and no one of note was brought to justice, the anger proliferated – and so did the rumours, and the easy fixes to the country's woes implied by them. In February 2011 *Der Spiegel*, the respected German news magazine, reported that Greek citizens had deposited €600 billion in Swiss bank accounts (about three times the country's 2011 GDP). It was a comic book figure, slated as 'completely unreal' by the governor of the Greek central bank in parliamentary testimony, but it has stuck. In coffee-house conversations about the crisis today, you still hear the question asked – when are they going to 'catch' the 600 billion in Switzerland? Nothing has had a more corrosive effect on social cohesion and the credibility of the political system than its failure to crack down on tax evasion.

The reasons for this failure are diverse and deeply rooted. One area where the underlying problem is starkly visible is that of information technology and its inability to achieve results in the absence of the political and administrative will to use it. Which brings us to Dr Diomedes Spinellis.

George Papandreou is a well-known digital enthusiast. When the leader of PASOK became prime minister in October 2009, he hoped to unleash the forces of e-government to streamline bureaucracy, cut waste, increase transparency and – not least – improve the state's abject record in the fight against tax evasion. One of the first innovations that the Papandreou government introduced was the opengov platform for the selection of high-ranking government functionaries, from general secretaries of ministries to governors of public hospitals. To avoid the traditional practice of party leaders appointing close associates or failed parliamentary candidates who more often than not were entirely unsuited for the jobs at hand, it was decided to place calls for the recruitment of high- and mid-level officials in public view, on the internet. Applications would be submitted online and – in theory – the minister would choose the person with the best qualifications for the job: pretty standard practice for a normal developed country, in other words, but downright revolutionary for Greece.

Because it was ill-prepared, but also because the party machine of PASOK knew how to turn attempted reforms into its own instruments, the opengov experiment went awry. Critical appointments took far too long, and all too often the person chosen had much stronger party than professional credentials.[3] But there were also some notable successes – individuals picked on merit, who would have had little chance of getting the job under the old system. One of them was Diomedes Spinellis, an IT prodigy who taught software engineering at the Athens University of Economics and Business, and who in November 2009 was put in charge of the General Secretariat of Information Systems (GSIS) at the Ministry of Finance.

Spinellis has always been fascinated by electronics and computing. He speaks about software programs like they were old friends, not as if he were the ghost to their machine but as if they partook of the same substance. It is an unseasonably warm day in late November, and we are having a speed-lunch on campus. Outside the gates, African vendors of counterfeit goods hawk their wares. Inside there is graffiti singing the praises of class hatred and the walls are plastered with posters of the youth wings of the various political parties. Afterwards, he has allowed me to sit in on one of his classes ('it's not like you needed my permission,' he quips; it's true: people come and go freely into the university building and even into classes).

'My writing and arithmetic skills can at best be described as mediocre,' he tells me. 'With computers, I always got along well. Whatever I can do well, they help multiply its positive effects.' As a teenager in the early 1980s, he learned programming from lessons published in a magazine on electronic circuits that he read avidly. He and a friend, who went on to work for Apple, would write down code on school exercise books and show it to each other for feedback. Then they turned to renting computers, at 100 drachmas (€0.29) an hour, to practice.

He went on to study Software Engineering at Imperial College London (the subject did not exist at the time in Greek universities). He earned a Masters and a doctorate there, but despite prospects for a high-flying career abroad, he decided to return home, and began teaching, first at the University of the Aegean and then, since 2000, at the Athens University of Economics and Business. 'My goal was to show that one could achieve similar things academically in Greece as they would if they remained abroad,' Spinellis tells me. 'I was able to publish papers in the most demanding journals in my field, put out a book with one of the top publishers which won prizes and was translated into six languages and I was invited to the best conferences to present my work. It may take some extra work to achieve things from inside Greece, but it can certainly be done.'

By 2009 Spinellis was at the top of his game academically, one of most highly cited Greek scientists internationally. He was married with children, and enjoyed getting away from the Athenian daily grind by trekking in the mountains surrounding the Attic basin. Unfortunately for his peace of mind, he had caught the public policy bug, and Papandreou's opengov experiment allowed it to manifest itself. The tasks awaiting the soft-spoken, socially awkward, sheepishly humorous forty-something at the Ministry of Finance would prove his most challenging yet.

Of these tasks, none was more urgent than the reorganization of the GSIS in order to transform it into a tool for bringing to light the income and assets that Greek taxpayers hid from the government. Spinellis found a system of tax administration in shambles. As he explained in a TEDxAcademy talk in Athens in September 2012, evaluation based on targets and results achieved was an alien concept. Convoluted regulations and decisions requiring dozens of signatures ensured inertia and an absence of accountability. Public sector procurement procedures were impossibly time-consuming and the requirements imposed were often useless, meaning that necessary systems upgrades took forever. Last but not least, for many employees in the tax agency, the use of IT was, as he put it, 'a mountain to climb'.

Nikos Tatsos, a professor of Public Finance at Panteion University, former Greek ambassador to the OECD and a man weighed down by thirty years' experience as an adviser to finance ministers, has seen it all in Greek tax administration – most of it time and time again. He has witnessed countless ministers coming in starry-eyed and full of dreams of making their mark, only to be slowly ground down by the bureaucratic apparatus. 'You cannot go in there using a regular army,' he says. 'You've got sharp-shooters shooting at you left and right. It's a guerrilla war, and you need to use irregular methods to succeed.'

Spinellis has used similar language. At the TED event, he spoke of fighting a 'guerrilla war' to try to get things moving. He used the opengov platform to hire a team of five to staff his office, using a software program he wrote to rank the nearly 1,000 applicants according to their qualifications. He and his team used open source software wherever they could to upgrade systems and improve transparency without going through the clogged official channels of public procurement, which took ages and cost exorbitant sums.

'In all the meetings we had on technical assistance, which was part of the deal between us and our creditors, you had the foreign technocrats on one side with their laptops and our guys, the officials from the ministry, looking for things in stacks of paper,' Spinellis recalls. As he says, the open source software solutions were particularly critical in unclogging the system: 'The data centre was put up for tender in 2002; it is only now [in late 2012] that it is going online. Elenxis [a critical IT tool for centralizing and monitoring the auditing process] was put up for tender in 2005 and it is still not fully operational.'[4]

One area where there was immense room for improvement was the cross-checking of taxpayers' data to uncover discrepancies between their declared income and their lifestyle. For example, take a well-off Athenian doctor with an allergy to giving out receipts who declared an annual income of €10,000, below the tax-free ceiling. If he drove to work from his villa in the upper-tier district of Ekali to his practice in Kolonaki in a Mercedes S-Class vehicle, chances were he was hiding something.

The expensively bought and laboriously installed Taxis IT system had amassed a formidable volume of data like this since it went online in 2001 but, upon arrival, Spinellis found that no one was making use of it. As for everything else, there was a committee for electronic cross-checking, but he says it had never been convened. There was even information about which drivers had not paid road tax and which businesses had not paid VAT, not needing any cross-checking, that just lay there unused, as if the country was not on the brink of the worst fiscal crisis in its post-war history.

The new head of the GSIS put the committee to work. This was part of a wider effort by the Finance Ministry under Papaconstantinou to determine taxpayers' income indirectly from their assets and expenditure. As Professor Tatsos notes, the design of the policy was flawed, because it left too much out – for example, it allowed a person to buy a home, a car or even start a business without having to explain where he got the money. Still, it was a step in the right direction.

The cross-checking soon started producing results. One particularly fruitful line of enquiry related to the so-called 'business compensation' received by owner-managers of a certain class of small businesses. A number of owner-managers received part of their income as dividends from profits and another part as salaried compensation for their management role, a legal accounting measure to reduce the company's taxable profits. Then, however, they conveniently forgot to include the salaried portion of their income in their tax statement – something the Taxis system was able to trace. Such revelations and others were passed on to the 300-odd tax offices across the country for the relevant cases to be pursued.

A word here on Greece's tax offices: there were still 290 in January 2011, a number which the government struggled mightily to reduce to 118 by the end of 2013. If Kafka had been Greek, his masterpiece would probably have been entitled *The Tax Office*. The number of such offices had little to do with the requirements of efficient tax administration; it reflected instead the alacrity with which parliamentarians and ministers catered to the needs of their electoral constituencies. They were – and still are – notorious for their long queues, chaotic operation and an atmosphere thick with hostility and existential despair. To visit one is to take part in a minor Absurdist tragicomedy, where the hapless protagonist is tossed around like a basketball from official to official, from floor to floor, always hoping that he has the necessary paperwork and always finding out that there is some arcane document that he or she lacks, because of which their case cannot be settled.

As Spinellis has repeatedly said,[5] at the point when he sent off the data uncovered by the cross-checking to the tax offices, he would completely lose track of it. He soon became worried that no use was being made of it at all. To tackle the situation, he created a monitoring system within the GSIS that would assign cases to specific tax offices and check on their progress in closing them. The system started operating on 1 January 2011.

By September of the next year, according to figures that he made available on the GSIS website, the state had collected more than €762 million in extra revenue as a result of using the available data. This may sound like progress, but another figure puts it in perspective: at the end of 2010, the sum total of Greeks' outstanding debts to the taxman was €38.7 billion; three years later it had climbed to €62.3 billion.[6] The rock kept being pushed up the hill only to fall back down bigger.

One of the main reasons was that until very recently, the tax service was obliged by law to audit every business operating in Greece. 'It was a mistaken logic. What we are doing now instead is auditing a specific sample, chosen through risk analysis,' says Haris Theocharis, another Imperial College alumnus – one with extensive private sector experience, in Greece and internationally – who headed the GSIS between 2011 and early 2013. 'The goal is for the system to consider the taxpayer by default honest and to examine specific cases for compliance; until recently the default view of the taxpayer was that they are dishonest.'

Theocharis had been picked by Spinellis as his top adviser in the GSIS. He then succeeded him, after Spinellis resigned in October of 2011, citing 'personal reasons' for his decision. Few people bought it – unless he meant that he took fuel smuggling, and the state's blatant indifference to its perpetuation, very personally indeed.

According to myth, Hephaestus, the Olympian god of fire and metallurgy, son of Zeus and Hera, was born so ugly and disfigured that his mother cast him from the mountaintop into the Aegean Sea. A few years ago, Singular Logic, a leading Greek software company, developed a software tracking program of the same name, to help combat the illicit trade in heating fuel which was estimated to cost the government up to €500 million annually in lost revenues.

When the Hephaestus program was developed, the rate of taxation on the consumption of transport fuel was almost double the rate for heating fuel. This allowed distributors to buy heating fuel and sell it illegally as transport fuel, pocketing the difference instead of turning it over to the state treasury. In 2008 the New Democracy government hired Singular Logic to run Hephaestus and use the data it gathered in the battle against this and other forms of fuel smuggling.

The concept was simple: heating fuel distributors were required to buy fuel at the high tax rate and sell it at the low rate, the tax authorities pledging to reimburse them within forty-eight hours for the difference. But the only way to get their money back would be to declare all their transactions on Hephaestus. This allowed the government to monitor the heating fuel distribution chain from the customs office to the consumer and to spot any irregularities.

When PASOK came to power in 2009, the outsourcing of the management of the system was repealed because the cost – around €15 million over two years – was thought too high. Hephaestus was brought in-house, to be run by the GSIS. Spinellis added an important element to its functioning: if the data showed that a petrol station applying for a reimbursement owed taxes, the GSIS demanded that the tax debt be settled before it paid out any money to the debtors. This could not be done while Singular Logic ran the system, because it was argued that the government could not give out information about taxpayers' debts to a private company. When it was put into practice, it proved a sure-fire means to add desperately needed revenue to the government coffers. Tackling fuel smuggling was high on Prime Minister Papandreou's priority list. It seemed like the time had come for this long-festering wound to be cauterized.

Like his divine namesake, though, this Hephaestus was destined to be disfigured. With a little-noticed intervention, the Finance Ministry abolished the obligation of buying at the high rate, starting on 1 January 2011. The move effectively eliminated the incentive that fuel distributors had to register their transactions with Hephaestus. One argument put forward was that it was not achieving what had been hoped against the smugglers. When I asked Spinellis how the decision could be justified from a public policy perspective, he was at a loss to respond. 'When something is not working as well as it could, you fix it,' he pointed out. 'You don't get it rid of it.'

Theocharis, who was part of the committee that recommended the decision as an adviser to Spinellis and who had objected to it, mentions another element that may have influenced the committee's deliberations: 'There were questions about mistakes in the system which led to some reimbursements that should not have been made. Certain people in the ministry signed for these reimbursements to be authorized, and were therefore personally responsible.' As he explains it, it is standard practice in Greece's legal culture not to distinguish, in cases where the public interest is harmed, between error and malicious intent. In other words, whereas in most European countries a public official is judged differently if the damage that he has caused stems from an honest mistake rather than a premeditated plan, in Greece the approach is more utilitarian: only the outcome counts. This makes officials reticent to put their signature on decisions, especially ones authorizing the expenditure of public funds, and contributes to the lethargic pace at which public administration moves.

As a result of the legislative amendment, even though fuel distributors were still legally obliged to report to the system, a growing number did not do so. It was a vital blow to Hephaestus as a tool for tracking the smugglers and for making petrol stations pay their back-taxes.

Even before this, suspiciously little interest had been shown by the authorities in making use of the wealth of data that Hephaestus made available. Andreas Drymiotis, a respected former executive at Singular Logic who later served as an adviser to Prime Minister

Papandreou on IT issues, said in a TV interview in January 2012: 'Since 2008, the company that ran the system kept uncovering cases that were worth looking into, in the so-called 'exception report' [...] To my knowledge, not a single audit took place.'[7]

'The problem was that there was no clear ownership of the responsibility to make use of the data and look into the suspected infractions,' explains Theocharis, who had been the person responsible, on the technical side, for the transfer of Hephaestus from Singular Logic to GSIS. These were complicated issues, as he points out, potentially involving both tax and customs violations, and each directorate sought to avoid taking them on, claiming they involved matters beyond their competence. 'Questions of competence between different agencies create the worst problems in Greek public administration,' he notes. 'It's not that everybody wants ownership; it's that nobody does.'

A few months after the Finance Ministry decision to scrap the mandatory nature of buying fuel at the high rate, the reluctance of the tax enforcement authorities to act finally proved too much for Spinellis. The bureaucratic straw that broke the camel's back came on 26 August 2011. GSIS had uncovered 3,500 cases of heating fuel distributors who had not registered their transactions with Hephaestus between 1 January and 30 April 2011. It had sent the relevant data to the General Secretary of Tax and Customs Affairs, Yannis Kapeleris, who was responsible for imposing the appropriate fines. Instead, Kapeleris issued a directive suspending the requirement of imposing fines until such time as the matter was resolved through new legislation.

A few weeks later, Spinellis tendered his resignation. It was widely believed and reported that the cause was the unwillingness of the enforcement apparatus of the ministry to crack down on the fuel smugglers. A newspaper story to that effect[8] led to an investigation by the newly instituted Office of the Financial Prosecutor, which ended up indicting Kapeleris for breach of duty, a felony, claiming that his actions may have cost the public purse 'a minimum of €15 million'. Kapeleris denies the charges, which seem hard to prove. The case was still pending when this book went to press.

Theocharis claims that Spinellis was eager to return to teaching and academic work, which he felt he had left for too long. He has warm words for his former boss. 'He achieved a lot. Among other things, he created a new mentality, where party affiliation plays no part in personnel decisions. It is a mentality that I have tried to maintain.'

As his successor admits though, Spinellis thought he was not achieving enough – otherwise the lure of the academy would have been much easier to resist. He, Spinellis, indirectly admitted as much to me. 'I would have been much happier at my post in the autumn of 2011 if there was a General Secretary of Tax and Customs Affairs who would call day and night asking for data and offering ideas about how to combat tax evasion. It is well documented that this was not the case.'

Faced with a history of failure in tackling tax evasion related to the misuse of transport oil as heating oil, in October 2012 the coalition government led by Antonis Samaras bit the bullet and equalized the tax rates imposed on the two categories of fuel. This eliminated the opportunity for illegal arbitrage on the part of the smugglers, and the government also hoped it would bring in additional revenue, budgeted at €500 million.

Things did not quite turn out like that. The rate equalization led to a 30 per cent increase in the price of heating oil. For struggling Greeks, facing another year of recession and with their incomes already significantly shrunken, this was unsustainable. A heating oil benefit that was instituted was ignored by most beneficiaries – only €80 million out of an available €260 million was handed out – because they could not afford to pay out of pocket for the fuel and then wait to be reimbursed. Demand collapsed: in the first two months of 2013, only 374,000 tonnes of heating oil were sold, compared with 1.1 million in the same period in 2012. The net increase in tax proceeds from the consumption on heating and transport oil was only €40 million, less than 10 per cent of the projected amount.[9]

Instead, there was a mass reversion to fireplaces and woodstoves, where people burnt everything from processed wood from broken-up furniture to trees illegally logged in the forest. Given that woodstoves emit about the same amount of particle pollution as 3,000 oil furnaces, the result was that Athens and other cities were turned into open-air gas chambers in the winter months, as a pall of smog descended upon them. On cold, windless days, when the air became thick with woodsmoke, there was a notable increase in cases of asthma and bronchitis. Meanwhile, there were indications that the smuggling of tax-free shipping oil had increased significantly after the equalization of the rates in the other two categories.

Thus did yet another round of the government's war against the smugglers end in stalemate, with the civilian population the only clear loser.

Spinellis's struggles with the old guard at the tax agency did not end with his resignation. On an early December evening a couple of months after he had left the GSIS, he spoke at an open discussion forum on 'Tax Evasion and Social Justice', held at the War Museum, a block away from the government district of downtown Athens. In his speech, he presented his case for a wholly new, politically independent tax agency. This agency, according to his proposal, would handle all revenue – from taxes, customs offices and social insurance contributions – and would have the authority to shape the rules and regulations pertinent to tax administration, to perform audits, to impose and collect fines and to engage in arbitration in contested cases.

It was a radical proposal, based on the judgement that the existing apparatus is so rotten as to be unreformable and that a new tax administration has to be rebuilt *ex nihilo*. But these constructive ideas were not what dominated public debate the next day. What drew the flak was Spinellis's reference to widespread corruption among tax officials, which he used as an argument to show that the existing mechanisms could not be reformed piecemeal. The former general secretary mentioned, in particular, what was known in tax administration circles as the 4-4-2 system, whereby a tax fine of €100 was typically divvied up under the table to net the taxpayer a 40 per cent discount in the amount payable, with another 40 going to the tax auditor for his 'services' and only 20 ending up in the state treasury. He also talked about the practice of paying a cut to the tax auditor involved in cases where the government offered sizeable tax rebates to a taxpayer. Spinellis said the rate of the kickback was typically 8 per cent, only to be corrected by another panel member, Nikos Lekkas, the head of planning and auditing of the tax police, who said that the rate had been increased to 10 per cent.

The revelations caused uproar – much of it hypocritical in the extreme – and led to another investigation by the Office of the Financial Prosecutor. They also produced an indignant response from the tax officials' union, which sued Spinellis for slander. The relationship of the union leadership with the former general secretary and his band of wired warriors had never been warm. The old guard viewed the GSIS team and its innovations 'the way the Indians used to view the train', as Professor Tatsos puts it. Spinellis' reaction came via his Twitter account, through which he called on citizens to send in personal testimony of corrupt practices by tax officials so that he could use them in his defence. This case, too, was still pending at the time this book went to press.

According to Babis Nikolakopoulos, president of the tax officials' union, Spinellis' attack was a smokescreen to cover up his own failure and that of the political leadership of the Finance Ministry over the years to simplify tax legislation and to streamline tax administration. This failure, in his view, is not just a matter of incompetence. 'There is no political will to combat tax evasion, because there is a whole system that is served by lax enforcement, lack of transparency and corruption,' he tells me. Thus, as he explains, tax officials are left to bear the brunt of public anger in tax offices across the country for the avalanche of taxes and the countless hours of waiting that taxpayers have to endure, which are the direct cause of the wilful inertia of their political superiors.

This gets to the heart of the impasse. Both Spinellis and Theocharis told me they had no complaints about the commitment of the political leadership to crack down on tax evasion, and that the problem started at the plumbing level, when the time came for the officials on the ground to implement the policy priorities of the leadership. Part of this was down to the failure of the leadership to follow up on these priorities on an operational level. But as Theocharis puts it, 'the issue of political will that is continually talked about is often brought up with intent to deceive, to hide the real issue', which, according to him, is the inability of the existing apparatus to get the job done. Professor Tatsos concurs wearily: 'I have seen politicians who wanted things to change, fought hard and achieved nothing.'

Talk to a union leader like Nikolakopoulos and other tax officials, on the other hand, and you get the reverse picture. His is a world in which overburdened and underpaid officials have long advocated tax and tax administration reform, to free up auditors to do actual auditing, instead of wasting their time settling claims and being yelled at in tax offices. Their proposals keep going nowhere, they say, because those at the top are unwilling to change a system that works well for them and their political clients, if not for the financial well-being of the state.

The sad fact is that both sides have a point: in a system of governance where every government reshuffle is tantamount to regime change and everything begins anew, ministers and general secretaries have proved unwilling or unable to simplify the self-contradictory monstrosity that is the tax system and to shake up tax enforcement. But all too many tax officials have been more than happy to swim in the murky waters their superiors left behind, and union leaders have shown little inclination to make examples of the corrupt in employee ranks.

In fact, put on the defensive by widespread criticism and angry at deep wage cuts that have reduced their take-home pay by more than 40 per cent since 2009, the tax officials' union has become increasingly hostile to reform initiatives. In February 2012 union members tried to prevent colleagues from participating in exams for a new, specialized auditors' body – another Sisyphean pursuit of reformers through the years – the creation of which they opposed, clashing with riot police in the process. When the European Commission's Task Force for Greece, offering technical assistance among other areas in tax administration, came to the country, the federation of tax officials' unions refused to meet with its members, arguing that they would not collaborate with foreign occupiers.

Professor Tatsos, veteran of umpteen committees on tax reform, aborted efforts to upgrade the skill set of the ministry's auditors and other stories of white knights falling into black holes, paints a revealing picture of a machine that has taken on a life of its own and that sucks the life out of all who serve it. As he tells it, since exams were instituted in the 1990s for the hiring of public employees, Greece's best and brightest out of those who chose to go into public service tended to prefer the Finance Ministry, because it offered salaries way above anything on offer elsewhere in government service. 'These fine minds are wasted in a place where there is no strategic thinking, where no one sees the bigger picture and fresh minds are not allowed to contribute meaningfully until they reach a certain level in the hierarchy, which takes twenty years,' he explains. 'By that time, they have lost the ability to think, to process data. Young people get buried in the system.'

This bureaucratic abomination, which cannot be sidestepped, and which so far has swallowed up or spat out anyone who has attempted to reconstruct it, is creaking dangerously in the Age of the Memorandum. Tax evasion is as prevalent as it ever was, and the inelastic needs of the government for revenue are being met by violating some of what Tatsos calls 'the most basic tenets of taxation'. 'There is retroactive taxation, we are taxing gross instead of net income, we are repealing elementary tax exemptions, in general we are ignoring taxpayers' ability to pay,' he points out. 'We are doing this in a panic, and we will pay for it.'

On 7 November 2012, as part of the package of cuts and reforms demanded by Greece's creditors in order to release a mammoth €31.5 billion tranche of the second bailout, the government led by Antonis Samaras created the new post of permanent general secretary for revenue in the Ministry of Finance. It was the post that Greece had pledged to create, after much haggling and no little prodding from the troika, when it had agreed to its second bailout in February of that year.

According to the relevant statutes, the person chosen for this crucial job – by the cabinet, following the recommendation of the Minister of Finance, for a five-year term that can be renewed only once – must be someone of 'recognized stature', preferably with a postgraduate degree in tax administration, with extensive experience in tax affairs (preferably in the private sector) and the management of large organizations, and with a knowledge of foreign languages. The job contract includes quantitative and qualitative performance targets, both for the whole five-year term and for each successive year. Failure to meet these targets can result in dismissal. Success in surpassing them will mean a bonus, in the form of a percentage of the additional revenue collected.

The responsibilities of the office include the formation of the annual strategic plan for public revenue, the setting of qualitative and quantitative targets for the tax offices under its supervision, the evaluation of these units based on these targets and the dismissal of those in charge of them if they fail to meet them. In addition, the new permanent secretary has increased authority to make legislative and administrative recommendations to the minister on matters impinging upon his area of competence, to collect taxes owed, to move funds between tax offices as he or she sees fit, to take measures – including disciplinary action – against corruption within the tax agency and to organize training and specialization programmes for tax officials. Significantly, the secretary is forbidden from sharing information about which individuals or businesses are being audited, even with the Finance Minister.

On paper at least, it looked like a meaningful reform. If all went according to plan, the permanent secretary would be someone eminently qualified. He would enjoy a broad mandate and considerable freedom of movement. Combined with the reorganization and drastic downsizing of Greece's over-extended network of tax offices, it was hoped that whoever filled the new post would lead a quiet revolution in Greeks' relations to their tax responsibilities.

In January 2013, immediately after the Christmas holiday period, it was announced that the first permanent secretary for revenue would be Haris Theocharis. It was a heartening sign for the reformist camp. Theocharis, who would also retain control over GSIS, was clearly qualified, and chosen over candidates with far better party political connections. But the hostile briefings against him, even from within the government camp, began from day one. More significantly, despite renewed pressure from the troika, the government continued to resist the surrender of competences – including, vitally, control over the tax police – to the new office. A high-ranking member of the government anonymously told the press in March 2013 they were concerned whether giving this much power to 'an unelected person' was 'consistent with the democratic ethos' – the ethos which perennially allowed politicians to use the tax authorities to protect clients and corner their enemies.[10]

This has been a trend since the beginning of the Great Crisis: whenever it came time to implement what looked good on paper, the political system never missed a chance to disappoint. Spinellis, for one, is not optimistic. 'We committed ourselves to creating this post in January [2012]. Why did it take nine months for it to be enshrined in law? It is a worrisome sign,' he says.

In a country where tax evasion remains widespread and the well-connected still believe they are above the law, it will take a person of extraordinary skill, courage and integrity to succeed in this extremely sensitive role. Even that, in fact, may not be enough. The political system will need to accept that any short-term gains stemming from the ability to influence the tax police will be reduced to rubble by the tidal wave of public rage that will engulf everything if some small measure of tax justice is not, finally, seen to prevail.

Spinellis these days is devoting most of his time to his students at the Athens University of Economics and Business. Yet he has not entirely left the political fray. As we are walking into class, he points out a notice on the wall. It is a statement from one of the extreme left student groups, berating him for taking their picture as they forcibly prevented the holding of elections at the university for a new governing council mandated by higher education re-form law passed in 2011. 'Students' belonging to the leftist group had invaded the classroom where he teaches that day, abused him verbally and threatened him with violence. A student from his class tells me he is a good teacher, but dismissively places him in the 'them' category – those belonging to the system, both because of his term in the Ministry of Finance and because he supports the implementation of the higher education reform (discussed in chapter 10).

In class, which is nearly 100-strong, he is his usual mild-man-nered self, though not averse to throwing out those who are provocatively not paying attention. The subject is Java program-ming, so, as far as I'm concerned, he could be speaking Aramaic. Yet there is a lot of student participation. I notice him handing out little pieces of paper to those who answer questions. One of the students tells me these are pieces of code, given as a reward for correct answers. 'They write the sequence somewhere on a website I've set up and earn points for the class,' Spinellis tells me, geekily gleeful. 'Since I started doing it, a lot more hands are going up.'

Computer code is not all he's trying to get people involved in. Back when he was still at the Ministry of Finance, he had started talking to people about creating a citizens' movement against corruption. Once he returned to civilian life, he lost little time in pursuing his idea.

The result was www.teleiakaipavla.gr, a website that chronicles corruption across the country, through reports by citizens who write of their experiences, not only with the tax authorities, but other well-known loci of public sector malfeasance – city planning offices, health and safety inspectors, insurance funds and, above all, public hospitals. The reports do not name names, but they say where the incident occurred, what the issue was, how much was requested as a bribe and how much was given. There is also a 'good news' segment, where people send in accounts of positive experiences they have had in dealing with the public services. It is telling of the low expectations Greeks have developed over the years that most of the 'good news' refers to doctors or officials who refused to accept a bribe – i.e. it is 'news' when a public employee turns out not to be corrupt. 'We plan to expand it to identify places that give out receipts and places that don't,' he tells me.

Initiatives like this are essential if Greece is to become a normal country when it comes to taxation and public administration. But outside pressure can only do so much. It is only when politicians feel public opinion breathing down their necks that they will be forced to make good on the reforms that they have passed under duress. It is only when consumers make it clear that they will not pay for services without a receipt and those audited refuse to settle under the table that things will change on the ground.

Haris Theocharis will have a critical part to play in rebuilding the public's shattered trust in the tax system and those who run it. Without a minimum level of trust, tax evasion will remain the dominant strategy for too many Greeks. Such trust, Theocharis insisted to me, can only be built gradually, with setbacks and errors along the way. 'One of our biggest problems is that we have a Platonic ideal of how things should be, and we reject anything that anyone proposes that falls short of that,' he says. 'We must learn to take small steps forward.'

Crucial to rebuilding a sense of fair play – a 'tax conscience', as it is commonly referred to in Greece – is cracking down on tax evasion by the rich and powerful. New laws passed since 2010 have made it harder to shift profits to low-tax jurisdictions, while technological improvements have upgraded the methods for targeting companies and individuals engaging in large-scale evasion. But investigations into the finances of individuals on the Lagarde List were still progressing very slowly in 2013, as were audits of the 54,000 transfers of deposits abroad by taxpayers between 2009 and 2011.

Critics also accused Theocharis of buckling under external pressure when, in August 2013, he intervened in a major case involving transactions with intermediate companies based in tax havens by one of Greece's most politically well-connected firms. The tax authorities had investigated the case and imposed a record fine well into nine figures. The Secretary of Revenue was accused of issuing an administrative circular specifically to absolve the company of wrongdoing. In truth, the problem lay in the relevant law itself, which compensated for years of inaction against corporate tax avoidance with draconian clauses of questionable constitutionality, and beyond Theocharis's competence to fix.

The role of technology will continue to be critical in the years to come. Theocharis says that these days, any lingering resistance in the ranks of tax officials to the digitization of tax administration has been 'defeated by reality': 'The lines are so long, the people needing to be served are so many, that whenever we tell officials that something can be done electronically, they jump at it.'

What is proving more of a challenge is educating the public. In 2012, for the first time, all tax statements over €12,000 except for those of pensioners had to be submitted electronically. In 2013 not even pensioners were excluded. Theocharis speaks to the media as often as possible and is active on Twitter, trying to explain the new way of doing things and minimize the frictions of adjustment (as well as explaining the bewildering succession of new regulations that the ministry keeps producing).

In addition, despite many years and large amounts in European structural funds, the tax service is still far from having a full picture of the income and assets of each individual taxpayer. Local land registries are still not computerized, while a national land registry is still being compiled and will not be completed for years to come. That means that an auditor who wants to check whether a taxpayer owns more property than he or she has declared would have to contact all 258 local land registries with handwritten notes, and wait for a reply which may be indefinitely delayed.

On these and many other fronts, the battle to ensure that all Greeks are equal before the tax laws will continue in the years to come.* It has become an existential one for the Greek state; if tax evasion is not brought under control and government revenue does not increase to normal Eurozone member-state levels, its ability to provide services befitting a developed country will be decisively undermined. In some ways, as we will see in the next chapter, it already has been.

---

* That battle, however, will take place without Haris Theocharis. In June 2014, as this book went to press, he was ominously forced to resign, citing – like Spinellis before him – 'personal reasons'. Government officials made little effort to hide the fact that he was in reality being let go, in clear contravention of the spirit of the new position. As a non-political head tax collector, he was an easy choice to become the scapegoat for the government's poor showing in the European elections.

3

The Torn Safety Net

The Greek state's shocking failure to collect taxes did little to restrain its spending urges. Between 2001 and 2006, government spending as a percentage of GDP in Greece remained slightly below the Eurozone average. Between 2007 and 2009 it exceeded it, reaching, in the last of these years, 54 per cent, as against 51.2 per cent in the Eurozone as a whole. Meanwhile, in the same year, its tax-to-GDP ratio was a mere 28.9 per cent of GDP, one of the lowest in the euro area.[1]

In the heady days before 2010, the state's eye-popping inadequacy in enforcing the tax laws, and the yawning deficits this produced, were papered over with public borrowing. Enough people benefited from tax evasion of various kinds and there was enough money sloshing around for public sector jobs and social benefits that there was no real pressure for fiscal house-cleaning.

The Age of the Memorandum has changed this irrevocably. Especially after the first few months, when the troika got wise and stopped believing that part of the agreed-upon fiscal retrenchment would come from cracking down on tax evasion, the Greek government had to take extreme measures, both on the revenue and on the spending side, in order to meet its deficit targets. This meant that the free-riding and the free benefits of some, which could no longer be financed in the bond markets, would now be paid for by squeezing the rest.

What a squeeze it has been. The Greek public sector has gone through a draconian austerity programme, perhaps the harshest of any advanced economy ever. In 2009 it ended the year with a budget deficit of 15.6 per cent of GDP, or, in absolute numbers,

€36 billion. The primary deficit alone — without taking into account debt-servicing payments — was €24 billion, over 10 per cent of GDP. In 2012 the budget deficit had fallen to 6 per cent of GDP while the primary deficit was a mere 1.5 per cent of GDP. In 2013 Greece was on track to post a primary surplus. According to projections made by the IMF in October 2012, the cyclically adjusted balance of Greek government finances — that is, the fiscal position as seen when taking the recession out of the equation — will have improved by 17.5 per cent of GDP by the end of 2013 compared to where it was in 2009.[2] No other economy, either advanced or emerging, comes remotely close.

The size of this adjustment is all the more remarkable if one considers that Greece's GDP has been shrinking rapidly in this period — by a total of almost a fifth in the period from 2010–12 alone and by about a quarter from 2008–13. In the projections of the initial Memorandum, Greece's output was forecast to fall by 4 per cent in 2010 and 2.5 per cent in 2011, while returning to positive growth of 1.1 per cent in 2012, when unemployment was projected to peak, at 15.3 per cent. In fact, in the summer of 2012 the unemployment rate passed the 25 per cent mark. For the year as a whole, Greece's economy shrank another 6.4 per cent, and it was projected to shrink by around 4 per cent more in 2013.

This, then, has been an adjustment programme that has exacted a heavy price. To give some examples: pensions — not high for most of the elderly to begin with — have been cut twelve times between 2010 and 2012; successive VAT rises have brought the standard rate up to 23 per cent, tied for third highest in the EU; repeated fuel tax hikes have turned Greece from one of the countries with the cheapest petrol in the EU to the third most expensive one (data from August 2012); extraordinary taxes upon extraordinary taxes have been levied on personal income and property. The list goes on.

Greece's return to economic reality after its long holiday from History was never going to be easy. It did not, however, have to be this brutal. The failure to tackle tax evasion was the biggest factor. But the way spending was cut also exposed the dangerous dogmatism of Greece's official lenders, as well as a domestic political class which neither had the will nor knew the way to build a more effective, slimmed-down state apparatus. Instead, we have witnessed rushed last-minute cuts to achieve deficit targets demanded by the troika on pain of cutting off funding, cuts that have struck indiscriminately, have often destabilized vital government agencies, disrupted services and have seemingly been guided above all by the doctrine of not hurting one's clients – be they powerful oligarchs in the media, construction and energy, employees of parliament, unionized workers at the former natural monopolies, or influential professions like lawyers, engineers and journalists.

In an influential 2009 paper,[3] Greek economists Theodore Pelagidis and Michael Mitsopoulos write of 'numerous rent-seeking groups' that 'curtail competition in the product and services markets, increase red tape and administrative burdens, and actively seek to establish opacity in all administrative and legal processes in order to form an environment in which they will be able to increase the rents they extract'.[4] These rent-seeking groups, which oppose all efforts, each in their own sphere, to open up the economy, are called 'Vikings' because they have been raiding an increasingly defenceless Greek state and walking away with ever-increasing spoils.

The most vulnerable members of society did not feature in the cosy arrangements between the 'Vikings' and their allies in politics and the media. Already before the crisis, the outsiders – households of underpaid private sector employees with children, the long-term unemployed, those without health insurance – were left largely to their own devices. But strong family networks and a healthy economy meant that they always had something to fall back on – an undeclared job at the family business until some other opportunity turned up, some pocket money from one's parents and grandparents, medical insurance under another family member's plan.

Since 2010, as the official welfare state has been torn to shreds, these informal networks of support have also been battered by austerity and recession. Nowhere has the cost of these developments been more terrible than in health care.

I met Polydoros Yannibas as he was coming out of his first session of chemotherapy, at the oncology wing of 'Sotiria' public hospital near downtown Athens. It was a Wednesday afternoon – the time of the week set aside by doctors, nurses and secretarial staff of the oncology wing since June 2012 to offer free care to uninsured cancer patients.

I had already got to chatting with Polydoros's brother, George, who was waiting outside the chemo ward to pick him up. George had told me that Polydoros had been a football star in his youth. He had played for Apollon Athinon, a historic Athenian football team that has recently, like most of the country, fallen on hard times.

I asked George how Polydoros ended up depending on charity to get treatment for a life-threatening disease. George explained that his brother had worked for a while in the public sector, at a job that came with generous benefits, which he had taken the unusual step of quitting. He had started his own business, which went bust a long time ago. A few years back, he had fallen out with his girlfriend with whom he was running a small eatery in the downtown district of Pangrati. The business being in her name, she had sold it and he claims he had been cut out of the deal.

In February 2012, in his late sixties and without health insurance, he began experiencing pain in his left arm. He visited an orthopaedic doctor, who gave him an X-ray, concluded the problem was in the nape of his neck and prescribed a course of anti-inflammatory drugs. The pain got worse. He went back to the doctor in early summer, who insisted on his original diagnosis and prescribed swimming in the sea, massages and more, heavier anti-inflammatories. By the end of August, the pain still not having subsided, his brother took him to get a CT scan, which revealed a tumour in his left lung, which had been growing for months. It had eaten away at his ribs and was now putting pressure on his spinal column. If it had been left untreated a little while longer, he would have been paralysed.

In September, Polydoros Yannibas began a course of radiation treatment at a private hospital. The doctor who oversaw the treatment acted as guarantor: if his patient was unable to pay for the sessions, he would pay instead. Not having paid in enough in social insurance contributions for a full pension, Polydoros had applied since April for a basic old-age benefit for the uninsured that included medical cover, but it had yet to come through. Complicating things further, the doctor told them radiation would not be enough; chemotherapy would also be required, the cost of which would range up to €10,000 – way beyond George and Polydoros's means.

Through a family friend, they found out about the social health centre at Hellenikon, in the southern suburbs of Athens. Set up in December 2011, in the space of a few months it had become a kind of coordination centre for the rapidly expanding network of voluntary health-care initiatives. It offered in-house services, from examinations to free drugs, to whomever it was able to. More complicated cases that could not be handled there were referred to hospitals, diagnostic centres and private doctors who had made commitments to pitch in.

That is what happened with Polydoros. His brother went down to Hellenikon, showed them the necessary paperwork – documents demonstrating lack of funds and the biopsy results – and got a reference to visit the voluntary cancer clinic set up in 'Sotiria' hospital. 'The system is completely broken,' George tells me. Motioning around us, he says: 'This thing here, it's like a light guiding us.'

When Polydoros came out of the chemo ward, he looked tired and frail. His eyes were moist, his hands full of blisters. They had to leave quickly, but he was eager to talk, so he invited me to his place the next day, in the district of Vyronas on the foothills of mount Hymettus.

Konstantinos Syrigos, the head of the oncology wing at 'Sotiria' and the man responsible for setting up the volunteer initiative, became aware at the beginning of 2012 of the growing number of cancer patients who had no access to care – either in the form of exams, treatment or necessary medicine. 'People started coming to us saying, "I am sick, please do what you can, but I have no insurance" and my hands were tied,' he tells me. 'We also had patients who had started treatment and who would then disappear. When we called them, they said their insurance booklets were no longer valid.'

Most among the fifty or so cancer patients benefiting from the initiative at 'Sotiria' when I visited were men and women who a few years ago had belonged squarely to the middle class. Many owned small businesses or were otherwise self-employed, people with strong families, attached to their community.

Being self-insured became a trap when the crisis hit. In straitened economic circumstances, they were forced to choose between paying their staff or paying dues to the insurance fund of the self-employed and many elected to forgo the latter. When they were forced to shut up shop during the recession, their unpaid dues came back to haunt them: without an insurance clearance certificate, they could not apply for indigent status, a classification offering basic coverage. Indigent status was also not available to sacked private sector employees who had any sort of property to their name (far too many, given the extremely high incidence of homeownership in Greece), even if they derived no income from the property because they lived in it. They, too, were left out in the cold.

'What shocked us, as doctors, was that for many of them, their cancer was not their first priority,' Syrigos says. He is an imposing man not given to sentimentality, but it is clear that what he has seen in the last few months has deeply affected him. 'You would think that people diagnosed with cancer would quit everything and devote themselves to dealing with it. But many of the patients we've seen had been aware of their disease for months and were doing nothing about it. They were too busy trying to feed themselves and their kids.'

Beyond the volunteer work of the 'Sotiria' staff, pharmaceutical companies and even private citizens donated medical equipment and drugs. I asked Dr Syrigos whether they were looking for a bigger sponsor, in order to expand the programme. His reply was intriguing: 'This is a major dilemma. On the one hand, we know we are in it for the long haul, so we are looking for a more durable solution, through a permanent sponsor. On the other hand, if we are able to offer such a solution, outside the official institutions, then there will no longer be an urgency in government to solve it officially.' Such an official solution has proved elusive.

The government cannot forgive the debts of those who owe money to their insurance funds across the board so that they can acquire indigent status. This, at a time when the credibility of the pensions system is in tatters, would kill off any incentive the insured have to continue paying their dues. Already mostly bankrupt, Greece's social insurance funds cannot afford further revenue losses.

Later that day, I'm walking around the ward where the clinic is held with Vangelis Sarris, one of the physicians who volunteer their time, a solicitous young man with a trimmed beard and an earnest manner. A few people are undergoing chemotherapy or radiation treatment, while anxious relatives are waiting outside, consulting with the doctors or chatting with the chirpy secretary, who helps relieve some of the tension.

'When Mr Syrigos came to us with the idea, all the doctors of the oncology wing, without exception, gladly volunteered. So did many from the nursing and the secretarial staff,' Sarris tells me. The clinic begins at 2.30 in the afternoon and lasts until the last patient leaves. Beyond cancer specialists, the oncology wing includes dermatologists, psychiatrists and others who are also actively taking part. There are even collaborators outside the hospital, like the radiotherapy unit of Attikon university hospital.

At some point in my conversation with Syrigos, when I referred to the initiative at 'Sotiria' (the name means 'salvation') as philanthropic, he cut me off. 'This is not a philanthropic effort,' he insisted, brooking no disagreement. 'What I am doing is part of my obligation. Philanthropy is something that goes beyond your obligation. These people have a right to be treated; they have a chronic illness for which they are not at all to blame. A civilized society must take care of its most vulnerable members. It commits a crime if it allows people who can be treated to die.'

Dr Sarris makes a similar point when I ask him what motivated him to participate in the clinic. 'I cannot help people pay their debts or put food on the table. But I *can* help them with their health problem, and I consider it my duty as a doctor to do this. A doctor is not someone who only offers his services when he is paid.'

Another doctor with a noble conception of his calling and the sense of moral urgency to put his principles into practice is Dr George Vichas, the cardiologist who in December 2011 started the Hellenikon social health centre, through which Polydoros Yannibas was referred to 'Sotiria'. Throughout that year, Vichas had been monitoring a disturbing trend similar to the one Syrigos had noticed: many of the patients in his IKA surgery in the mornings (IKA is Greece's largest pension and health insurance fund) would stop visiting for long periods, and then would reappear to tell him they had lost their insurance cover.

'I remember one case in particular that really shook me up,' he tells me, sitting in the paediatrics surgery of the health centre in Hellenikon on a cataclysmic night of pouring rain and howling winds. 'It was a man with a very serious heart condition. I had not seen him in a really long time and he had come to tell me he could no longer visit me. This was a person who needed regular observation and daily medication. When he came to me after three months without having taken his medicine, he was at death's door.'

Before the crisis, he says, it was very uncommon to find people who could not get access to basic health care. Those who lost their jobs could find others that offered health insurance. Until they did, they could almost always depend on family support to pay for their medical needs. The rare cases that fell through the cracks 'belonged to a different category – they were substance abusers and so on', he points out. His heart patient, by contrast, was an engineer, with a wife and small children.

Galvanized by such cases, Vichas went to the mayor of Hellenikon with the idea for a social health centre for the uninsured and the poor. The mayor immediately consented, handing over use of a building near the old US military base and agreeing to pay the utility bills. By December, the centre was up and running, with seven doctors and fifteen citizen volunteers helping with administrative matters, the small in-house pharmacy and anything else that needed seeing to.

When I met him, eleven months later, the operation had dramatically expanded: it included thirty in-house doctors, eleven dentists, eight or nine psychologists and seven reflexologists. The pharmacy had grown considerably in size, thanks to anonymous contributions (the policy is that no one can advertise their donations and no one can contribute money). Ten doctors had agreed to receive patients referred from the centre at their private practice, as had one private hospital, two maternity clinics and over twenty-five diagnostic centres across Athens.

Demand for the centre's services has gone through the roof. As Vichas told me, between December 2011 and August 2012 they registered 1,200 doctor visits. In September–October it went up to 1,300 visits; in November, when we spoke, in a single month it reached more than 700. The wave of need was rising by the day, and would continue to: twelve months later, in November 2013,

1,463 people visited the Hellenikon social health centre.

These astonishing numbers were not caused only by the burgeoning ranks of the uninsured, which a top government healthcare official estimated at over 3 million in the autumn of 2013.[5] 'In the last month,' Vichas says, 'we have been getting visits also from people who have insurance, but who cannot afford the new co-payment levels. This was not part of our original mission, but we held a general meeting about this twenty days ago and we decided that we could not turn away pensioners who get 300 euros a month and cannot afford to pay for the medicine they need.'

The bespectacled cardiologist, whose mild expression hides an undercurrent of quiet indignation, warns of difficult days to come. 'The coming winter and the period after that will be very rough,' he predicts. 'We are living through a humanitarian catastrophe.' But there is also a note of hope amidst the ruins of the welfare state. 'The only way out for Greek society is for solidarity to spread everywhere. It's not just about supporting each other. It is also a vital element in the effort to overcome what is happening to us. If we allow ourselves to despair, we become instruments and we cannot fight back. In that sense, what is going on here in the social centre makes me very hopeful for the future.'

Polydoros Yannibas started playing football without his parents knowing. Back in the early 1960s, Greek football was still not a professional sport. When his father caught him playing he would try to beat his notion of sense into him. It was to no avail: at sixteen, Polydoros joined the lowly neighbourhood team in Vyronas. 'The team president was the neighbourhood coffee-house proprietor. The general secretary was the local barber and the general manager was the local taxi driver,' he recalls, nostalgic amusement lining his worn features.

Though he was a scrawny kid who played in boots two sizes too big, Polydoros quickly stood out. He was soon spotted by 'fishermen' – as football scouts were known back then – from

Apollon Athinon. One summer evening less than a year after his debut, a formally dressed visitor arrived at the family pastry shop. He introduced himself as a representative of Apollon and, with Polydoros watching anxiously from the back of the shop, told his parents that their son was wanted in the big leagues. Polydoros's mother, whom he describes as a fearsome woman of Cretan origins, initially dismissed the man. But he was able to win her over, to the point where she browbeat the president of the local team, the coffee-house proprietor, to consent to the transfer, with the aid of a kitchen knife that she thrust menacingly into a chopping board in front of him.

Polydoros played as a left full-back with Apollon from 1963 to 1974. He developed fast, the demands of football multiplied and he quickly abandoned any plans he (or rather, his parents) had for a higher education. He played for the national youth side and, later, for the national armed forces side. He was even selected for the men's national team, but never got to play. The closest he got was a game against Wales: he had put on his jersey, had received his instructions and he was about to go onto the field, when the coach took him aside and told him to change back. '"You were done in by the powers of darkness," the coach told me,' he remembers. It was the custom then for the national squad to be picked almost exclusively from the dominant Athenian teams, which did not include Apollon, and in those days there were no substitutions. 'After that, I said I did not want to be selected again,' he says.

While still a footballer, the person who had arranged his transfer to Apollon got Polydoros an office job at PPC, the state electricity monopoly. The job paid 1,800 drachmas a month, compared to a 1,000 drachma bonus that players got only when the team won (they received no fixed salary). But the new work environment did not agree with Polydoros. 'I remember in the first week, there was a group of guys in their late twenties to early thirties, and they were discussing when they were going to retire. That really disappointed me,' he tells me. 'There was a kind of infectious laziness that I could not live with.' Around the same time that he stopped playing football, he also left PPC, quitting a job from which he could not be fired and which offered generous health-care and retirement benefits.

Polydoros preferred the adventure of starting his own business to the mind-numbing security of a lifetime job in the public sector. His chosen field was kitchenware, imported from Italy. He built up a network of saleswomen who went door to door selling these items and business was going well. But then, in the mid-eighties, as he was increasing the quantities imported to hold them as inventory, a law was passed imposing major financial burdens on importers. 'This is how the government destroys small business. It's still doing it today,' he tells me bitterly. He could not afford the new levy; he had to fold.

To add insult to injury, he was audited, and, though he claims they found nothing out of order, they asked him for a bribe in order to clear the case. 'I have always been against giving or receiving bribes, so I refused,' he says. Things got so heated that he beat up the tax collector and even held him at the edge of a fourth floor veranda threatening to push him off. The final verdict in the case, six years after it was initiated in 1984, came down hard on Polydoros. He did not settle his debts with the taxman until 2004.

After he shut down his kitchenware business, even though he had not reached the contributions required to retire, Polydoros did not contribute one cent more to the insurance fund of the self-employed. His activities were either part of the informal economy, or he was an invisible partner in them. In the nineties he devoted himself to illegal bookmaking related to horse racing. He claims he made money from this, but that he spent it all over the place instead of saving up.

At the end of the decade, with what was left, he decided to open a canteen, along with his live-in girlfriend (his one marriage had ended in divorce). In keeping with his allergy to the formal economy and the state, he kept his name off the books and signed it over to her. It was a decision he would come to regret.

A few years later, with the canteen doing well in the time of the Athens Olympics boom, her twenty-something son came to work at the shop. Polydoros claims that, against his wishes, she put the young man in charge of the cash register and that, a little while later, he caught him stealing. When he told her this, she sided with her son. This, he says, was the beginning of a slow and steady deterioration in their relationship, which resulted in her taking over the canteen without paying him his share, him cashing a cheque with her signature without her knowledge, and their dispute ending up in court. 'I realized how stupid I was, trusting in people, in one's word of honour instead of what's written down on paper,' Polydoros says. 'With me, when I said something, that was it – there was no going back on it. But others were not like that.'

Meanwhile, getting on in years and knowing that he had done little to provide for his old age, he bought a private health insurance policy in 2005. About a year before he found out about the cancer, however, he let it expire, because, money-wise, 'that's when the real problems were beginning'. He and his brother George owned a property on Marathonos Avenue in the eastern suburbs of Athens that they had rented to a local shopkeeper, an arrangement that in pre-crisis years brought in €3,000 a month. His brother also owned a bistro in Vyronas which added to the family income. In 2006 George had heart surgery at a private hospital. 'It was costly', Polydoros says, 'but we had no problem paying for it then.'

Greece's relentless recession put an end to their comfortable situation. The shop on Marathonos Avenue went under. After the business closed down, the brothers tried to sell the premises, but there was no interest. Meanwhile, traffic had plummeted at George's bistro and it was hanging on for dear life.

When I talked to him, Polydoros was expecting that the basic-pension-and-health-cover benefit that he had applied for would come through in the coming months. With it, he hoped to pay off the cost of the radiotherapy sessions and whatever further treatment his disease would require. But the cancer had advanced too far. In April 2013, he succumbed, another life needlessly cut short in the years of the torn safety net.

The Greek government lost control of health-care spending in the first decade of the twenty-first century – especially during the second half. By 2009 it had reached 9.9 per cent of GDP – above the OECD mean and up from 8.2 per cent of GDP in the year 2005.[6] Around two-fifths of this was private expenditure – a level among the highest in the developed world, which grew impressively throughout the decade in absolute numbers. According to a 2006 study,[7] of those two-fifths, about 30 per cent, or 12–13 per cent of total health spending, was spent outside the formal economy. These were cash payments beyond the reach of the tax authorities, which included the notorious *fakelakia* (the term means 'small envelope' in Greek): bribes to doctors to get good rooms in hospitals, faster service, or just extra fees under the table for surgeries and other procedures.

But it was *public* spending on health care that really exploded. Pharmaceutical expenditure, including medical supplies, by the state quadrupled from 2000–9, from €1.3 billion to €5.2 billion. Expenditure by public hospitals jumped from €3.9 billion in 2005 to €7 billion in 2009, while state spending on lab exams and diagnostic centres in the same period climbed from €1.6 to €2.6 billion annually.[8] Greeks had CT and MRI scans for breakfast (by far the most per capita in the OECD), along with far more antibiotics than was good for them. Greece was – and still is – the country with the greatest density of doctors in the developed world, though it is also extremely short on GPs and they are very unevenly distributed, in favour of urban centres and at the expense of the countryside. Public hospitals bought equipment at prices many times greater than they were sold in other EU countries, with no incentives to control costs. Behind all this excess stood the Greek state, paying for it all and asking few questions about the efficiency or the equity of its spending.

When the men of the troika came to town, they identified health care as a centrepiece of the effort to get government spending under control. Wielding their axe freely, they set hard budgetary constraints within which the country's public health-care system would now have to operate. As a result, by 2012 the government's health-care expenditure fell to 6 per cent of GDP (it was 6.7 per cent of GDP in 2009). At that time, in 2010, the country was already two years into a recession that the troika's unyielding austerity policies were about to make a whole lot steeper. GDP began to fall precipitously, which meant that the spending cuts required to meet the targets on health care grew inexorably.

Health insurance was the area most affected by the troika's insistence on deep cuts, combined with disastrous implementation of reforms on the Greek side. When ESY, Greece's version of the National Health Service, was being set up in 1983, the plan was for all health insurance funds to merge into a single body, as was happening at the time in Spain and Portugal. In typical fashion, the law that emerged was maimed by special interests and did not meet the expectations of those who designed it. A national system of health-care provision was created, but the so-called 'aristocratic funds' – those with more generous benefits, belonging to privileged sectors like the public utilities, the banks, the legal profession and others, the 'Vikings' of their day and ours – successfully resisted their integration into a single insurance entity. In subsequent years, more attempts were made to fulfil the original vision of a single health insurance fund, but none managed to overcome the concerted opposition of the privileged professional sectors and the doctors and health-care suppliers who benefited from their relationship to them – a relationship financially backed, often to a scandalous degree, by the government.

Greece's official creditors were not concerned about the political cost of clashing with these powerful groups. They forced the hand of the Papandreou government and, in early 2011, after nearly three decades of inertia, a law passed integrating the country's four largest funds, covering about 90 per cent of the insured, into a singly entity: EOPYY. But the way the old dream of a unified fund was realized guaranteed that it would turn into a nightmare.

Anastasios Philalithis (his family name means 'lover of truth'), professor of Social Medicine at the University of Crete, was a partisan in the original battle for the creation of a single insurance fund for health care. A Jordanian Greek with an MSc from the London School of Hygiene and Tropical Medicine and a PhD from the University of Athens, he was the main author of the preamble to the law setting up the Greek health service and a major player in health-care policy in the PASOK governments of the 1980s. So what did he think about the EOPYY experiment? 'The merged funds were heavily in debt. There was no business plan to make the new fund viable. Where was the money going to come from?' he asks.

The speed with which the new entity had to be created made a long period of administrative chaos inevitable. In a July 2013 report, the Inspector General of Public Administration wrote of a 'disheartening' situation in a regional EOPYY office consisting of 'huge volumes of files' filled with debts incurred by the insurance funds, which have 'flooded the agency's spaces' and which the minuscule staff, 'despite its seemingly superhuman efforts', cannot possibly process in time. The report noted that the particular EOPYY office had yet to process payments for suppliers of health services for the entire period between June 2010 and December 2011 – in total over 45,000 files. As far down the line as the summer of 2013, EOPYY still had no way of directly knowing if an individual insured by one of the funds merged into it was up to date on his contributions and hence eligible for compensation for services they had consumed. The new entity – more like a mega-broker than an insurance fund in its own right – started off with only forty staff and still, in late 2013, did not have its own HR department. Its salary processing was still handled by IKA, its biggest constituent fund, with a staff of thousands, which EOPYY paid for the service.

The initial plan was for the government to subsidize EOPYY at a rate of 0.6 per cent of GDP annually. This was low enough as it was, but it was soon revised downward to a paltry 0.4 per cent, with no consultation, in the search for last-minute spending cuts to mollify the troika on the eve of the second bailout. Kyriakos Souliotis, a member of the younger generation of Greek health economists and the vice-president of EOPYY until September 2012, is clear in his assessment of the circumstances in which the fund was conceived: 'in such a fiscally challenging time, such a project, though it is in the right direction, does not have the financial support it needs.'

This is putting it mildly: the 'primary' deficit of EOPYY in 2012, its first year of operation, was €1.3 billion (during that year most of the 'aristocratic' funds were also dragged kicking and screaming into merging with it). At the same time, EOPYY inherited from the four merged funds aggregate obligations of €3.5 billion incurred between 2009 and 2011.[9] This tsunami of debt was only likely to increase further, not just because of administrative inability to cope but also due to the equalization of benefits across the different merged funds. This had meant, for example, that farmers, who had for years paid contributions of €15 a month, suddenly got access to top private clinics on the same terms as private employees insured by IKA, who had been paying in many times that amount.

The collapse of economic activity made a bad situation a lot worse. Skyrocketing unemployment and falling wages meant that revenues from insurance contributions dwindled. In addition to the months-long delays in payments that it caused, this huge debt meant that the fund 'lost much of its negotiating powers vis-à-vis private providers regarding prices', Souliotis says.

The troika-mandated cap on government health-care spending has provided strong incentives for cost control. But these have not been translated into well-designed structural reforms focusing on cutting waste and protecting the worst-off. The knee-jerk manner in which EOPYY was created, with little care given to fortifying it with monopsony muscle, or to establishing rules for rationing benefits according to cost and medical effectiveness, has prevented it from assuming the curative role it should have. 'There is still no control over where the money goes. EOPYY lacks the necessary technocratic tools to restrain spending in the right way,' Philalithis says.

More generally in post-Memorandum health care, cuts occurred like acts of God, without rhyme or reason. For every case of wasteful spending trimmed through electronic auctions for medical supplies or better monitoring of prescriptions, there were hospitals left without basic supplies. 'These days, hospitals have closed budgets, which were set arbitrarily, without taking into account the number of patients cared for or anything else. The budget limits cannot be exceeded and this leads many hospitals to run out of money for buying necessary supplies halfway through a given month,' Syrigos, the 'Sotiria' oncologist, laments.

As a result of all this, for all the insured but especially for those insured under the new mega-fund, reform became a synonym of hardship. There were recurrent shortages of many pharmaceutical products, including medication vital for cancer patients and other chronically ill individuals. Pharmaceutical companies that were owed large sums, or that were paid in Greek government bonds that suffered a haircut in the first restructuring of Greece's debt, or that found the new price controls too stringent, simply stopped providing certain drugs to the Greek market. Doctors and pharmacists, who in normal times offered their services and products on credit and were then reimbursed by the insurance funds, now refused to do so, sometimes for weeks on end, invoking the ever-mounting levels of unpaid debts. People with chronic ailments had to pay upfront, often large sums they could ill-afford to part with, and then wait for EOPYY to conjure up the cash to reimburse *them*. This at a time when people have far less to spend out of pocket on health care compared to earlier times, were more keen to access publicly provided health care and were more likely to get sick, because of the well-documented adverse health effects of unemployment, job insecurity and loss of income.

But there is a light dimly visible on the horizon. Despite a slow start, the Samaras government has undertaken valiant efforts to fix the design flaws of EOPYY, settle its past debts and control current expenses, notably through a push to increase the prescription of cheap generic drugs (the share of the market in Greece is particularly low by European standards).

The country also, finally, has credible, detailed data on the costs of health care, thanks to a large extent to the efforts of Lykourgos Liaropoulos. A poor kid from the mountains of Arcadia who won a scholarship to attend Athens College, Greece's most elite private school, and then another one to study in the US in the early sixties ('the greatest decade the world has ever known', he tells me), this stout economist with the curt manner and the dry sense of humour has been around from the very beginning of the post-junta debates on health planning. He nevertheless retains his sanity.

This is a particularly impressive achievement if one considers that, as Greece's long-time health envoy to the OECD, he has fought an exhausting campaign of trench warfare with Ministry of Health officials since the early 2000s in order to get them to help compile the necessary data that would allow the country to conform with the OECD's System of Health Accounts. The SHA homogenizes statistical reporting on health-care spending across the OECD, allowing meaningful cross-country comparisons and better assessment of the effectiveness of health policies within each member state. After years of obstruction and indifference, of facing down officials who pulled numbers out of hats and of pushing ministers and general secretaries to get their act together, finally, with almost every other OECD member having completed the task, Liaropoulos and his team reached the promised land: in April 2013 they presented the Greek SHA and had it incorporated into the country's official statistics.

Having precise numbers will help Liaropoulos give concrete shape to the big idea that has been on his mind the last few years: national health insurance. At its core, it is about disconnecting access to health care from one's employment situation, a concept he developed by studying the economic, fiscal and human tragedy that was the pre-Obamacare US health-care system.

'It will be funded by general taxation,' he tells me, perhaps over-optimistically. 'Employee and employer contributions will be significantly lowered, which will make Greek business more competitive and increase GDP, which means a greater tax intake.' As he explains: 'Insurance is meant to act as a buffer in tough times. There is no logic to a system which leads you to lose your insurance when you lose your job during a recession.'

The professor thinks it will take a while for his idea to sink in, because of a combination of public resistance, intellectual laziness and administrative inertia (also, because currently there is nowhere near enough revenue available to fund it). But he believes it is a reform whose time has come. The one major precondition for its successful implementation, in his view, is the restructuring of the tax system to combat mass tax evasion. 'Only 1–2,000 households declare an income of over 100,000 euros in this country. This cannot go on,' he says. The point is clear: if this situation does not change, the state will have neither the money nor the inclination to pay for national health insurance, given that it would likely lead to redistribution not from the rich to the poor, but from honest taxpayers to tax cheats, including wealthy ones.

The loss of access to health care is the most blatant sign of the torn safety net. But the pain of austerity and recession is felt in many other ways as well.

In the backyard of KYADA, the City of Athens Homeless Shelter and Solidarity Centre on the corner of Piraeus and Sofokleous streets, people had begun gathering for the midday meal distribution – long lines of the hungry men and women of Athens, old and young, the perennially destitute as well as the until-recently well-to-do.

The shelter organizes two of the sessions, one at noon, attended mostly by Greeks, and one at five in the afternoon, attended largely by illegal immigrants as well as Greeks who are in trouble with the law, such as drug users. It is known that in the afternoon session personal information is less eagerly requested by the authorities. In between the two sessions, at around 3 p.m., the Archdiocese of Athens runs its own meal-provision service.

By the end of 2012, about 1,300 people attended the shelter's two daily meal services. Applications for the 'Social Grocery Shop', a programme run by the shelter in collaboration with a major supermarket chain that offers 200 poor households or individuals food for half a year, have shot up from 486 in the first six months of 2011 to 780 in the second half of 2012. At the main offices of KYADA there is also a storage room with donated food supplies which municipal employees say are never enough to cover growing needs, and a medical team offering basic care and some essential vaccinations. The in-house doctor prescribes medicine that can be procured a few blocks away at the KYADA-run 'Social Pharmacy', which is supplied through contributions by companies and private citizens.

'It is the hungry I am most worried about; that is the real emergency,' says George Apostolopoulos, the earnest, perpetually harried head of KYADA. 'There are unemployed people, pensioners, wage-earners whose wages have fallen dramatically, even public sector employees whose pay is docked to pay off bank loans.' There are even members of the upper class, from posh districts like Kifisia or Kolonaki, who attend the daily meal-provision services or who come to get food supplies, he says. Some of them tell their social circle that they are only getting the food to distribute it to the needy, ashamed to admit their predicament.

According to the latest data available from the Hellenic Statistical Authority[10] (to the extent that they can be trusted given the gaps between real and declared income in many Greeks' tax statements), 23.1 per cent of the population of Greece were at risk of poverty in 2012.[11] This was up from 19.7 per cent in 2009.

Childhood poverty is higher than the population average, at 26.9 per cent, up from 19.3 per cent in 2005. Inequality is also on the rise. The richest quintile of the population pulls in 6.6 times as much income as the bottom quintile. This makes Greece the second most unequal country in the EU.

Strikingly, more than half (52.1 per cent) of unemployed men are poor. This is a reflection, again, of the scandalous indifference of the Greek welfare state to the plight of its most vulnerable citizens. Unemployment benefit lasts for at most twelve months in Greece, and it is not for everyone. Employees who get fired before they have paid in a sufficient amount in contributions to the unemployment insurance fund, undeclared workers and full-time employees officially showing up as contract workers so that employers are spared insurance costs, are all ineligible. In mid-2013 less than one in ten of the 1.35 million unemployed Greeks received unemployment insurance. On the orders of the troika, as part of the deal for Greece's second bailout in February 2012, those who do get it in its basic form receive only €360 a month.

If a year passes and no job has been found – something that is increasingly becoming the norm in the Age of the Memorandum[12] – the state has very little to offer. There is a twelve-month, means-tested unemployment assistance benefit for the long-term un-employed, for what it's worth. What it *is* worth is €200 (it has remained unchanged since 2003). In pre-crisis years, eligibility was limited to those with an annual income of less than €5,000.[13] Unsurprisingly, in 2009 only 1,420 people received it. In January 2012, with long-term unemployment rampant, the income criterion was raised to €12,000. In November 2012 the age range of eligibility was expanded to include those between 20 and 45 years old, though the income cut-off was reduced to €10,000 – effective as of 1 January 2014. In 2013 only 23,300 people received long-term unemployment assistance from the government, at a cost of €56 million. The new policy is projected to cover 41,700 people in 2014 – still less than 5 per cent of the long-term unemployed.[14]

Was it not clear to those in charge before 2009 that clientelist politics were leading Greece straight off the fiscal precipice while making a mockery of the country's pretensions to be a modern, progressive welfare state? And why didn't anyone do something about it?

In their recent book *Understanding the Crisis in Greece*,[15] Mitsopoulos and Pelagidis, the economists, explain how, in the context of an ill-informed public and powerful media closely connected to the 'Vikings', legislators make the rational choice to play along and to keep the economic rents flowing. They know full well, after all, what happens to the few foolhardy souls that have dared to strike out on the path of pro-market, anti-statist reform: they have been consigned to political oblivion, at best ridiculed as quaint and unable to grasp the 'Greek way' of doing things, at worse attacked as agents of foreign powers or extremists out to impose alien economic models on a country that was not made for them.

Nothing proves the authors' point as perfectly as the failed pre-crisis effort to reform the Greek pension system.

4

Pensions, Retired

Platon Tinios is an unlikely source of threat to the social order. A floppy-haired professor in his mid-to-late fifties, he is descended from the privileged enclave of the Greek colony of Alexandria in Egypt and was educated at Oxford and Cambridge. These days, he lives with his wife (also an economist) and their cats, two of which are named Maynard and Lydia, after John Maynard Keynes and his spouse, in a neoclassical two-storey house in downtown Athens with a lovely enclosed courtyard.

Yet this phlegmatic academic is something of an underground hero for the small minority of liberal, reform-minded Greeks, and a *persona non grata* for the Greek political establishment. His ostracism is the direct result of his most important contribution to public policy, the Report on the Economy & Pensions that he authored on behalf of the Spraos Committee in 1997, commissioned by the then prime minister, Costas Simitis.

The study, which came to be known as the Spraos Report after the venerable chairman of the committee, John Spraos, professor emeritus of Political Economy at University College London, was the first serious domestic attempt to outline the complexity of the issues and the extent of the crisis facing the Greek pension system. It set out, in crisp Anglo-Saxon-style prose that seemed like a different language from the abstruse metaphysics of the usual coterie of pension experts, the absurdities and blatant inequities of the system, and the unsustainable trajectory it was on. The report also presented the available options for reform and explained why some would be preferable to others. It was meant to serve as a 'contribution to social debate', as its subheading stated, from which there would emerge a radically reformed, fairer, simpler and financially sustainable pensions system.

For these and other crimes against the Client State, the Spraos Report was summarily tried and executed in the court of public opinion, by wilfully ignorant journalists, ideologically fossilized professors and ruthless union chiefs. These men, Spraos and Tinios – went the verdict – were dangerous extremists, trying to terrify the population into giving up on social insurance and leaving pensions in the hands of that perennial bogeyman of contemporary Greek politics: 'private interests'. After its execution, the remains of the report quickly vanished from circulation, never to reappear.

While Spraos returned to London in 1998, Tinios stayed on as economic adviser to the prime minister, through the failed Giannitsis pension reform of 2001, until 2004 when PASOK lost the elections to New Democracy. Since then he has played no role in shaping public policy on pensions.

The story of how Spraos and Tinios were vilified reveals much about how the Greek pension system slowly and predictably imploded, taking the public finances down with it. More than that: the story exposes a political system so beholden to special interests and a state administration so incapable of effective implementation that it is a wonder that the collapse did not come sooner.

As with all good stories, it is best to begin a little before the beginning.

Costas Simitis had first met John Spraos in Geneva during the rule of the colonels, when the professor was head of the anti-junta committee in London, where he taught. Hailing from a wealthy family from Asia Minor which settled in Greece after the *Catastrophé* of 1922, as a teenager he took active part in the resistance against the Nazi occupation of the country. In the early part of the Greek civil war, he was arrested and beaten for selling *Rizospastis*, the newspaper of the Greek Communist Party. He had lived in London since 1946, when he had moved there to study.

In 1985, when Simitis was named Minister of National Economy by Andreas Papandreou and tasked with stabilizing a fiscal situation that was lurching towards the cliff, he brought Spraos with him as his chief economic adviser. Spraos founded the Council of Economic Advisers, modelled on the White House body of the same name, and held intense and open discussions about the nature of the country's economic problems and the direction that policy should take.

Simitis, though successful in averting a full-scale fiscal crisis, was defenestrated in 1987 by Papandreou when electoral politics demanded more populist policies. In January 1996, however, when Papandreou was forced to resign from power because of illness, Simitis ran to succeed him on the basis of his work in 1985–7 and won. Cementing that parliamentary victory by winning the national election he called for September of the same year, he immediately set out to achieve the reforms he had been preparing for a decade to make Greece more competitive and to ease its path into euro membership, which was the defining national vision of that time. To aid him in fulfilling his grand plans, he called again on Spraos, who had just retired from UCL, naming him head of the 'Committee for the Examination of Long-Term Economic Policy', or, as it came to be known and loathed, 'the Spraos Committee'.

'The idea Simitis had was that the ministries of the Economy and Development would be too bogged down in dealing with short-term problems and would not have the time to study the long-term structural challenges the country faced,' recalls Tinios. The committee chairman greatly valued Tinios's expertise and felt he was not made adequate use of at the PM's office, so he appointed him to the committee and elevated him to the role of main associate. Spraos and his posse of ambitious technocrats quickly set to work, and produced four reports in the space of a few months, on agriculture, bureaucracy, the tax system and incomes policy. But it was the fifth one, on pensions, that would stimulate a flurry of public debate, or what passes for it in Greece.

The Greek social insurance system had already, by that time, caught the eye of Greece's EU partners as a potential source of trouble. Kevin Featherstone, director of the Hellenic Observatory at the London School of Economics, has written that in the run-up to Greece's adoption of the euro, the Germans in particular put pressure on Simitis to reform the pension system as a means to facilitate Greece's convergence with the criteria of entry.[1] An IMF report commissioned by the conservative Mitsotakis government in the early 1990s had also warned of the coming Apocalypse if action was not taken swiftly on pensions.

None of this was news to the Greek political class. As Tinios noted in the pensions report he authored for the Spraos Committee, calls for the reform of social insurance had been issued as far back as 1958. A report had come out that year written by Evangelia Papantoniou, deputy head of IKA, Greece's largest pension fund, a pioneering woman in a male-dominated field and one of a slew of left-wing economists present at the creation of IKA, under the Metaxas dictatorship in the late 1930s. Papantoniou — mother of the controversial Yannos Papantoniou, who served as Economy Minister under Simitis — had written:

> There is complete inequality of protection, to the point where the constitutional principle of the equality of citizens has been completely forgotten [...] There is a need for a system that will combine the necessary with the possible and that, getting rid of the unacceptable perception that its purpose is to safeguard privileges at the expense of the many, will use available means to tackle need. [...] Study is required that will take place without the pressures of haste and surrounding noise, a long-term program of action. Above all what is required is the guarantee of cross-party agreement.

The 1958 report referred to fixing the pension system as 'particularly urgent'.

The Spraos Report (as the pensions study came to be immortalized) did not offer a specific blueprint for the overhaul of the system. What it did was give a detailed account of its pathology, both from an equity and an efficiency perspective, and of its unsustainability as a fiscal burden, especially given the drastic deterioration of the demographic picture that was already expected at the time. This account today reads as a chilling prediction of the catastrophe to come. It also reads as damning critique not only of the inertia that allowed it to happen, but also of the continuing inability of policymakers, even after the signing of the Memorandum, to offer the radical solutions that could lead to a rebuilding of trust in the system.

In its opening pages, for example, the report stated: 'for it to be fruitful and effective, the debate must be honest, it must not deal in evasions and it must deal with the problem as a whole. However painful this may be, it is the only guarantee that the problem will not keep coming back to trouble the insured and to serve as a constant source of insecurity.'

On the issue of apportioning the burdens of adjustment between present and future generations, it said: 'Until now, every debate on social insurance ended up burdening the "absent generation" of the employees of the future. Today's younger generation, however, is already "debited" with unemployment, the public debt and will have to deal on its own with deteriorating demographics. Its further encumbrance will jeopardize the future of the Greek economy as a whole.' It should be noted that at the time, public debt and in particular youth unemployment numbers were nowhere near the eye-watering levels they have reached in the Age of the Memorandum.

While cautioning against hasty decisions, the report also warned that the time for debate was not unlimited. As it pointed out: 'The window of opportunity that perhaps exists now will be followed, in the period until 2005, by the retirement of the largest generation of Greek pensioners with the highest accumulated benefits in the history of Greece. *The sooner corrective measures are taken, the smaller the extent of the necessary correction* [my italics].'

Then came the analysis of the problem. The challenge of an ageing society, faced by most advanced economies, was complicated by a social policy apparatus that failed in its basic function of social cohesion and had been turned instead into an instrument for the protection of the privileges of client groups at the expense of the rest of the population. These privileges, enjoyed primarily by employees of the public sector, the DEKO (state-owned companies) and the state banks as well as the members of certain professions (journalists, engineers and lawyers prominent among them), included higher pension benefits, lower contributions and many loopholes through which to slip out of work into early – sometimes very early – retirement. Some of these funds, whose total number was always a bit of a mystery, were able to provide these perks because of their healthy finances, often achieved thanks to the imposition of arbitrary levies on users of their services (for example, part of the price that a company paid for placing an advertisement in a newspaper went to the journalists' insurance fund). Others depended to an increasing extent on the government budget to make up the difference between their revenues and their obligations, thus sowing the seeds of macroeconomic mayhem. The fragmentation of pension management into many autonomous subsystems, as the report recognized, obscured the issues facing the system as a whole and prevented the surpluses of the healthy funds from supporting the ones that were in deficit.

Faced with all this, the report called for greater discipline. For example, it proposed the elimination of the concept of arduous jobs, which sent workers to early retirement without giving incentives for more health and safety in the workplace (and which was extended to job categories which were anything but taxing to one's health, like hairdressers and TV anchors). It also proposed tightening the eligibility for disability pensions (another avenue to early retirement that was massively exploited) and ending anachronistic benefits, like those for widows and unmarried daughters. In addition the report called for measures to increase the participation of women and immigrants in the labour force and for the rationalization of pension financing through government borrowing. Overall, it emphasized that the only three ways to improve the sustainability of the system given the coming ageing crisis were higher contributions, lower benefits or a raised retirement age.

But Tinios and Spraos did not stay solely within the parameters of the existing system. In the spirit of the times – the World Bank had produced its famous 'Three Pillars' report on pension reform in 1994[2] – it asked, positively inclined but without giving its own specific response, whether Greece would benefit from moving from its monolithic and unsustainable Babel of a system to a new, three-tier model. The first pillar of this model would be a basic pension guaranteed by the state in the context of occupation-based schemes; the second would be funded by employee and employer contributions; the third would be optional and would be funded by individual contributions to private accounts. Despite the caution with which they approached this topic, it would be this part of the report that would come back to haunt them.

On 16 October 1997, three days after the Spraos Report had been officially presented, Christos Polyzogopoulos, president at the time of GSEE, the General Confederation of Greek Workers, made an unintentionally prophetic statement. The Spraos Report, he said, 'essentially says that if its recommendations are not implemented, the system of social insurance will collapse by 2010. But the social insurance system, as a sub-system of the wider economic and social system, will collapse after the collapse of the State Budget [capital letters, significantly, his] and the economy as a whole.'[3] Polyzogopoulos meant this as a counter-argument to Spraos. He thought he was demonstrating the absurdity of the idea that social insurance could ever go bust. As Spraos himself told me in his North London home when I was researching this book, many of the opponents of reform 'actually believed that the promises made by the system could be kept, because the state could prop it up indefinitely'.

As things turned out, it was precisely in 2010 that Greece was cut off from the bond markets and forced to seek emergency financial assistance to avoid default, in large part because the pension funds broke the budget. Since then, 'the economy as a whole' has been in a state of freefall, and social insurance 'as a sub-system' has been brought to its knees.

At the time, however, this seemed like a far-fetched dystopian fantasy rather than a realistic prediction. Instead, the guardians of a system that more than any other personified the inefficiency, the injustice and the unsustainability of Greece's political economy went on the attack against what they perceived as the dark vision informing the Spraos Report. As was their custom, they wildly distorted the content of the report, and did not hesitate to go beyond policy disagreement into their preferred mode of personal denunciation.

The most influential of the smears came from the popular Ios (meaning 'virus') column of the left-wing newspaper *Eleutherotypia*. Subtly entitled 'Mr Spraos, Mr Piñera and Mr Pinochet' and decorated with a photo-collage pitting the left-wing, anti-junta Greek professor next to the Chilean military dictator, separated by tanks, this 'investigative' piece purported to uncover the iniquitous truth behind all that clever talk about sustainability and inter-generational solidarity.[4] It began thus: 'Mr Spraos calls himself a leftist, but the model he proposes to fix pensions has a rather dark tinge. The changes promoted by his "Committee" for the pension system include no original Greek element. They are exclusively based on the privatization method imposed by the World Bank on Chile, in the beginning of the '80s, at the time of the harsh imposition of military dictatorship. What is impressive is that the final proposal is nothing but an exact translation – word for word – of the Chilean option.' The authors of the article go on to accuse Spraos of attempting to surreptitiously copy the Chilean model without anyone uncovering the vile source of his inspiration, and they refer to the model and its three pillars as beloved by all the think-tanks 'dealing with privatization and the demolition of the welfare state'.

There were other, even more revolting attacks. *Rizospastis*, the newspaper of the Communist Party that he had been arrested and beaten for distributing during the civil war, in a news analysis entitled 'A Monument of Social Darwinism', called the report 'terroristic' and likened Spraos to a 'killer' trying to solve the pensions problem through measures that will lead workers to an early demise![5]

'I had tried to put the issue in as simplified a manner as possible,' Spraos recalls. 'So I said "the problem exists because we're not giving birth and we're not dying", i.e. fertility rates were very low and life expectancy was going up. And the conclusion they reached was, "he wants to kill us off".'

Tinios, too, felt the ire of unreconstructed lefties and groups privileged by the existing system. He was attacked in the media for his role in writing the Spraos Report, and even received anonymous threats. 'In the first few days, there was a numb feeling, cautious responses, with New Democracy in particular coming out favourably' he remembers. 'Then there was an organized reaction, a main element in which was the *Eleutherotypia* article, and which also included personal attacks on Spraos, as an outsider, someone who would lead pensioners to early graves and so on. This changed the climate completely.'

What was perhaps even more shocking to Tinios was that the committee members distanced themselves from the contents of the report, almost disavowing any knowledge of them. These included the then head of the Council of Economic Advisers and future crisis-era Finance Minister Yannis Stournaras, and the PM's adviser and subsequent Minister of Labour Tasos Giannitsis, who would go on to author the last serious pre-crisis pension reform plan four years later, only to see it crushed by the same forces that brought down Spraos. 'We had had at least two meetings of the committee with the full text written down. Most of the comments of the members, with the exception of Spraos, related to missing commas and things like that,' Tinios recalls. 'Afterwards, Giannitsis in particular acted as if he had never been a member of the committee.'

Speaking to me, Giannitsis says that 'the committee, and in particular, its head, were undermined from day one by ministers who were loath to allow independent analyses of matters under their purview over which they did not exercise control. For this reason, what in other countries was an established mechanism providing governments with unbiased expert advice, has never taken hold here. The media, political parties and the unions also set themselves against the very idea of having such a committee making proposals on such significant issues.' Asked if he could have done more to defend the pensions report when it was issued, he replies, 'It was not my role. I was an adviser to the prime minister.'

Simitis himself cowered in the face of the storm and did not support his old friend. In fact, according to Tinios, the prime minister's office bent over backwards to give the impression that the report had no official status. Within months it was withdrawn from the single bookshop where it could be found in Athens. Since then it has acquired a status akin to *samizdat* literature, officially unavailable but passed around in photocopies or digital copies and discussed among friends of the quiet revolution it espoused, which was so brutally suppressed by the *ancien régime*.

The government's timid reaction led the opposition itself to pull back. 'New Democracy thought that there was something else behind the report, a serious effort to change things. When it became clear that the government had no intention of backing

Spraos and treated him as a foreign element, they too went quiet,' Tinios explains.

One of the few men to speak up in favour of the Spraos Report after the onslaught was Manos Matsaganis, an Economics professor who was then politically affiliated with the hard-left Synaspismos party – which today forms the core of SYRIZA – but who had recently begun serving as an adviser to the Minister of Finance. Writing in *Avgi*, the party organ of Synaspismos, he excoriated the stance of many of the report's critics as 'a mix of bad intentions and ignorance', which combined noxiously with the 'sloppiness as well as the irresistible tendency towards sensationalism of journalists from the entire spectrum of the press, even the "serious" news-papers'.[6] He lambasted the *Eleutherotypia* article in particular as indicative of the worst aspects of 'a certain type of leftist culture' which engages in 'the trial of intentions, the superficial study of facts, the summary conviction and public censure of the convicted'. As he explained in his column, a three-pillared model could be anything from the neoliberal Chilean version to the social-democratic one implemented in Sweden, with a generous basic pension and a socialized, defined-benefit system of contribution-based pensions. In fact, as he pointed out, the Spraos Report expressly stated that in a European context the Chilean model was neither desirable nor possible.

'The Pinochet article was what drove me to write that column,' Matsaganis remembers. 'I got so pissed off about it'. He goes on: 'It was obvious to me that something had to be done about social insurance, otherwise the whole system would collapse and our children would get no pensions, which is not much of a left-wing ideal. But even if the system had been viable, those on the centre-left should still seek to reform it, to remedy the unequal treatment of different groups of citizens. I also believe that issues of viability themselves *are* issues of equity, between different generations.'

The progressive professor, who today teaches at the Athens

University of Economics and Business and is a member of the Democratic Left, the Synaspismos offshoot which joined the coalition government after the June 2012 elections, has harsh words for his old comrades. 'The opposition strategy of Synaspismos towards Simitis was ridiculous. Instead of criticizing him for not moving forward with progressive modernization, they criticized him to the extent that he did move forward with it.'

I asked Spraos how he, a lifelong leftist, felt about being targeted by what the Greek left had turned into. 'I consider myself to be on the left, further to the left in fact than what is known as centre-left,' he tells me. 'I believe that you cannot make the poor less poor other than by making the rich less rich. It is easier in a growing economy, but I believe in the redistribution of income and of privileges at all times. That's what being left means to me. The pension system, in the final analysis, was anti-left because it allowed a very unequal distribution of benefits. And yet I was the one who was attacked as an enemy of the people – in 1985–7 as well as in 1997 – by those who believe that you can spread benefits all over the place without ever being called to account. These are pipe dreams, not to be taken seriously.'

But why did Simitis himself fail to stand up for what he clearly believed and had been working towards for the best part of ten years, since he had left the post of Economy Minister? It cannot be that he did not expect the frontal assault from the motley gang of rent-seekers, ideologues and media bullies. Why did he retreat without a fight, decisively undermining his government's reform momentum?

Tinios believes it had a lot to do with PASOK, the old guard of which never reconciled itself to real structural reform and always considered Simitis a pretender rather than the true heir of Andreas Papandreou. 'From the beginning they lost no opportunity to remind him who's boss, to make sure he knew that he was in office but not in power,' he says. Matsaganis, for his part, points out that even the 'modernizers' backing Simitis within the party did so only because of a 'survival instinct' and were among the first within PASOK to mobilize against pension reform.

As for Spraos, he is more forgiving, saying Simitis had always planned for the committee's findings to stimulate debate, not to be translated immediately into policy. But when pressed, he admits that the prime minister 'let me know on a couple of occasions the kind of pressure he was under' to put a muzzle on the committee. He could have pushed harder for a public dialogue; in the absence of a robust civil society to take up the discussion, the report was left in a drawer and neglected, like so many before it. 'That was for me a source of disappointment,' he concludes.

Despite this decidedly inauspicious start, fixing social insurance remained a goal of the government. After his narrow re-election in 2000, Simitis, with Giannitsis as Labour Minister, gave it another go. The proposed bill had dispensed with the more radical experimentations of the Spraos Report – three pillars and all that – and concentrated instead on a tightening of the existing system to give it a lease of life for another few years. Measures included increases to the retirement age and to the required insurance period for a seniority pension, a reduction of the replacement rate of reference earnings and means-testing for minimum pensions.

The reaction, once again, was brutal. GSEE called a general strike. The press had another bout of populist hysteria. Giannitsis' colleagues in the cabinet, who had been kept in the dark about the specifics of the reform bill, swiftly deserted him and Simitis once again caved, withdrawing the bill. The law that was passed in its place was a compromised piece of legislation risibly ill-equipped to arrest the slide of the system into ignominy and bankruptcy. 'The effort was doomed from the start,' Giannitsis says. 'At that time of national euphoria, with high growth rates and with Greece entering the single currency, even top government members thought it was crazy to worry about ten years ahead. This was symptomatic of a political system and a society fundamentally opposed to change.'

Perhaps he is right, and a more courageous stance in support of Spraos four years earlier would not have made a difference to his reform effort. But the failure to fight against the forces of inertia in that first skirmish more or less ensured that they would give no quarter in round two. Whatever the case, pension reform died a slow, agonizing death in those four years. The repercussions for Greece would be cataclysmic.

On 12 July 2010, two months after the signing of the Memorandum, the Greek parliament passed Law 3863/2010 for the reform of the pension system. The Memorandum itself made reference to the need for pension reform and even laid out the principles on which it should be based. The law was hailed by experts and even the IMF itself as a milestone, and was the most significant piece of legislation on pensions in a generation.[7]

Its most radical break with the past was its adoption, to be implemented in 2015, of a two-tiered system of social insurance. It was made up of a (very) basic pension of €360 awarded to almost everybody (with the exception of the uninsured above a certain income level) and a proportional, contributions-based pension dependent on earnings and the number of years spent in the workforce. There was no provision, however, for a privately managed third pillar (private insurance contributes a tiny percentage of retirees' income, lagging behind the rest of Europe).

The law cut benefits by extending back the earnings period relevant for their calculation and capped indexation at the level of inflation. It raised the retirement age for all and cancelled a number of special clauses offering opportunities for an early exit from employment for favoured groups. It thus dampened some of the more egregious inequalities in this respect between different groups of the insured. It also offered incentives for longer careers through accrual rates that rise with the length of working life, promoted the drastic reduction of the class of arduous professions and instituted disability verification centres and random checks to combat bogus disability claims. In terms of both efficiency and equity, in other words, with the troika's gun to its head, the Greek government took bold steps forward. Echoes of the Spraos Report, and of Giannitsis' reform effort, littered the text of the bill.

And yet – if anyone expected national bankruptcy to jolt Greece's politicians out of their old, clientelist ways, the pension reform law provided a useful wake-up call. Showing a passion for negotiation that eluded it when it came to the incomes of less privileged groups, the Papandreou government got the troika to acquiesce to the preservation of the separate insurance arrangements of doctors, lawyers, engineers, journalists and employees of the Bank of Greece, which allowed them to retire on far better terms than the rest. It also left untouched the overly generous benefits secured by employees of banks, public utilities and the press who had been hired before 1983. The 'acquired rights' of firemen, police and military officers were similarly unaffected, irrespective of hiring dates – at least at this early stage.

Even in the Age of the Memorandum, in other words, the political system was doing its best to protect politically influential professional interests at the expense of the rest. Singled out for punishment in an almost sadistic way were the young – men and women who had recently entered or were just entering the labour market who would have to work longer (were they lucky enough to find a job) for lower benefits. And all this to protect 7.3 per cent of total retirees, who, as Stefanos Manos, the liberal former Economy Minister and head of the 'Drassi' party calculated,[8] received more than 50 per cent of all retirement income.

Despite these substantial flaws, the government could claim at the time to have returned the pension system to a fiscally sustainable path. Before the reform, Greece's pension costs were projected to jump from 12 per cent of GDP, where they stood in 2007, to over 24 per cent in 2060 – by far and away the worst ratio in the European Union.[9] The objective of the measures included in Law 3863 was to reduce the increase in pensions costs over the next fifty years to only 2.5 per cent of GDP, so that it would reach 15 per cent by 2060. In case developments threatened to confound these expectations, there was even a provision allowing future governments to change the parameters of the system by ministerial fiat so as to bring it back on track.

Yet since then, as the recession has destroyed jobs on an industrial scale, cut down wages and hence contributions and starved the state of tax revenue while increasing demand for welfare services, the pensions crisis has deepened alarmingly. The haircut imposed on holders of Greek debt as part of the country's second bailout in March 2012 was also a body blow to the finances of the insurance funds, which had invested heavily in Greek government bonds. As this book went to press, pensions had been reduced eleven more times after the initial cuts in 2010. Public anger at the cuts has been a driving force of the anti-Memorandum tide in Greek politics. But the nebulous, ill-informed nature of public debate has meant that this anger has not honed in on the true scandals.

For example, in the frantic final days before the signing of the second Memorandum accompanying Greece's second bailout in February 2012, it was leaked that the Papademos government planned to make up the shortfall in the spending cuts demanded by the troika by imposing focused cuts on the generous pension arrangements of PPC and OTE, the former electricity and telecoms monopolies, as well as the banks. The matter seemed to have been settled, but then calls were placed to the right people, the right sort of pressure was applied, and the government changed the policy, imposing uniform cuts on all pensioners instead. People were furious at the cuts and some lonely voices tried to highlight the nefarious logic of it.[10] But their analysis was drowned in the general outcry, and all anyone remembered was that the old had suffered another blow to their income. PPC, OTE and bank employees were seen as victims like everyone else, though they retained many of their advantages against the rest.

As this book went to press, efforts continued to unify the system, which remained highly fragmented, entailing high administrative costs and unnecessarily complicated planning. Furthermore, as Tinios remarked in a speech in Athens in October 2012, 'a superficial conception of the Greek system of pensions would perhaps consider the existence of a plethora of separate insurance institutions – funds for main and supplementary pensions, lump-sum cut-off payments – as a kind of risk diversification. [...] But a careful reading leads to the conclusion that the final guarantor of all the funds and the insurance agencies, the last line of defence, regardless of the legal status or the organizational form, is the same: it is in all cases the state.'

It defies belief that, despite the manifest inability of the government to protect retirees from sliding into penury, policymakers have failed to push for the creation of a supplementary third pillar run by the private sector. As Giannitsis puts it, 'given that the state has wrought such havoc with the finances of the funds in the interests of preferred social groups, and given the corrupt practices recorded in their management, the insured should have access to their own accounts, administered by serious, well-regulated private companies.'

In addition, as Tinios noted in his speech, the law offered a way out for the so-called '*Polytechneio* generation' – those who came of age around the time when Greece threw off the yoke of the colonels in 1974.[11] Its members got to retire with their generous benefits intact.[12] In some cases, like that of mothers of underage children, the new legislation even led to a reduction of the retirement age. Thus, in 2010 and 2011, there was a rush for the exits from the world of work, especially in the public sector and especially among women.

Meanwhile, poverty and inequality among old people in Greece remains disgracefully high and, if anything, the situation is getting worse. According to Eurostat data from 2011, 29.3 per cent of people over sixty-five are at risk of poverty in Greece, compared with a European average of 20.5 per cent.[13] Law 3863 included a clause stipulating that, for those insured for at least fifteen years, the sum of the basic plus the proportional pension would not fall below the sum total of fifteen minimum daily wages. At the time, that came to nearly €500 a month. But the slashing of the minimum wage in February 2012 as part of the deal for the second bailout means that the new floor for pensioners is €392.70 – barely above the basic pension itself.

In an essay in the liberal, reform-minded *Athens Review of Books* in February 2010, Matsaganis explained a central structural reason why pension reform had failed to materialize over all those years. 'The benefits of reform,' he wrote, 'are spread among social groups that are either under-represented on the negotiating table (private sector employees, the young, women, immigrants) or completely absent (the coming generations). On the other hand, those who benefit from the existing system are over-represented in the unions, the parties and the various political and social lobbies, and they seem determined to defend their privileges tooth and nail.'

Three years later, the positive effects of Law 3863 notwith-standing, this structural obstacle to the necessary overhaul of the system remains in place. The rent-seekers retain a great many of their privileges, and the cause of pension reform has been tied in the public mind inextricably, in a suffocating grip, with more years of drudgery and fewer entitlements at the end of it. Without rad-ical political reform the future of Greek pensions will remain mired in perilous uncertainty.

Sitting under a tangerine tree in Tinios's courtyard on an unusually warm October day, swatting away tiger mosquitoes, I listen to him talk about his efforts to prise pension data from the unwilling hands of Labour Ministry functionaries, who treat every bit of information as if the survival of the state depended on its remaining secret. The troika may have forced Greek bureaucracy to modernize its data-gathering methods so that the effect of policy can be precisely quantified, but access to this information is still barred to academics or journalists (unless members of the troika themselves give it to them).

Since he left government service, Tinios has continued to do research and to publish on pensions, and he is arguably the country's top expert on the subject. Despite this, and despite the fact that developments have vindicated his warnings in the most dramatic way, successive ministers of Finance, even those who are personal friends like George Papaconstantinou and Yannis Stournaras, have not called to ask for his input. Evangelos Venizelos, who invited him to his office in 2007 when he made his first bid to lead PASOK, had requested that he arrive very early and leave through the back door, lest any prying eyes see him.

'I feel like the invisible man', he tells me. 'No one wants to be connected to me because they fear that they will immediately be tarred as enemies of the people.'

Spraos concurs: 'The mark of Pinochet has not washed off. It has stuck, and it is very effective. You cannot easily escape it.' I ask him if he sees parallels, in terms of the tendency to shoot the messenger, between the Spraos Report and the troika-imposed reforms and cuts of 2010–12. He does, observing that 'we Greeks are always looking for some nefarious outsider to blame'.

Tinios blames the fact that he has been marginalized in part for his inability to compromise with the political limits of reform. 'If I had said "yes" on a few occasions more, my career would have evolved much better than it has,' he says.

In fact, as he tells me, if he knew how little influence he would have, he would never have returned. 'When I left Cambridge to do my military service, the World Bank had asked me to join them after I was done. I chose instead to come home and occupy myself with IKA and all the rest of it because I thought I had something useful to contribute. Turns out that I didn't; I was just collateral damage.'

Spraos, who spent almost his entire professional life outside

Greece, is, perhaps for that very reason, less gloomy. He says he hopes the current catastrophe will 'teach us to take precautions in time', like his report had tried but failed to warn people to do, and he believes that the biggest part of the fiscal adjustment has, as of the autumn of 2012, already been achieved. He recalls his time in the Ministry of the Economy in the mid-1980s, saying that the 'extremely strict' policies imposed at the time, which opponents savaged as ruthlessly as the current programme is attacked these days, saved Greece from catastrophe and served as a launching pad for Simitis' quest for the prime minister's office a decade later.

I put it to him that back then the Greek government had three crucial advantages compared with its successors during the Great Crisis. The external environment, in particular the tumbling prices of oil, helped soften the blows of austerity. Greece still had its currency, the devaluation of which gave a much-needed boost to the economy as it tried to adjust to the new, stricter conditions. Most important of all, public administration had not rotted to the extent that it had by May 2010. He remains undaunted. 'Things *are* much harder now. But the fact that an adjustment of such magnitude was achieved in these conditions is even more telling of the progress that was made.'

Whether that progress, in pensions and in the economic system as a whole, will survive the outsized social cost it has produced, remains to be seen. This is particularly true in the case of labour reform, the subject of the next chapter.

5

The Return of Class War

The date was 20 July 2012, a Friday, before daybreak. In a few hours the sweltering summer heat would be bearing down on western Attica but, at the time, it was still cool. The dozen union members picketing the gates of the Hellenic Halyvourgia steel plant in Aspropyrgos had no idea what was coming. They were there to safeguard a strike that was about to enter its tenth month, making it the longest in the modern history of Greece.

At around five o'clock in the morning, a fleet of police trucks carrying close to 300 riot policemen stormed the gates. Resistance was futile. Six of the pickets were arrested. The leaders of the strike were woken up and rushed to the scene, flanked by Communist Party and SYRIZA members of parliament. They tried calling members of the cabinet to ask them to intervene. During the nine months of the strike, responsible ministers had proved pliable to pressures from the union and reticent about criticizing its actions. Now, the ministers – of Labour, Justice, Citizen Protection – were not answering their phones.

In the next few days, there were more skirmishes on the grounds of the factory, between the strikers and the police and also between pro- and anti-strike workers. Demonstrations were held by the factory union and its supporters at the site, in Athens and in a number of towns and cities across the country. Newspapers and politicians of the left vented their frustrations in angry tirades about the repressive apparatus of the state crushing the just struggle of the workers. But everyone knew the game was up. A week after the police action, the union voted to end the strike, 272 days after it had begun. Their only condition was the withdrawal of the police from the grounds.

It was the dramatic denouement of a bitter stand-off which pitted a venerable industrialist, pummelled by consecutive years of heavy losses, against a workforce facing wage cuts that would relegate many of them to the ranks of the working poor. The story of the strike – the terms offered by the owner of Hellenic Halyvourgia, which were rejected by the factory union in Aspropyrgos but accepted by the union in the company's other main plant, in Volos; the role of the Greek Communist Party, which controlled the union in Aspropyrgos; the internecine strife between workers at the two factories and between supporters and opponents of the strike in Aspropyrgos – brings out many of the crucial themes in Greek labour relations in the Age of the Memorandum. With a recession showing no sign of ending and with the troika pushing for a radical restructuring of the labour market in the direction of greater flexibility, unemployment soared after 2009 and class tensions intensified.

But how did we arrive at the showdown of 20 July? What did the management of the steel plant offer the workers, and why did they reject it with such vehemence? To find answers to these questions, we have to travel back in time, to the years of affluence during the first decade of the twenty-first century and beyond.

Yannis Manesis, the father of the current owner of Hellenic Haly-vourgia, founded Halyvourgia Volou – later renamed Halyvourgia Thessalias – in 1963, when the steel industry in Greece was just beginning to modernize. Volos is a port city in the region of Thessaly, about 300 kilometres north of Athens. Competition for a plant licence near the capital was too fierce, but the Minister for Industry, a former mayor of Volos, was willing to grant one in his hometown, where unemployment was wreaking havoc.

In the years that followed, protected by stiff tariffs on imports, the sector embarked on a robust upward trajectory. Business leaders like Dimitris Aggelopoulos, president of Halyvourgiki and a close friend of Prime Minister Andreas Papandreou, steered the industry with a steady hand.

Even after Aggelopoulos's murder in 1986 at the hands of the left-wing terrorists of '17 November' and after tariffs were repealed following Greek entry into the European Economic Community, the sector's expansion continued, buoyed up by booming house-building activity and a plethora of large-scale infrastructure projects. Annual demand rose from an average of 1 million tonnes in the 1980s to 1.3 million tonnes in the 1990s, and then to a peak of over 2.5 million tonnes in 2006.[1]

In 2004, Halyvourgia Thessalias, then run by Nikos Manesis, son of the company's founder, took over a rival's steel plant in Aspropyrgos, on the western outskirts of Attiki, which had been the first one to operate in Greece. The new company was named Hellenic Halyvourgia. It was the second largest player in an oligopolistic market of mainly three, in a country where public works funded by the EU continued unabated and where the adoption of the euro and the liberalization of retail banking had led to new highs in housing loans and house building. Domestic demand for steel was further increased in the aftermath of the 1999 Athens earthquake, in which 143 people perished. The tightening of the building code that resulted meant that for a given volume of construction material, 15–20 per cent more steel would be needed for specifications to be met.[2]

The good times could not last for ever. In 2009, as the rest of the global steel industry was beginning to recover from the Lehman shock, the first worrying signs appeared on the horizon of the Greek economy, whose closed nature protected it from the first wave of global contagion. By the end of the year, with the storm clouds darkening over the new government and the country, annual steel demand in Greece had fallen to 1.5 million tonnes. The next year, it plunged further, to 1.1 million, and the year after that, 2011, to 700,000 tonnes. In 2012 it plummeted to 365,000 tonnes– a level not seen since the 1960s, and lower than the annual production capacity of the Aspropyrgos plant of Hellenic Halyvourgia alone.[3] The big steel players, who had over-invested in previous years expecting the boom to continue, now found themselves in real trouble.

According to management sources at Hellenic Halyvourgia, Manesis had already done all he could by the summer of 2011 to cut operational costs without firing anyone and without reducing wages. The company's borrowing had reached an all-time high and it was on its way to a fourth consecutive loss-making year. As described by its financial statements, it would end up €48.9 million in the red in 2011, after losing €15.7 million in 2010 and €31.2 million in 2009 – a total of €96 million in those three years alone.

During that fateful summer, with the flow of customers' lorries slowing to a trickle, Manesis sat down with his two sons, Yannis and George, both in their thirties and active in the running of the company, and tried to figure out what to do. The consensus view was that the recession would only get worse and that if the company continued on the course it had charted, it was heading for the rocks.

The outcome of the deliberations was a proposal presented by Manesis to workers in both Volos and Aspropyrgos that would reduce wage costs without resorting to dismissals. For a period of four months employees would work five-hour instead of eight-hour days, leading to a 37.5 per cent cut in take-home pay. This way, people would continue to work five days a week, which meant that they would not be turned into part-timers, which would entail a loss of insurance cover. Manesis also promised to revert to the previous terms of employment at the end of the four months (end of February 2012) and not to fire anyone.

The factory unions in the two sites reacted in a markedly different way. In Volos, where the Manesis family went first and where they were better known because the company was born there, the employees, following extended discussion, voted to accept the offer.

In Aspropyrgos, the executive council of the union was controlled by PAME, the militant federation of employee organizations under the control of the Greek Communist Party. The union president, George Sifonios, a fifty-two-year-old smelting operator with a grey beard, a lisp and a rigidly Communist world-view, was adamant from the moment he heard the proposal: he would fight it with every resource at his disposal. Manesis explained to the union leadership that he was not bluffing and that if the five-hour working day was rejected, he would have to sack 180 workers – half the plant's workforce. It was in vain. The sixty-four-year-old blue-eyed blue-blood could not get through to the class-conscious proletarian, who saw the contradictions of capitalism laid bare before his eyes. According to people present at the fateful meeting, one of the union representatives told Manesis: 'You won't shut down this factory; we'll shut it down for you.'

I met Sifonios on a bright December day, fourteen months after the beginning of the strike. The weather was mild, so we sat outside on some wooden benches in Navarinou park, a city block in the leftist district of Exarcheia that was taken over by activists, dug up and planted a few years ago, to prevent it from being turned into a car park. Though it was a working day, we were meeting in mid-morning, because the plant, after being forcibly reopened in late July, had been shut down again in November, for three months, because of lack of demand. Sifonios, along with the rest of the remaining workers in the production line – about 200 – were furloughed, receiving 50 per cent of their wages plus another 10 per cent from the unemployment office.

'Wages at the plant are set by the collective agreement negotiated by the Panhellenic Federation of Metal Workers for the entire sector. What they wanted was to get the signature of the workers on an agreement to fix wages at the firm level,' he tells me. Faithful to the PAME line, he insists that Manesis did not just do this for his own benefit; he was acting, instead, as the advance guard of his class, pushing for the decentralization of wage bargaining and the weakening of union influence. 'It is no accident that they chose the toughest factory, the most class-based, the most organized,' Sifonios says. 'They figured that if they broke us, resistance from the rest would crumble.'

Beyond the issue of deviating from the sectoral wage agreement, Sifonios and his acolytes were sceptical about the numbers presented to them by Manesis. 'Production was up 40 per cent compared to 2009; the company was exporting,' Sifonios tells me. 'Manesis claims he was exporting at a loss. That cannot be. Who wants to increase production if they are losing money?'

It is, indeed, the case that turnover (not production) had increased between 2009 and 2011, as the company increased its exports, in particular to North Africa and the Near East, at a time when world steel prices had risen significantly. But steel is not much of an export sector – the finished products are too heavy, hence too costly to transport across great distances. It can only be sold to nearby countries, at low margins. What little economic and geographic scope there was for exports was limited further, in the case of Greek steelmakers, by continual increases in the price of industrial power, which was twice as high as that paid by some of their regional competitors. Hellenic Halyvourgia was not making windfall profits by exporting. It was merely trying to recoup a small part of the colossal losses caused by the collapse of domestic demand and to get access to much-needed liquidity to cover its operating costs without resorting to more high-interest borrowing.

None of this moved the executive council of the union. They held a general meeting of the 360 workers in Aspropyrgos in mid-October in which they presented Manesis's proposal in the terms that Sifonios described it to me more than a year later. A vote followed on whether to accept the proposal or not – not by secret ballot, as stipulated in the union charter, but by show of hands. Workers who later turned against the strike claimed the vote by show of hands was deliberate intimidation on the part of the leadership. Sifonios says it was a 'clear-cut, democratic process' and that the 'strikebreakers only remembered it was a violation of the charter five months later'. In any case, the decision was a near-unanimous 'no'.

At the end of October, as they had warned, management went ahead with the first round of redundancies. A labour law that had been passed the previous year by the Papandreou government had raised the limit of dismissals allowed per month from 2 per cent of the workforce to 5 per cent. Eighteen people were fired on 31 October and another sixteen on 1 November. On 31 October the union called a twenty-four-hour strike in protest through another show of hands – only three employees did not raise theirs – and, assisted by PAME troops, occupied and picketed the gates of the plant. It would not open again for more than nine months.

In the first weeks and months, the overwhelming majority of the workforce backed the strike. The strike-support mechanism of PAME went immediately into full swing. Banners were hung, a pot making *fasolada* (a traditional Greek bean soup) and other meals for the pickets was set up and bags full of groceries as well as a stipend of €100 per week began to be distributed to all workers participating in the strike. The strike leaders also organized cultural performances in the grounds of the factory, including sketches by the well-known actress and Communist Party deputy Eleni Gerasimidou.

As the days passed and the strikers held out, there was an outpouring of solidarity from unions, student organizations, schools and citizens' groups across the country, and even from abroad. People visited the gates of the plant and brought money and food, including pensioners who could barely spare a dime and farmers who donated what they could not sell at the market. Drivers passing by honked their support.

The union leadership, along with PAME cadres from neighbouring factories, had taken control of the gates of the plant complex – illegally, as Manesis claimed – which they had barred with lock and chain, preventing the entry of company executives, customers' lorries and even employees of a separate company active on the 29-hectare grounds. They also held demonstrations outside ministry offices in Athens, to spread their message of unremitting class struggle.

Soon, they concluded that none of this was aggressive enough, so a new tactic was adopted to increase the pressure on management. With the invaluable help of PAME and the Communist Party, which recruited hundreds of cadres and student members of KNE (the youth wing of the Party), they organized visits to the company headquarters, in the leafy suburb of Kifisia a few kilometres north of downtown Athens. Well-to-do old ladies, wives of the wealthy and powerful out with their kids and other denizens of the area saw columns of workers marching through the streets, chanting about bringing down the bosses. Some had probably never seen workers demonstrating before.

'We went eight times to Kifisia,' Sifonios recalls. 'We called the bosses and told them we wanted a meeting. Since they were not coming to Aspropyrgos, we went to them.' Manesis agreed to see them on the first two occasions. During the second meeting, in December 2011, according to the union president, the owner complained that the union was overstating the amount of pay that would be cut and misinforming the workers. 'He said, "It's not 500 euros a month, which you shout about, it's 580." So I said, "Why don't I give you 700 a month, and you tell me if you can make do with that." He banged his hand on the table and stormed out. He never met with us again.'

Pressure was building on Manesis. At the beginning of December he fired another sixteen people, bringing the total to fifty. The union was demanding that they all be rehired and that the reduced hours proposal be revoked. On the political front, George Papandreou had resigned as prime minister in early November, after his short-lived call for a referendum on the austerity and structural reform programme that would accompany Greece's second bailout and the restructuring of its debt. He had been replaced by the technocrat Loukas Papademos, who had to shepherd an array of brutal new measures through parliament, including wage and pension cuts and radical changes to the labour market, facilitating dismissals, reducing the influence of collective bargaining and slashing the minimum wage from €751 to €586 per month.

The Minister of Labour, George Koutroumanis, a former president of the union of insurance fund employees and the person who would be the primary pointman on (read: political victim of) labour reform, had little inclination to further damage his clobbered populist credentials by coming out against striking steelworkers. He and the assistant minister, Yannis Koutsoukos, another PASOK deputy who would quit his ministerial post in early February in protest over the labour reform measures that the government was about to pass, tried to get Manesis to soften his stance.

The industrialist, with public opinion against him and the government pushing him to compromise, began to offer concessions. In six tripartite meetings between representatives of management, the union and the government held at the Ministry of Labour during December, he and his representatives made a number of different proposals trying to appease the union. He went as far as to offer to rehire all but seven of those who had been let go and to revert to the pre-strike work-schedule and pay as soon as the strike was called off.

Sifonios rejected the proposals, insisting that all of those who had been fired be reinstated. Speaking to me a year later, he insists it was the right thing to do. Those who had been fired were 'workers at the forefront of the struggle', he tells me, who were thus considered 'subversive elements' by the owners. Management sources reject this. According to their version, workers were let go on social criteria, with the young, the newly arrived and the unmarried first in line. These were often the employees management was most keen to retain, as they told me, but their strict adherence to the social criteria was the reason why almost none of the dismissals was successfully challenged in court.

On 3 January, the sixty-fifth day of the strike, in a fiery speech outside the Ministry of Labour after another failed negotiating session, Sifonios called on his fellow workers to join him on a trip to Volos, to the other plant of Hellenic Halyvourgia, whose employees had accepted Manesis's terms.[4] They apparently needed some schooling on false consciousness and the nature of their class interests, and the time had come for them to receive it.

On a cold winter Saturday almost a year later, on which a curtain of rain seemed to have descended over the whole of continental Greece, I visited the Volos steel plant of Hellenic Halyvourgia. Life there continued for the most part as it had since the beginning of the Great Crisis. The lorries were loading up with scrap and delivering it to the gigantic industrial furnace, where it was melted at temperatures exceeding 1,600 degrees Celsius, purified through the use of lime and then emptied in liquid, bubbling form into a 100-tonne fireproof cauldron. Ingredients like silica were added to it in this hellish state so that it would achieve the prescribed chemical consistency. Then it was processed and cooled to produce billets, steel bars 12 metres in length from which the finished products – steel rods, coils and wire mesh – would be manufactured at the company's rolling mill a few kilometres away.

Despite having accepted the need for a five-hour working day, the workers of Hellenic Halyvourgia in Volos, both at the steel plant and at the rolling mill, were never subjected to it. The strike in Aspropyrgos meant that all of the company's production was transferred to Volos. As a result, instead of the plant there being reduced to operating only eight hours a day and five days a week, it would keep to the schedule it was on – eight-to-nine hours of production during the week and forty-eight hours straight at the weekend, when power is cheaper (this schedule was already significantly shrunken compared to the days before the crisis, when it operated for seventeen to twenty hours even on week-days). There were no redundancies at the Volos plant. Instead, in the months since the strike at Aspropyrgos began, there have been thirty-four new hires.

For Thodoris Glavinis, president of the company union in Volos, a chain-smoking thirty-nine-year-old with an easy smile and Everyman common sense, avoiding job losses was the top priority from the start. He tells me the following story to illustrate his point: 'The other day, I was arriving at the plant for my shift, which started at six at night. At the traffic lights in the intersection near here, I saw an old friend. He asked me where I was going and I cursed my luck about having to go to work. He said: "Are you kidding me? Do you know how long it's been since I had a job?" I felt ashamed.' Glavinis also relates the story of one of the new hires, a man in his early forties, who had recently approached him and tried to kiss his hand. As the man told him, when he brought home his first paycheque, his wife started weeping. He had been looking for a job for more than three years.

The plant in Volos, just like the one in Aspropyrgos, had felt the slowdown in demand since 2008, so it was no bolt from the blue when Manesis visited them with his proposal. The union held three general meetings on the offer and they extracted from management commitments that no one would be fired, that people would continue to be paid for their time on leave and that workers who had received loans from the company would not have to pay anything back during the four months when their wages would be reduced. The spreading scourge of unemployment, as factory after factory shut its gates in the area, played a crucial role in the deliberations.

At the third general meeting, when the vote would be held, the union membership met at the Volos Centre of Labour Unions, but

Glavinis did something unusual: he asked the president of the centre and the rest of the council to abstain from making statements. He also barred journalists from the meeting. He wanted only the workers of the company to participate in the process, and to prevent party politics and media misreporting from derailing it. The vote turned out overwhelmingly – about 95 per cent, he says – in favour of accepting the proposal.

That Volos continued working created an obvious problem for Sifonios: so long as Manesis could transfer production to the Volos plant, he would be able to weather the strike in Aspropyrgos. It was the latest episode in a relationship between the two unions that had been fractious from the start. As Glavinis recounts, the Volos union had approached their counterparts when Manesis had taken over the Aspropyrgos plant, but they had been rebuffed on more than one occasion. 'They told us that they did not cooperate with unions run by DAKE and PASKE,' he says, referring to the union blocs affiliated with New Democracy and PASOK respectively.

In October 2011, when the Volos union was mulling over the proposal, Glavinis claims he repeatedly tried to get in touch with his fellow union leaders in Aspropyrgos, but they could not be reached. They only contacted him after the Volos union had made its decision, in order to criticize it. After the strike began in Aspropyrgos, the Volos union sent funds and food supplies. Their counterparts initially rejected these, Glavinis says, though they then changed their minds. Sifonios is contemptuous about the offer of aid. 'What am I to do with a case of food? Don't they see the harm they do to workers' rights?' he tells me.

In early January, when a delegation led by Sifonios hopped on a bus and travelled up to Volos to exhort their fellow workers to join in the strike for the first time, Glavinis had gathered his members at the gates to hear their visitors out. 'When Sifonios started going on about the class struggle and all that, some of our guys heckled him,' Glavinis recalls. 'They told him that each union had made its own decision and that they trusted their union leadership.' Tension built, and he cut the meeting short to prevent scuffles from breaking out.

After a few more demonstrations outside the plant gates in the next few weeks that got nowhere, the PAME people decided on a more proactive approach. Glavinis was informed that a large contingent was coming up to Volos to forcibly shut down the factory. This, he recalls, infuriated the workers, particularly once it became clear that many of those who came were not their colleagues from Aspropyrgos, but PAME cadres and Communist students from nearby towns and cities. Everyone except those working their shift – even those with Communist sympathies – gathered at the gates, lit braziers in empty barrels and waited to give the raiders a piece of their mind. Squadrons of riot police also arrived on the scene. When the forces of PAME came, they quickly realized than any commando operation to capture the steelworks or the rolling mill would be to no avail. There was a stand-off that lasted around five or six hours; angry words were again exchanged, but no blows. After that, PAME did not attempt another visit.

Glavinis thinks the different approach taken by the two unions is, among other things, a matter of age. 'The average age of our executive council is thirty-five. It's a new generation, with fresh ideas, a different mindset,' he tells me. But it also played a part that Volos was a smaller community. 'We run into each other in town,' he explains. 'I couldn't face my co-workers and have them ask me why I made decisions that cost them their jobs, when everybody knows how bad things are here.'

The strike in Aspropyrgos may have allowed the steelworkers in Volos to avoid the implementation of the initial offer by Manesis, but the ever-deepening slump meant that they could not escape entirely unscathed. In October 2012 the Volos union made a deal with the owner for an 18 per cent reduction in wages, again for a period of four months. After it ended, Manesis asked for a two-month extension, which they rejected, as the result of which he unilaterally instituted a four-day week for all employees, meaning even less pay and no health insurance.

Glavinis seemed confident about the wisdom of the decision to accept the 18 per cent cut, saying the steelworkers of Volos will continue to support the efforts of the company to survive the crisis. But many of his members were more doubtful. In the vote on the 18 per cent cut, about 100 employees opposed it – more than a quarter. Glavinis himself opposed its extension in February, and the Volos union reacted angrily to the unilateral action of the company, leaving open the possibility of a strike. In the new era of decentralized bargaining and ever-weakening unions, peace in the workplace will depend on the perception of employers as socially responsible, not out to exploit the advantage the new legislative framework affords them. The more demands for wage cuts multiply, the harder it will be for that perception to be maintained.

Eleni Katavati is a forceful personality. She has a piercing, determined voice and a no-nonsense manner. When she remembers certain episodes of the nine-month strike, the voice rises in indignation, as if she is reliving the moment.

An executive secretary who has worked for twenty-seven years at the Aspropyrgos plant (she had been hired as a telephone operator by the previous owner), she was one of only three employees who opposed the original decision to go on strike. She thought Sifonios had not negotiated with Manesis for a better deal and that he preferred confrontation to compromise. In time, she would emerge as his prime rival for the allegiance of the workers.

'He dragged us into a strike because PAME wanted it, not because we did,' she tells me, sitting in an office at the Aspropyrgos plant site. Katavati is one of the few who have continued on the job after the decision to suspend production in November 2012. The sprawling site itself has that unmistakable ghost-town feel. Outside the steel factory, heaps of scrap lie exposed to the elements, waiting for the day when they can be purged by fire and forged into steel. Inside, the cranes and magnets lie still, and the smelting handler's station, manned in normal times by Sifonios, is empty, its window panes covered in soot. Storage areas which used to be filled to the top with finished products are almost entirely empty.

In the early days of the strike, Katavati was a lonely voice against it. She claims that this was because the steelworkers had been 'emasculated by PAME' and the material support it was offering them, feeling an obligation towards the strike leaders – 'the best supermarket would be envious of what the PAME lorries brought in at night', she says. It is nonetheless the case that they overwhelmingly backed the decision to go on strike before any bags of groceries had been handed out and, as she herself admits, at least at first, they had faith in Sifonios.

Katavati started agitating in the general meetings of the union against the role PAME was playing in perpetuating the strike. 'Kotronis [a PAME trade unionist from a plant belonging to another firm] and the PAME lawyers would huddle with our union leadership and they would coach them about how to present to the rest of us what the company owner had proposed to them,' she recalls. She was jeered, called a 'flunkey of the employer' and other charming epithets, but she persisted.

She remembers the December offer – to revert to the previous wage agreement and rehire all but seven of those dismissed – as the beginning of a turning point. Sifonios and the rest of the leadership committee had gathered the workers outside, beneath a shed because it was raining, and they were claiming victory. Facing the usual heckling, Katavati proposed that they accept the deal and continue to fight for the reinstatement of the rest of their colleagues who wanted their jobs back – the numbers of which the union leadership deliberately overstated, according to her – from the inside. But the leadership, by her account drunk on the concessions it had won, argued that Manesis was terrified and that if they stood firm, he would relent and rehire the rest of the workers as well. There was another show of hands and it was decided that the strike would continue.

After that, Katavati intensified her efforts. Slowly but steadily, she developed a following. At the end of February, when Sifonios made another one of his visits, along with a few hundred of his closest comrades, to the company headquarters, he was surprised by a counter-demonstration of about thirty people, led by Katavati, shouting into a bullhorn until her voice grew hoarse. She claims that when he saw her, a smile froze on his face, but maybe it was the wintry weather that did it. Whatever the case, after that PAME stayed away from Kifisia.

Meanwhile, parliamentary elections were approaching, a factor never conducive to reasoned dialogue. Management, as well as Katavati and Glavinis, the Volos union leader, accuse PAME of persisting with the strike not for the good of the workers, but for the electoral benefit of the Communist Party. Whether that was the calculation or not, it is certainly true that the Party brought the full weight of its propaganda mechanism to bear on the battle between Manesis and the Aspropyrgos union. Hundreds of activists were assembled in front of the factory gates whenever Sifonios wanted a show of force. The Communist media reported day and night on the 'heroic struggle' of the steelworkers. An association of the wives of the workers was set up to keep the men's morale from faltering. Elementary-school children were brought to visit and they made sketches of Manesis as an evil plutocrat holding bags of money and making the workers suffer.

The targeting of the company owner by the Communist Party and other groups on the far left cannot be dismissed as mere rhetoric. In post-junta Greece, harsh words against members of the 'ruling class' have occasionally been followed by bullets. Politicians, newspaper publishers, industrialists like the steel man Dimitris Aggelopoulos, and bankers had all been gunned down for, in some manner or other, betraying the interests of the people, as interpreted by '17 November' and other left-wing terrorist groups. Particularly at a time of growing misery and a rabid search for scapegoats, political 'statements' like the banner that appeared in a rally by ANTARSYA, an extraparliamentary Marxist group, calling for Manesis to be strung up, were almost criminally incendiary. The industrialist and his sons received threats and had to travel around in armoured vehicles.

The Aspropyrgos strike became such a potent issue that not even the far right could resist weighing in. As the elections approached and their prospects for entering parliament for the first time were looking better with each passing day, the racist ultranationalists of Golden Dawn sent a delegation down to the plant in February to demonstrate their support for the striking workers and thus shore up their support among the working class. Party spokesman Ilias Kasidiaris, who later that year became internationally famous for slapping a female Communist deputy on live TV, led the brawny, black-clad delegation, which donated crates of canned goods with stickers sporting Golden Dawn's chilling slogan: 'To clean up the filth'. Speaking to the assembled crowd, with Sifonios by his side applauding, the shaven-headed Kasidiaris, who on most days loathes communists only marginally less than foreigners, said Golden Dawn had supported the strike 'from day one' and that the only reason they had not been able to visit earlier was because they, too, were working people and their work schedules did not allow them to.[5] It was another meeting of extremes, another coalition of political polar opposites that has been witnessed in other major fronts in the Age of the Memorandum. When I asked him about it, Sifonios admitted to having been caught off guard by the visit of Golden Dawn, and claimed unconvincingly that he was clapping 'ironically'.

Throughout this period of rising virulence, Katavati kept pushing the steelworkers in Aspropyrgos to 'open their eyes' and to rise up against the occupation (as she called it) of the plant by PAME. Her constituency grew, even though Sifonios would line up their fired colleagues – 119, by the end of May – to deride her. 'The employer's flunkeys', as the PAME people constantly referred to them, even tried a few times to enter the premises and go to work, only to be pushed back by the pickets.

By the beginning of June, seven months into the strike, the division in the ranks could be seen on the street outside the plant. Sifonios's sentries, eternally vigilant, guarded the gates against any potential incursion. A few metres down the road, in front of a BP petrol station, the Katavati crowd massed every day in silent protest against the continued strike. There seemed no end in sight to the stalemate.

Then, two things that happened in the space of two weeks shifted the balance of power decisively against the strikers.

On 21 May Manesis filed a lawsuit against the union, requesting that the strike be ruled illegal. The case was heard on the 29th and on 5 June the verdict was announced, in favour of the plaintiff, on the (procedural) grounds that the decision to go on strike had been made with a show of hands, not by secret ballot, and that management had not received twenty-four hours' notice.

This did not mean that the union and its political allies were about to throw in the towel. The Communist Party put out a statement blasting what it referred to as 'class justice'. The PAME troops prevented employees from going to work. Sifonios had been re-elected as union president a few weeks earlier and had called a vote – by secret ballot this time – on 28 May (after the lawsuit had been filed) on the continuation of the strike, which he had won handily (204 in favour, 42 against). Katavati accused him of election rigging – she spoke to me of multicoloured ballots, the sacked and company pensioners called in to vote. But her objections, even if true, would take months to be heard in court.

A few days later, dozens of anti-strike employees managed to slip past the picket line, cut the chains securing the gates and make it onto the site. In reaction, PAME sent three times as many people to the entrance of the plant to hem them in and to verbally abuse them. 'They had climbed onto the gates and were shaking them, they had such rage,' Katavati recalls. In the end, she called the police, to make sure, as she tells me, that she and the others would make it out unharmed. But even though the strike had been ruled illegal, the police could do nothing to prevent Sifonios and his supporters from reoccupying the gates. As a lawyer from PAME explained to the officers, this was a *new* strike, called by the new executive council elected in May, and no court had pronounced a verdict on *it*.

The rule of law being a malleable commodity in Greece, something more was needed for things to move. It occurred on 17 June, when the country went to the polls for the second time in six weeks and elected Antonis Samaras, leader of New Democracy, as its new prime minister.

Samaras had already declared his intentions in relation to the strike. Questioned by Katavati in a televised town-hall-style pre-election meeting on 1 May about it, he had said that 'it is an abuse for people to want to work and not to be allowed to'. As June gave way to July, however, his Minister of Employment, Yannis Vroutsis, was getting nowhere in his efforts to broker a resolution. The days passed and press reports began appearing which quoted anonymous company sources on the imminent closure of the plant. Sifonios spoke of 'blackmail' and 'rumours' spread to break the will of the striking workers.

Finally, on 19 July, Katavati went to the public prosecutor's office and delivered a letter, signed by all the employees who were against the strike, demanding enforcement of the 5 June court decision. In a sign of the extent to which events that followed were determined by politics, Samaras was reported to have intervened in person in order for the riot police to storm the gates. The right to work is 'sacred', he was reported as having said, and the government 'would defend it with all means at its disposal'.[6]

*

According to the original formulation of the insider–outsider model of the labour market, those in employment use their insider status and the cost to firms of labour turnover to exact rents from their employers (higher wages, more job protection etc.) and thus make it harder for outsiders, i.e. the unemployed, to find work. The theory was advanced in the 1980s to explain, among other things, persistently high unemployment in the European Economic Community, and it was later amended to include other categories in the outsider class. One of the more prominent examples were workers on temporary contracts in Spain, primarily young, unskilled and non-unionized, who were let go by the hundreds of thousands during downturns so that employees on permanent contracts could be protected.

Greece was a special case of the insider–outsider model prior to the crisis. A recent paper by Manos Matsaganis sums it up nicely.[7] According to it, the Greek labour market can be divided into three distinct categories: insiders, outsiders and 'midsiders'. The 'hyper-protected' insiders, as he refers to them, 'comprise about 1 million workers employed in the union strongholds of the civil service, public utilities, and – to a lesser degree – in formerly state-owned banks'. The outsiders include 'possibly as many as 2 million persons precariously employed on a temporary or part-time basis, immigrants in the shadow economy, women and young people trying to enter or re-enter the labour market, the long-term unemployed and others lacking access to secure jobs and associated benefits'. The third class consists of the 'under-protected "midsiders" […] consisting of about 1.5 million workers formally employed in private firms'. As Matsaganis explains, these employees 'occupy an intermediate position: they enjoy more limited job protection and less generous pay and benefits compared with insiders, but remain within a (more or less) legal framework – thereby being less fully at the mercy of employers than is the case with outsiders'.

Wage bargaining was highly concentrated before the Great Crisis. Since 1992, the national minimum wage was set through negotiations, usually every two years, between the third-tier organizations of employees and employers. From that floor, the 'social partners' in each sector, the second-tier federations at the national level and the first-tier organizations at the local level, added what further increases they could agree on. If they could not agree, they resorted to mediation and, in some cases, arbitration, invariably favouring the employees' organizations, which sometimes ended up with even bigger increases than they were asking for. The national minimum wage applied to everyone, and national and local sectoral agreements also tended to extend beyond unionized employees, to all those working in the particular industry. There were also some – no more than a few dozen – firm-level agreements signed every year.

In the run-up to the crisis, during the Eurozone years, this institutional setting conspired with the inflationary effects of the new currency to produce wage increases that outstripped productivity gains. The last national minimum wage agreement before the crisis, signed in April 2008, set the minimum monthly salary at €739.57, which in Greece's case was not multiplied by 12 but by 14 (including summer leave benefit and the Christmas and Easter bonuses). This, as the IMF pointed out, meant that, even at the end of 2011 Greece's minimum wage was substantially higher than that of its closest competitors – 50 per cent higher than Portugal, and 17 per cent above Spain. Unit labour costs increased by over 35 per cent in Greece during 2000–10, compared to less than 20 per cent in the euro area as a whole.[8]

Real wages in the same period, however, had actually failed, by a small margin, to keep up with productivity,[9] and compensation in Greece on the eve of the crisis remained well below the European average, in particular in the private sector. According to the European Commission, the average real wage in Greece in 2009 was 84 per cent of the EU-15 average. The labour market reforms instituted from 2010–12, which in every instance were politically contentious in the extreme, even within the ranks of the governments that had to pass them, have led this percentage to slide back by the end of 2012 to 68.5 per cent, a level not seen since 1993. At the same point in time, the purchasing power of wage earners in Greece was down to levels last recorded in 1997. The Greek minimum wage is now, after the axe taken to it in February 2012, one of the lowest in the EU and the lowest in the EU-15 group.[10]

There is no doubt that adjustments were needed in the labour market. But the policy of internal devaluation through wage suppression, which is one of the few things the three members of the troika strongly agreed on – former ECB chief Jean-Claude Trichet was said to bring a chart with Greece's unit labour costs relative to the rest of the Eurozone to Eurogroup meetings – was pushed too hard. The result, in a closed economy overly dependent on domestic consumption, was a collapse of economic activity, which caused a flood of unemployment.

In this context, with recession turning into depression and reforms stripping employees of basic protections against the arbitrary behaviour of employers, it is no surprise that the strike in Aspropyrgos lasted as long as it did and enjoyed support for so long from public opinion. People saw jobs vanishing, pay and working conditions worsening – by 2012, hundreds of thousands of salary earners were getting paid after weeks or months of delay – and the striking steelworkers seemed to many to be taking a stand against all this, not just for themselves but for everyone. While the Communist Party overplayed its hand at Hellenic Halyvourgia and paid an electoral price for it in the June elections, the leftists of SYRIZA, employing a less stultified version of the doctrine of class struggle, soared to second place.

The absence of an export base and the excessive reliance on domestic demand, which was devastated by wage cuts and endless layoffs, was not the sole reason for the failure of the policy of internal devaluation. Equally important was the stubborn resistance of prices to follow wages on their downward spiral. Greece before the Great Crisis was not an economy that allowed free rein to market forces. From road haulage to legal services, from pharmacies to the beer market, milk and cruise shipping, some combination of legal restrictions, regulatory inertia and incumbents' political connections ensured that before the Great Crisis, competition was stifled at the expense of the consumer.

The troika was well aware of this. In its report on Greece's original bailout request, the IMF noted that 'competition in internal markets is impaired, particularly in network industries (with large public sector participation) and liberal professions, but other industries have also oligopolistic features that keep margins high. Weakly contested domestic markets result in high costs and poor underlying productivity.'[11] In September 2012, an internal IMF report about the Greek fuel market was leaked to the *Wall Street Journal*.[12] In it, according to the newspaper, the IMF's Athens team argued that restrictions on competition in Greece's oil-refining industry, a duopoly controlled by two of Greece's most powerful families, the Vardinoyannis and Latsis clans, is costing Greek consumers more than $1 billion a year.

Dominant players in various markets were encouraged to continue using anti-competitive practices to keep out potential new entrants by the slow, ineffective response of the competition authorities to complaints. In one prominent case, the Greek Competition Commission in December 2013 revealed preliminary findings showing that the incumbent 'had adopted and was pursuing an integrated, long-term and targeted policy of excluding and limiting the potential for growth of its competitors'. The investigation had lasted twelve years.

In other sectors, innovative, internationally unique regulations were thought up to protect domestic producers from foreign competition. In the milk market, for example, a presidential decree had determined that the shelf-life of pasteurized milk could not exceed five days, a restriction that the OECD called a 'strict deviation from standard EU practices', which 'shields the markets from imports' and 'leads to high and increasing prices'.[13]

The troika proved much more successful in getting Greek governments to push down private sector wages than in leavening the anti-competitive sclerosis in product markets. If this was a sin of omission, another aspect of the failure of internal devaluation was a sin of commission – namely, the insistence of Greece's creditors, against the will of Athens, on dramatically increasing VAT and other forms of indirect taxation, especially on fuel. The standard rate of VAT climbed from 13 per cent to 23 per cent (tied for second-highest in the Eurozone), while consumption taxes on petrol and heating fuel surged upwards.

As a result of all this, in 2010, the first year of the bailout, despite a recession approaching 5 per cent of GDP, the annual inflation rate was 4.7 per cent – nearly triple the euro area average. In 2011 GDP shrank by 7.1 per cent, but prices rose another 3.1 per cent. Even in 2012, despite a further collapse in Greek incomes, the price level continued to rise, albeit marginally.

The cost of the failure to keep down prices while wages plummeted, in terms of the standard of living, the depth of the downturn and the perception of the adjustment programme among Greek public opinion, has been incalculable.

Besides the woefully mishandled policy of internal devaluation, Greece's international creditors did not have much of plan to deal with its competitiveness slide. Despite some reforms at the margins, the country's business-throttling bureaucracy and its chaotic legal system have remained set in their dysfunctional ways. Hellenic Halyvourgia offers one of innumerable cases in point.

In 2004 the company applied for a licence to build a pier onto the Gulf of Eleusina, at the southern edge of the Aspropyrgos plant, from where it could take delivery of the scrap and offload its finished products onto ships chartered by its customers. This would save time and money, as the company would no longer have to use the slow and costly services of the port of Eleusina. It would also reduce traffic congestion and pollution in the area, since the need for the convoys of lorries delivering raw materials to the factory and transporting products to the waiting ships in Eleusina would be drastically reduced.

The process to get approval of the environmental terms lasted four years, and required signatures from four different ministries and from different departments within each ministry, from various levels of local government, from the antiquities service and many others. This was only the beginning. In the summer of 2008, the prefecture of Western Attica filed suit against the project with the Council of State and construction was suspended. The reason given was that the chosen site should be used for leisure and cultural activities, even though it is a strip of land right in the heart of the area where there is the greatest concentration of heavy industry in the country. Far from dismissing the case, after two-and-a-half years, the high court ruled in favour of the plaintiff. There followed another extended round of applications, legal opinions and so on, until in February 2012 the (modified) environmental terms were again approved.[14] But just as work was about to begin, the municipality of Aspropyrgos filed another suit with the Council of State. As this book went to press, the project was still frozen, a decade after it had been set in motion.

Even if workers agreed to work without pay, no sane investor would want to step into this quicksand of ceaselessly proliferating paperwork and ever-lurking legal challenges, and watch his time and money sink with agonizing slowness into nothingness.

Investment and the Deep Blue Sea

On 20 October 2010 the Council of State, Greece's supreme administrative court, issued a pair of decisions that caused major rumblings in the country's tourism industry. According to the decisions – 3396/10 and 3397/10 – the creation of Integrated Tourist Development Areas (ITDA) was judged to violate the Constitution.

The Council's verdict threatened to pull the rug from under a number of planned large-scale property development projects. Among them, it seemed to obstruct the further expansion of the biggest tourist investment ever to have taken place in Greece, the Costa Navarino luxury resort network in Messinia, on the south-western edge of the Peloponnese.

The case was the latest to pit the court's passionate defenders against its equally fervent detractors. In the view of the former, the Council, founded in 1929 on the model of the French *Conseil d'État*, was staying true to its steadfastly pro-environment jurisprudence. Since the establishment of the court's fifth section in the early 1990s, they argued, it had been a thorn in the side of unscrupulous developers and their allies in the executive branch. According to the latter, it was yet another testament to the judges' extreme environmental activism, which consistently undermined prospects for large-scale development projects.

Irrespective of the merits of the verdict, however, both sides presumably agreed on one thing: it came far too late. The law that formed the basis of the ministerial decision that was disallowed had been passed in 1997; the ministerial decision itself in 2001. By the time the Council's decision was made public, the first of four phases of development of Costa Navarino had been completed and the resorts were in operation.

That was only the tip of a juridico–bureaucratic iceberg of Himalayan proportions. By 2009, as construction of the first phase was nearing completion and a year before the Council's verdict was revealed to the world, TEMES, the development company undertaking the massive project, had had to collect over 3,000 signatures from all levels of public administration. In all, over twenty ministerial and joint ministerial decisions had had to be issued, as well as more than 600 licences and legal opinions, twenty-five decisions of the Messinia Prefectural Council and forty decisions of local municipal councils. A total of sixty trials had been held.[1]

More than any other case, that of Costa Navarino highlights the realm of existential horror that major investors enter when they decide to do business in Greece. But it is about much more than that: it is the story of a court that has stood almost alone among the institutions of government in the last twenty years in defending the environment against all who seek to profit from its degradation; of a tourist industry that got complacent, lost ground to Greece's cheaper neighbours, and is now seeking to reinvent itself; of a pristine piece of the Peloponnesian shoreline that has been irreversibly altered by an investment of unprecedented scale by the country's standards; and of a businessman whose life's vision was to turn his home region into a beacon of sustainable, high-end tourism, despite the innumerable obstacles in his way.

Vasilis Constantakopoulos, widely known as 'Captain Vasilis', or simply 'the Captain', was born in 1935 in the small village of Diavolitsi in Messinia and died on 25 January 2011. Dubbed the king of container ships by Lloyd's of London in the 1980s, he didn't even glance at the sea until he fled his native village for Athens in 1948, during the Greek civil war.

Those were hard times for Greece. Fratricide on a national

scale, which ended in 1949, had been preceded by three-and-a-half years of Nazi occupation. The country was poor and deeply divided. Constantakopoulos spent his adolescence in the capital selling milk and buttons during the day and going to night school in the evening. His parents hoped he would get a government job, which offered security and a steady income. But he had other plans.

'It just wasn't for me. Something gnawed on me that I would wither away,' he is quoted as having said about the prospect of life in the Greek public sector, in a glowing obituary.[2] The escape route he chose was the sea. In 1953 he joined a 450-tonne vessel with a 75-horse-power engine as an unpaid sailor. He spoke with deep reverence about his experiences on board, in particular about the early morning shift, from four o'clock to eight, when – as he said in a rare interview in 2006 – 'it was just you, the sky and the earth', and the introspection forced upon one 'made you a better person'.

Having risen over two decades to the position of master and having saved up about 30,000 dollars, Constantakopoulos decided in 1975 to buy a small cargo ship and start his own shipping company, Costamare. Over the years, and in particular after its successful entry into the container market in 1984, Costamare became a global empire. Run today by Konstantinos Constantakopoulos, the first-born son of the Captain, at the close of 2013 it owned and operated fifty-six container ships, and was building eleven more. It is listed on the New York Stock Exchange.

But the company's dizzying international expansion did not make its founder forget where he came from. He wanted Messinia to share in his success. Even before he became a shipowner and amassed untold riches, he would express his wish to return home and create something of consequence there. Gradually the idea formed in his head of building a major tourist resort, which would put Messinia on the map as a top Mediterranean destination, introduce its natural and cultural gifts to the world and create jobs for the local population.

Constantakopoulos was also an early adherent of environmentally conscious business practices. His love affair with the sea led him to become a founding member and to serve numerous terms as the president of HELMEPA, the Hellenic Marine Environment Protection Agency, an international NGO set up by Greek shipowners to improve safety at sea and reduce marine pollution caused by shipping. When he turned his attention to land, one of his concerns was that his project – despite its unprecedented scope – would respect its natural surroundings and help protect the immaculate coastline of Messinia from the kind of monstrous development seen in other parts of the Mediterranean, most notoriously in the Costa Brava. Still, the project was a major tourist development aimed at turning a profit and there were – and there remain today – critics who argue that it cannot blend harmoniously with the Messinian landscape.

Starting as far back as 1982, Constantakopoulos began acquiring parcels of land near the town of Pylos, home of the Homeric king Nestor and the site where the tablets that led to the decryption of Linear B script, the earliest attested form of Greek, were discovered. He bought the plots one by one, from what ended up being over 1,200 small landowners. He met with each one of them and got to know their concerns and their family situation. He established a uniform buying strategy, so that early sellers would not feel like they had been played for fools as later sellers took advantage of the rise in property values caused by the big development project. For twenty years, with few exceptions, no matter where he was in the world, he would speak to his real-estate broker on the phone twice a day – once at nine o'clock in the morning and once at nine at night.

By the mid-1990s, the seas ahead looked calm for the Captain's vast land project. He had bought most of the properties he needed; his second-born son Achilles, then aged only twenty-four and having completed his studies at the École Hôtelière de Lausanne, had just joined him as CEO of TEMES, the development company set up to bring Costa Navarino to life; and the government, after an obligatory decade or so of delay, was preparing to pass a law defining the conditions for the creation of Integrated Tourist Development Areas, thus establishing the necessary institutional framework that would allow work to begin.

Little did he know of the Odyssey that still awaited him before the bulldozers could begin shovelling up the pieces of Homeric earth that he had so painstakingly acquired.

In a 1999 academic paper, Nicholas Papaspyrou, then of Harvard Law School and a rising star of Greek constitutional law, wrote: 'The starting point of any analysis of the Council's stance in environmental issues is the absence of credible environmental policy in Greece. Regional and urban planning has been disorganized and poor, quality of life aspects have been neglected, and assessments of environmental impact have played little role in the scheduling of important public works. As a result, there has been a continuous deterioration of the environmental aspects of Greece's standard of living.'[3]

Article 24 of the Greek Constitution, enacted in 1975 to refound Greek democracy after the rule of the colonels, asserts that 'the protection of the natural and cultural environment constitutes an obligation of the State and a right of every person.' It goes on to state that the government must draft a land and a forest registry, restructure land planning on a national level according to the dictates of science and in the interest of 'the best possible living conditions', protect monuments and traditional settlements.

It wasn't until 2008 that Greece's politicians got around to passing a general framework law for land planning, which most experts considered deeply flawed. As for a land and a forest registry, despite generous EU funding and grand announcements by ministers at various times since the mid-1990s, they remain tantalising dreams, still a long way from completion. In the second decade of the twenty-first century, Greece remains the only country in the EU in which the rights of landowners, the boundaries of government property, the meaning of the term 'forest' itself, are lost in a legal fog.

In the absence either of a national plan or of regional plans for the use of land, without a clear legal demarcation of the boundaries of forests or a database of private owners of plots, the stage was set many decades ago for an anarchic orgy of indiscriminate construction. *Afthereta* – homes built without permits, mentioned with regard to Keratea in chapter 1 – had already begun springing up across the country, mostly in the cities and above all in Athens, the overflow of people toward which began in earnest in the 1950s. 'Greeks moved very rapidly to the urban centres,' says Rania Kloutsinioti, an architect and member of the National Council of Land Planning. 'These were people who were used to living in the countryside, near the land, so they felt they had an absolute need for a small accommodation, with a little garden where they could plant their olive trees and what not. That's how the story of the *afthereta* began.'

As time went by, the nature of lawless home-building changed. The *afthereta* were no longer the unassuming shacks of former farmers. They became bigger and gaudier. *Nouveaux riches* Greeks, unburdened by good taste or fear of legal consequences, built anywhere – on ridgelines, in the woods, next to the sea.

The process, too, became more sinister. Often clusters of illegal structures would crop up after suspiciously convenient fires wiped out the pre-existing forest. Overpopulated Attica suffered disproportionately from this. Between 1980 and 2009, the era of rising living standards and of the consequent vertiginous proliferation of house-building, Hymettus and Penteli, two of the three mountains enveloping the capital, were repeatedly targeted. Many spoke over the years of arsonists who were paid by ruthless developers to destroy hectares of forest invaluable both in itself and for the preservation of a liveable climate in metropolitan Athens. No such case was ever successfully prosecuted.

The way it usually worked was that when the smoke cleared, men would appear who would claim parts of the scorched earth. Some would come with *hodjetia* – deeds of ownership dating back to the Ottoman era and delineating the boundaries of the property in relation to place-names and nearby farms long swallowed up by the slow-burning fires of Time. Despite the dubious nature of their claims, with no forest or land registry to refute them, they were almost invariably vindicated in court, with the help of local political patrons eager to recruit them in support of this or that party.

Often, especially prior to the first mass legalization of *afthereta* in 1983, the aspiring smallholders would not even wait for any court to give them the go-ahead. They built first and asked for permission later. This, too, was almost always granted, as local government officials and parliamentary deputies representing the contested area pushed for the buildings to be granted access to telephone services, water and electricity.

The central government did little to combat illegal house-building. It seldom fought with any tenacity in court to retain the designation of lands as public. Indeed, at semi-regular intervals of about ten years, it offered mass amnesty to owners of *afthereta*, thus reinforcing the incentives for the practice to continue. Infamously, in 1994 the PASOK government offered to give access to power to illegal homes on 'social criteria'. The result was that droves of illegal homeowners suddenly developed heart conditions, cancer, diabetes and kidney disease, at least on paper, and were thus hooked up to the power lines of the Public Power Corporation. It was reported that 30–40,000 *afthereta* were legalized that year.[4] In addition, governments routinely approved the expansion plans of municipalities which brought the latest generation of *afthereta* in from the legal cold. Around 4,000 plans for the expansion of municipalities in Attica have been approved since the foundation of the modern Greek state. The first known public mention of the construction of illegal homes in Athens was in 1837.[5]

Over time, as cement climbed inexorably up the mountains of the Attic basin, governments attempted to bring the situation under control. But bureaucracy and a dearth of political will combined to prevent this. Inspections could only take place after a complaint was lodged and a final verdict on demolition usually needed a minimum of five years to be reached. Even then, after 1994 the act of demolition had to be carried out by elected prefects, who were keen to avoid this electorally onerous duty and almost always managed to do so, pleading lack of funds and other lame excuses.

More generally, the post-junta years saw the massive expansion of a uniquely Greek approach to land planning, which had its origins in the urgent need to house the masses of refugees from Asia Minor after the eviction of the Greek population by the Turks in 1922. In Greek it is called *ektos schediou domisi*, which can be translated as 'building outside the plan'. The Greek state, in a 1985 law, officially recognized the right of plot owners to build in areas outside planned settlements. Essentially, property owners were told they could build anywhere they pleased, so long as it was not an area of high environmental or cultural significance protected by law, and provided they met certain basic conditions, above all regarding the minimum size of the plot below which no construction was allowed. But even that limit – set at 4,000 square metres – was watered down in the legislation through a number of loopholes ('deviations', as they were called) allowing construction in smaller plots in a very large number of not-so-special special cases. In practice, owners of small parcels of land 'outside the plan' always found a way to deviate from the 4,000 square metre rule and to build their little castles even in plots as small as 100 square metres, often in the middle of nowhere.

All this is only a part of the chaotic situation that the fifth section of the Council of State, established in 1991 to handle disputes involving issues of environmental protection, had to contend with. The weight of these heavy responsibilities would fall on the founding president of the fifth section and the person who engineered its establishment, the controversial and brilliant Michael Dekleris.

Dekleris, a graduate of the Universities of Athens, London and Yale, had been a member of the Council of State since 1958. In that capacity, he was chosen as one of the eleven members of the Constitutional Court set up by the junta in 1973 (it never functioned). This, plus his ill-concealed scorn for politicians, made his appointment to head the fifth section a polarizing one. Little he would do in the eight years until his retirement would alter this assessment.

Using article 24 as well as EU legislation as his springboard, Dekleris went on the attack against anything the executive did that he considered threatening to his understanding of 'sustainable development'. The fifth section pursued its mandate forcefully, repeatedly refusing to override environmental concerns in the interests of economic development and relentlessly demanding that public administration decisions meet the requirements of adequate land planning. Large public projects were put on hold, urban plan expansions rejected, arbitrary land use changes and 'deviations' in *ektos schediou* construction blocked.

Dekleris saw himself as fighting against the degradation visited upon Greece's natural and urban environment by its client-based political system.[6] He was mostly right – his fifth section prevented plenty of atrocities, large and small. But critics say he went too far. Once, in a conference organized by the Technical Chamber of Greece, one architect quipped to Dekleris that if he had been around in the age of Perikles, he would have blocked the construction of the Parthenon. The criticism rests on two pillars: the unjustifiably wide scope he gave to the principle of sustainable development in determining the stance of the fifth section; and the overly intrusive nature of the decisions themselves, which strayed beyond mere invalidation and gave increasingly specific instructions to lawmakers and administrative officials as to what they could and could not do.

Dekleris's fifth section was a reaction – to some, an over-reaction – to the blatant indifference of Greek public administration for the country's natural and cultural heritage. As the case of Costa Navarino was to show, we are still living with the consequences both of that indifference, and of the occasionally exaggerated reaction to it.

In January 1997 the Greek National Tourism Organization (GNTO) issued guidelines for the creation of Integrated Tourist Development Areas – large-scale tourism projects which offer a wide range of activities for the visitor – and invited all interested parties to come forward with their plans. Only two investors appeared, and only one – Constantakopoulos – would get the green light for his project. Article 29 of law 2545/1997, which came a few months after the GNTO issued its call to investors, specified the terms for the creation of Integrated Tourist Development Areas (ITDAs). It stated that such an entity can be set up in the context of unified national, regional or sectoral planning or, failing that, within the framework of a national plan for this type of large-scale tourist investment.

The creation of the ITDAs was meant to be Greece's first step away from the 'sun & beach' model of mass tourist development. This model, founded on the country's incomparable summer charms – the dry, balmy climate, the transparent turquoise waters and whitewashed, cobble-paved island villages, the great food and drink, with a little ancient culture thrown into the mix – continues to define it in the eyes of the world to this day. It is a beguiling image, peopled by laid-back, life-loving hedonists, ready to school all comers in the virtues of Mediterranean living.[7]

The trouble is that, as a model for the continued health of Greek tourism, which makes up nearly one-sixth of Greek GDP, it has long outlived its usefulness. Overly dependent on a single season, with a declining product that was losing market share to enterprising neighbours like Turkey and Croatia offering the same package at lower cost, attracting low-income visitors who spent little ($146 a day, versus $200 in Italy and $162 in Turkey)[8] and often caused a great deal of mayhem, Greek tourism was so obviously ailing that even the government had noticed. It was hoped that resorts like Costa Navarino, which would include golf courses and tourist homes connected to the hotels, would extend the tourist season beyond the summer months, and attract a different kind of visitor: more affluent, better educated, interested not just in cheap thrills but in more fully experiencing the place they visited.

Based on the 1997 law, TEMES, the Constantakopoulos development vehicle, provided the government with a detailed plan of its intentions for the land it had purchased. It was time for the long march through the institutions to begin. Between 1998 and 2001, company executives were sent backwards and forwards countless times between the archaeological service, the forestry authorities, local urban planning offices, a number of ministries and, in many cases, a number of different departments within a given ministry. Some aspects of the planning, such as those relating to construction near the seaboard, provoked a deep sense of Sisyphean helplessness: moving forward on them required the assent of no less than fifteen agencies of government, many of which ignored any deadlines that existed on paper for making up their mind. Meanwhile, the 1997 law kept being amended to fix the many holes in its initial formulation, causing further delay.

In October 2001 a joint ministerial decision was issued designating three agricultural *ektos schediou* areas of south-western Messinia (Romanos, Rizomyloi, Pylos), nearly 400 hectares in total, as parts of the ITDA of Messinia, within which the Costa Navarino development would take place. TEMES also owns a fourth piece of land, in Kynigos, which is larger than the other three combined – about 650 hectares.

As set out in the joint ministerial decision, the planned resorts would include five-star hotels, the first signature golf courses in Greece, spas, convention centres, shops, bars and restaurants. Separate from the hotels but tied to them in varying degrees, TEMES planned to build and sell tourist homes.

After the 2001 ministerial decision, it took another two years for the Ministry for the Environment and Public Works to pass a regional plan for the Peloponnese which confirmed these boundaries, and another year for the government to decide to subsidize the investment, which it ended up doing with considerable generosity, offering €145 million of taxpayers' money.[9] Also in 2004, the ministries of the Economy and of Tourism issued another joint decision, ordering the expropriation of 26 hectares of privately owned land in Romanos and Pylos, belonging among other things to the only landowners who had refused to sell to Constantakopoulos. The way was now open: in 2005 the environmental impact assessment was approved, as were minor alterations to the boundaries and the zoning regulations of the ITDA, and in late 2006 the construction licence was issued and work on Navarino Dunes, the first part of the development, finally began. This despite the fact that five owners of the expropriated land appealed to the Council of State against the legality of the expropriation order.

In the years that followed, as the case meandered through the Council's Olympian deliberative process, the bulldozers in Romanos were hard at work. In January 2008, with the resort still far from complete, it was leaked that the judges, focusing on the absence of comprehensive prior land planning, considered particularly problematic because of the environmental sensitivity of the areas affected by the ITDA, would rule in favour of the plaintiffs on the expropriation order. But, crucially, they delayed the publication of the decision for more than two years. The engrossment process, to produce the officially valid final version of the verdict, took an astounding thirty-three months. In May 2010, four months before the authorized unveiling of the court's decision, Navarino Dunes opened its doors. If the verdict had been released sooner, it is doubtful that the resort would have been able to commence operation.

The need for meticulous land planning for development projects like the ITDAs is particularly pronounced in Greece because of its intricate, defiant terrain, full of daunting mountain ranges, delicately woven shorelines and thousands of islands, from the great, bumpy bulk of Crete to the tiniest slivers of sea-licked, wind-whipped Aegean land. Excluding various oceanic archipelagos, only Denmark has a longer coastline per square kilometre of surface area. 'Greek space is small scale. Large-scale development needs to be handled with extreme care,' notes Rania Kloutsinioti, the architect and urban planner.

Critics of the ITDA concept fretted from the beginning that it was incompatible with Greece's identity as a tourist destination. They argued that it would degrade the Greek coastline and blight the landscape through industrial scale interventions that would remove everything quintessentially Greek from the finished product. As Kriton Arsenis, a former environmental activist who was elected to the European Parliament in 2009, and who has long grappled with such issues, says: 'Instead of copying the tourism model of Tuscany or France, we copied the model of Thailand, which offers the same, globalized product in terms of architecture and landscape management wherever it is encountered in the world.'

The plans for the Messinia ITDA provided many sources of concern for those worried about preserving Greece's natural and cultural identity. Both the Romanos and the Pylos sections of the planned development were partly within or contiguous to environmentally protected areas belonging to the European Natura 2000 network, including the lagoon of Yalova, a fountain of local biodiversity, and the mesmerizing beach of Voedokilia.

In the wetlands of Yalova, more than 270 species of birds have been spotted, including 79 protected under European legislation as endangered. The area is also home to the African Chameleon, which can be found nowhere else in Europe, and the loggerhead sea turtle (*Caretta caretta*), which lays its eggs on local beaches. Pylos is also a cultural destination, with its own brand of traditional architecture. In this context, Constantakopoulos's desire to build the first golf resorts in Greece, his plans for a total capacity of 7,000 guests, hundreds of swimming pools and seaside tourist home settlements, were to some a potentially devastating blow to the unspoilt landscape, a source of major environmental harm and a threat to the architectural heritage of the area.

Local activists, plus a small number of academics, lawyers and journalists, raised these issues as Costa Navarino was fumbling its way through the bureaucratic maze. Some did so with fact-free vehemence. But others made legitimate points, asking, among other things, how the development would affect the rich eco-systems in the area and whether proper studies had been made about the region's water resources in relation in particular to the aquatic needs of the golf courses. Most crucially, they asked whether construction would take place near Natura 2000 areas, the precise terms for the protection of which remained scandalously unspecified by the government (Greece has been repeatedly sanctioned by the European Court for chronic failures on this front). The environmental track record of the executive branch being so abysmal, and the size of the Constantakopoulos project being so colossal, there was cause for the people of this sleepy, underdeveloped region to be concerned.

But the Captain's ambition was not restricted to the size of his hotels. To a degree unusual for a developer, his methods and vision for Costa Navarino were guided and constrained by his desire to bring it into harmony with the nature and culture of Messinia and to aid the local economy. The Turkish authorities had offered him the opportunity to build a similar resort in

2,000 hectares on the coast of Antalya, which would have been much less complex and probably much more profitable. He was not interested. The only place he cared about developing was Messinia.

In the run-up to the opening of Navarino Dunes, he frequently disagreed with the firms that would take over its management, like Starwood, on issues where he preferred a more traditional approach while they – traditional also, in their own way – focused on maximizing profits. Cuisine was one point of friction, with the chains' preference for a wide variety ultimately winning out over Constantakopoulos's taste for exclusively Greek food. The management companies, on the other hand, accepted the Captain's wishes that the majority of the hotel staff should be Messinians, even if many lacked the necessary experience: at the end of 2012, about 70 per cent of the 1,000 employees of Navarino Dunes came from the local population, according to TEMES (it remains to be seen, of course, whether this trend will be maintained now that the Captain is gone).

The Constantakopoulos family was determined to help the Messinian economy in other ways as well: Costa Navarino developed a line of agricultural and other products, from olive oil to figurines and ceramics, all produced by small local farmers and artisans. The hotels also offer plenty of activities in nearby villages and nature spots, where the guests can become acquainted with local food, culture and the beauty of the Messinian countryside.

To realize his vision of an environmentally respectful resort, the Captain hired the office of Alexandros Tombazis, Greece's foremost eco-architect, to build Navarino Dunes according to the principles of bioclimatic architecture. Everything in the construction process – from the natural materials chosen to the orientation of rooms, the insulation, the ventilation, the green roofs (5,000 square metres of them), the shading, the placement of the buildings within the plot so as to give the illusion of smaller size – was geared towards this goal. The developers are keen to point out that the resort's building footprint will be less than half what is permitted by law.

A wide range of measures was also put in place to conserve energy and water use and to reduce emissions. The irrigation needs of the Dunes resort, in particular, including the golf courses, are covered by using recycled water from a wastewater plant constructed for that purpose and from two reservoirs with a capacity of around 800,000 cubic metres. The reservoirs are filled during the winter months by utilizing some of the excess runoff from the local rivers which would otherwise flow into the sea.

TEMES also initiated a huge transplantation initiative for the olive trees – an emblem of Messinia with deep historical as well as actual roots – and citrus trees that had to be removed to make room for the infrastructure of the new resort. Some of the olive trees were many hundreds of years old and weighed over 10 tonnes. Agronomists, topographers and landscape architects have been working on this since 2004 and had transplanted, by the end of 2012, 10,000 olive trees. The final target is to replant 16,000 olive trees and 8,000 citrus trees.

A project this big was bound to alter – to *spoil* – the landscape to some extent. The Captain himself was known to remark that whatever man does, he cannot improve upon nature. But he and his son were committed to minimizing the effects.

This is not to say that all concerns have been allayed. For one thing, even if current development plans do not exhaust the legally allowable square footage, it remains an option in future, if the gods of profitability require it, to build more, or to allow other investors to build more. In addition, despite efforts to make water use sustainable, the cuts in the water supply that have long plagued the surrounding areas have got worse since the resorts opened for business, with some locals placing the blame on Costa Navarino.

But perhaps the more troubling part is that building the resorts in an eco-friendly way was mostly down to Constantakopoulos and his son: the ineptitude and indifference of public administration meant that, despite the mind-numbing regulations and the innumerable signatures required, a more ruthless developer could have wrought havoc upon the coastline of Messinia. As Kriton Arsenis, the MEP, points out, even though, by its very nature and size, Costa Navarino cannot but impose itself upon rather than fit seamlessly into the Messinian landscape, the Constantakopouloi 'went to great lengths to make the project sustainable. The worry is that the next ITDA investor won't be concerned with any of that and will cause much greater damage.'

After all, Romanos and the other areas were initially designated as parts of an ITDA in 2001 without prior land planning or an environmental impact assessment. There were no guidelines set on the architectural approach so that it would be in harmony with traditional local architecture, and the finished product is less successful on this front than on ecological criteria. Most disturbingly, the state has still not set up concrete biodiversity management regimes in the various Natura 2000 areas within or near the ITDA. In approving a project the size of Costa Navarino with this crucial regulatory framework left vague, the responsible government officials were allowing facts on the ground to be created that would subsequently be impossible to reverse.

'There is a sloppiness, a lack of defined goals or of an understanding of what we are called upon to manage as regards the Greek tourist product,' Arsenis says. 'Decisions are made on the basis of back-of-the-envelope planning, without an analysis of benefits and costs, and often leading to disastrous results, both for tourism and the natural and cultural environment.'

Beyond the dilemmas about the future course of tourism policy and the balance between development and wilderness protection, the story of Costa Navarino illustrates the deep flaws in the legal process. Individuals and groups who are opposed for whatever reason to an investment project can take their worries to court at little cost (it takes a mere €150 for a citizen to appeal to the Council of State). This makes sense from a democratic viewpoint, but – much like other rights in Greece – it is habitually abused.

A 2013 law increased the fee paid for injunction order appeals by companies involved in competitive tenders for public contracts, from €100 to 1 per cent of the budget of the contested project or up to €50,000. The Council had called for an increase in the fee in order to stem the torrent of frivolous suits that threatened to crush it under the ever-accumulating weight of backlogged cases. In early 2012, the number of cases outstanding in the country's supreme administrative court was a few dozen short of 32,000. The average delay in hearing a case that came before it at the time was five years.[10] The European Court of Human Rights has judged that in no court case should the verdict take more than three years to be handed down.

Similar – if not worse – delays plague Greece's lower courts. According to a Ministry of Justice explanatory report in support of a law aimed at speeding up legal proceedings, between 1997 and 2012 Greece has been condemned 360 times by the European Court of Human Rights for excessive delays in the administration of justice. In one of these cases, it took twenty-seven years for a verdict to be reached. The authors of the explanatory report write of a 'denial of justice', a condition that is deteriorating and that 'not only erodes the social fabric' and 'undermines democratic institutions' but also 'constitutes a drag on economic life and growth'.

One of the main culprits responsible for the wheels of justice grinding to a screeching halt is public administration itself. Ministries and government agencies routinely fail to meet deadlines for the remittance of case files to the Council of State for examination – often by great lengths of time and despite repeated calls from the court. The state also abuses the right to seek the reversal of lower court decisions, forcing high court judges to waste countless man-hours examining cases on the principles of which they have already handed down clear rulings. On public works involving a serious impact on the environment, the studies it commissions are often so shoddy and lacking in scientific credibility that they are guaranteed to be challenged in court, in many instances repeatedly until they are forced to get it right.

The creaky machinery of government, combined with an over-burdened legal system, in which anyone could appeal against anything at any time, throttle investment and breed corruption. In the 2010 edition of the World Bank's 'Doing Business' report, Greece ranked 107th in the world in the ease of registering property, 140th in the requirements for starting a new firm (it took 15 working days and 19 different procedures), 147th in the business-friendliness of employment regulation (see chapter 5) and 154th in protecting investors. As a result, Greece came in 109th out of 183 nations on the ease of doing business, and dead last of the twenty-seven member states of the European Union. Between 2007 and 2010, foreign direct investment (FDI) into the country averaged €1.7 billion a year, among the lowest levels in the Union. According to 2010 figures, although Greece's share of EU GDP was 1.9 per cent, its share of inward FDI stock was less than 0.5 per cent.[11]

Before the crisis, this troubled neither the government nor the domestic business community, the most powerful members of which were able to manipulate both the political and the legal system to grow fat at the expense of the more scrupulous or less well connected competition. Many of Greece's oligarchs had a tried and tested method for coming out on top, and staying there: they became big players in the country's murky media market, especially after the introduction of privately owned television and radio in the late 1980s, and used their newspapers, TV channels and radio stations to gain influence over ministers and officials. This guaranteed them first dibs in the allotment of government contracts, favourable tax treatment and easy borrowing from the banks. It also allowed them to use the justice system to entrap any helpless outsider who happened to beat them in a competitive tender – say, a foreign company unaware of Greek rules of engagement – in an eternity of appeals.

These days, the fundamentals of this unholy collusion have broken down. The media outlets of the oligarchs have seen their credibility and their finances collapse, as the banking system has gone bust and politicians have no public money to spend. Greece now needs FDI desperately, and FDI (indeed all kinds of DI), aside from a stable tax regime, requires a level-playing field, simple rules and regulations and a legal system that can enforce them fairly and expeditiously.

The oligarchs, like wounded beasts, will fight against these desired qualities with wild fury. But there is also another danger. Since the beginning of the crisis, politicians, businessmen and pundits have repeatedly spoken of the need to strip away obstacles to investment. There are many uncontroversial things that could be done – some already have been – to facilitate the procedure for starting a business, to simplify licensing, to expedite the legal process.

But it is still the same people governing the country who brought it to this low point, and their record on safeguarding the environment and the architectural heritage of Greece has been among their darkest legacies. Even before the crisis, they sought to bypass inconvenient Council of State verdicts by incorporating administrative decisions it repealed into laws, which are not subject to its jurisdiction. The politicians even amended the Constitution in 2001 to reduce the scope of the Council's oversight on environmental matters.

These days, as Kriton Arsenis, the MEP, observes, 'the logic seems to be that any law we come across that blocks a particular investment, we change it.' In the current clamour for private money to pour into the Greek economy at any cost, and with perennial naysayers providing a useful foil, it is not unlikely that investment projects will be greenlighted that will cause irreparable harm.

The Yalova lagoon has a dream-like quality. It is early February, dusk. Flamingos and great and little egrets float languidly in the marshy waters or potter about near the reed beds. Occasionally, a cormorant or a pair of ducks tear through the mist-coloured air that has turned the setting sun into a yellow-grey smudge. In the distance, binoculars reveal a majestic osprey, a species of eagle with a wingspan nearing two metres, resting on a tree branch. High above, multitudes of common starling criss-cross the sky, creating ever-shifting shapes of arresting beauty.

Fed sea water from the Ionian sea and freshwater from two small rivers, the lagoon is a rich ecosystem and a vital transit point for migratory birds – their first stop as they return to Europe each spring and their last place of rest before crossing over into Africa in the autumn. In the 1950s, when it was still a freshwater wetland, the government, engaged in a campaign to uproot malaria from Greece, had attempted to drain it. But underground sources from the two rivers kept providing it with water and the authorities eventually gave up. Then, in the 1980s, seawater started flowing in for the first time, causing unsustainable salinization. The lagoon was also becoming a repository of waste from all manner of human activity in its environs. It had even been proposed to turn it into an airport.

It was only in the 1990s that its significance – which increased as other nearby wetlands were successfully drained – was recognized and measures were taken to protect it from further harm. The Hellenic Ornithological Society started doing serious work there in 1997 – the year when the ITDA law was passed by parliament. Today, in the absence of a state body responsible for management and protection in the area, it remains the main line of defence for its precious flora and fauna. Sceptical at first about the Costa Navarino project, the Society then decided to collaborate with TEMES and influence developments 'from within'. But in 2012 the new board of directors of the NGO decided they would no longer accept funding from the Constantakopoulos family business, even though the need for it had become increasingly desperate.

It is a sign of the inevitable tensions that an investment the size of Costa Navarino creates in a region used to a slower pace and a much smaller scale. The old rumours that the Constantakopouloi were after the subsidies and had no plans actually to build the resorts, rumours fed by the bureaucratic delays and by the practice of many other hot-air salesmen in the recent history of Greek business, were proved false. These days, for the most part, the locals seem to have overcome their initial reservations, especially as many have either directly or indirectly benefited from the activity generated by Navarino Dunes. But new rumours still arise, without any need for corroborating evidence.

The 2010 verdict against it did not end up causing serious problems for Costa Navarino. The Council of State is not a constitutional court — it does not throw out entire laws, it only invalidates specific administrative decisions it finds of violation of the Constitution. TEMES altered its master plan so as to exclude the plots of the owners who did not want to sell, and moved on. The potential is always there, however, for new appeals against administrative decisions greenlighting new development in Pylos or Ryzomiloi. According to some legal experts, the Council of State precedent could be used to block all further development of the Messinia ITDA, though that seems highly improbable, not least because of the jobs and other benefits it has brought to the local economy.

If the development of Costa Navarino has stalled, this is less because of legal difficulties and more because of the effects of the crisis, in Greece and beyond. The company, buoyed by a series of international awards and glowing reviews (from Condé Nast, CNN, National Geographic, and many others), had hoped that 2012 would be the beginning of year-round operation for one of the two Dunes hotels. But the demand is not there yet. During the spring months in particular, the pre-election period(s) and the growing uncertainty about Greece's position within the Eurozone caused foreign tourists to stay away.

Initial plans to build two more hotels in the Romanos section have been replaced by a greater emphasis on building tourist homes and finding buyers for them. The same shift of focus is evident in the plans for Pylos, where the second golf course is already operational but where construction has been delayed on the Navarino Bay all-pool-villa resort, originally projected for completion in 2013. Though TEMES is also targeting buyers outside Europe – Russians prominent among them – the success of the tourist real-estate venture will depend on the level of demand among the European middle and upper-middle class, on whose incomes the long crisis has taken a heavy toll. But before all that, building more tourist homes will require further amendments to the relevant legislation, a process which, it should be clear by now, is far from speedy or straightforward.

The task now falls to Achilles Constantakopoulos to complete his father's dream. At the Captain's funeral, Achilles shared with the huge crowd, filled with simple folk as much as with the dignitaries of politics and business, some of the maxims that his father had imparted to his three sons. Some will be particularly useful to Achilles as he seeks to steer Costa Navarino into the future. 'When you have something difficult to do,' the Captain would say, 'once you decide it, you should be made of cement, and not budge an inch.' He would also tell his sons that he would curse them if they ever greeted one of their associates sitting down, and that a good name takes years to make and an instant to be unmade. Most important of all, though, he would always remind them of the duty that comes with privilege: 'He who has resources and can also dream, is obligated to create.'

Power Struggle

If government made a complete hash of business regulation and of fostering a climate conducive to investment in Greece, things became even worse when the state itself took on the role of entrepreneur. A lot has been written, and said, by politicians, the press, public policy professors and, more than anyone else, the people, about the dire business record of the Greek government. But nothing captures the soul-crushing perversity of life in the Greek public sector like a speech given by Panagis Vourloumis, at a time when he was president and CEO of OTE, Greece's largest telecoms company and a former state monopoly.

The speech was given in November 2006. It was the period after the 2004 Olympics, when the New Democracy government led by Costas Karamanlis boasted of the effectiveness of its programme of 'mild fiscal adjustment' (it turned out to be all mildness and no adjustment), the economy was growing at more than 4 per cent and talk of the coming reckoning was considered unfashionable, ill-mannered or just plain curmudgeonly.

Vourloumis, though, was not a man to sail with the prevailing winds. A veteran banker in his late sixties, he had been tapped by Karamanlis in 2004 to run OTE because of his reputation for able management, straight-talking and indifference to political pressure. This reputation had been mainly built in the late 1970s and early '80s when Vourloumis had served as governor of the state-owned Emporiki Bank, a position to which he had been appointed by Karamanlis's uncle, Constantinos Karamanlis.

On that November day, in the building that housed the stock exchange, he had been tasked with describing life in a Greek

DEKO (state-owned enterprise). He opened by saying that who-ever chose that topic was 'looking for trouble'. He pointed out that the precise number of DEKOs, many of which continued to dominate major sectors of the economy, from the railways to water to air travel, is a 'state secret'. But it was known that they employed a 'significant percentage' of the people in full-time employment in Greece and a growing proportion of the government's annual budget was used up to cover their mushrooming liabilities.

Then he embarked – so to speak – on his little parable. 'I have decided to liken the DEKO to a boat – a cruise ship, let's say.' On this ship 'there are life rafts for some, but not for everyone' and 'some pay for their ticket while others travel for free'. He elaborated:

> First class, deluxe in fact, is taken by the union leadership. Are they crew or passengers? It is hard to tell. They are paid well to travel without cares, they get special privileges too, like a cabin for their children. If they are lucky, the good ship DEKO is a stepping stone to the luxury ocean liner of parliament.

Turning his attention to the economy class, where 'space is elastic and almost limitless', he said:

> It is the dream of every Greek man and woman, particularly if she is unwed, to be taken onboard as a crew member on a DEKO. Good and regular wages, benefits, lifetime jobs, early retirement […] And most importantly, some time in the early eighties the crews mutinied and took over the economy class. Life there is comfortable and the pressure for a seat is irresistible. However much the port police tries to limit the size of the crew, it keeps on growing, to the point when they are hanging like monkeys from the rigging.

As well as the regular crew members, he went on, there are also the sailors on contract, 'who usually jump on board on the eve of some election. They go to the deck and their sole purpose in life is to get their papers and make it into the economy class.'

Then came the grand finale:

> The DEKO cruise ship travels for the benefit and the amusement of its crew. Transporting and serving the passengers is a secondary and incidental concern. A necessary evil, shall we say – and someone, after all, must pay. On the bridge the captain smokes his pipe and stares into the horizon with his binoculars. Now and then he turns his eyes to the deck, but he immediately turns away, disgusted. The sight of the far horizon calms him down. He lays out the course ahead to the helmsman: 'Stay away from the shoals of decisions, let the ship drift with the currents, keep it away from ports where the ship inspector and the registry lurk. What are you after? Do you want them to catch us without certificates, overbooked? Most of all, avoid storms: when you hear on the weather report that there is wind coming, ask for a sailing ban and cast anchor somewhere quiet until they pass. The ship-owning company wants no trouble. That's why they put us here and the bosses are elected by the crew. So, pay attention: what if the ship starts leaning to the side, what if the fuel is running out, what if we may capsize in a storm? We must cast aside these unpleasant thoughts – after all, we have been hearing these things for years and yet the ship is still plodding along, it is taking on water, but the pumps are working, we have the passengers to work them. Come, let us make our way around the next cape – elections – and then we'll see. The sea falls ill but does not die, and neither does Greece.'

Reactions from union leaders, politicians and the left-wing press ranged from the enraged to the apoplectic. But Vourloumis was onto something crucial. According to Law 3429/2005, a DEKO is defined as 'every limited company in which the Hellenic Public Sector has the capacity to exercise, directly or indirectly, decisive influence'. For the longest time, the stewards of the Greek state used that influence not in the interests of the national economy or of the consumers of public services, but to satisfy the demands of their clientele, by placing untold numbers of supporters on the payroll of these companies. The pay at these jobs was significantly better than in the private sector, it was impossible to be fired, the hours were shorter, retirement came earlier and pensions were far more generous. The immoderate cost of these marvellous arrangements was paid by 'the passengers', that is, the rest of the Greeks, either as consumers of the services of the DEKO, most of which used to be monopolies (some still are), or as taxpayers, an ever-increasing share of whose money was directed every year to covering the financial deficits of the companies and meeting the extravagant retirement benefits of their former employees.

Technological change and EU legislation in favour of liberalization created the first clouds on the horizon for the DEKO ships and the shipowners (successive Greek governments) in the 1990s. Since then, a long rearguard action has been in operation, in which the political system, the unions and the private interests that had a privileged relationship with the big state-owned companies did their best to create the appearance of living up to the country's European obligations, while at the same time preserving existing cosy arrangements. Nowhere had this strategy proved as effective, at least prior to the arrival of the troika, as in the electricity market, and the case of Greece's national power company, PPC.

In the waning days of the Karamanlis government, in late July 2009, Takis Athanasopoulos, the clean-cut sixty-five-year-old former Toyota executive who had been appointed chairman and

CEO of Greece's Public Power Corporation, received an uninvited visitor in his office in downtown Athens. The visit led to Athanasopoulos unwittingly being cast in a supporting role in an action-packed reality show which could have been entitled 'Trade Union Idol'. Nikos Fotopoulos, head of GENOP-DEI, the militant union of PPC employees, barged in with a number of his comrades, to demand an explanation for the fact that – as he claimed to have been informed – a meeting of the board of directors of the company had been held without notifying the workers' representative. The disputed meeting related to a decision on the competitive tender to build a new power plant fired by natural gas in the Megalopolis region of the Peloponnese, which ended up being awarded to METKA, a subsidiary of the Mytilineos Group, which is also Greece's largest private generator of energy.

The scene, which was shot and posted on YouTube by a GENOP film crew, is extraordinary. Fotopoulos, with his trademark two-week-old beard, in an untucked shirt and jeans, first homes in on three executives sitting in the ante-chamber of the CEO's office. He demands to know, in a rising voice, whether there has been a board meeting. When one of the executives attempts to escape, he orders him to sit back down. He marches from one hapless manager to the other, asking the same thing again and again. His interlocutors do not protest or respond. They look like they have shrunk into themselves.

He then moves into Athanasopoulos's office for the main event, and works himself into a frenzy. The man nominally in charge of the company tries to get a word in, but he is shouted down by Fotopoulos, who by now is screaming: 'Did you attempt a coup? Where did you attempt a coup? At PPC? At the company of the Greek people?' He goes on in this vein for a while, gesticulating dangerously close to the CEO's face and banging his hand on his desk, telling him he should be ashamed and reminding him that the military junta has been deposed. Later in the video, having calmed down a little, he utters the customary threat of legal action: 'GENOP will put you in the dock. You and all those others who act as rodents and rats in the interests of the private sector.'

A few months later the government changed hands and a few months after that, PASOK fired Athanasopoulos, who had been appointed by New Democracy. The top management of the DEKO always gets replaced when there is a transfer of political power – especially if, as in the case of PPC, the government is the majority shareholder. But Fotopoulos, the keeper of the flame, a fixture of the deep state, remained in place.

Nikos Fotopoulos has become an emblematic figure of what is known as 'Old PASOK'. He joined the party in 1978, as a firebrand young Trotskyite only sixteen years of age. PASOK itself was in its infancy, but, under the charismatic, turbulent leadership of Andreas Papandreou, it was already the second largest force in parliament and on its way to capturing power. The son of émigré parents who went to work in Germany – his father as a steelworker, his mother in textiles – and left him to be raised by his grandparents in the village of Agnanta in the Western Peloponnese, Fotopoulos developed from early on a devotion to the values of the working class – at least some of them.

Sitting in his office at GENOP headquarters in downtown Athens, flanked by pictures of PPC power plants, Aris Velouchiotis, Che Guevara and Lenin, he reminisces about those early days. 'I was always interested in public affairs, since junior high. I was class president and president of the student council. It came from the poverty we were living in. I joined PASOK to make the world better, more just. I believe in exactly the same things today – in class consciousness, in socialism.'

In 1986, a few years after PASOK won power, he got a job at PPC. He has always claimed that he didn't make use of political connections, though people who know how things were done back then dispute this. Pretty much immediately, he got involved in the union affairs of the company. After serving his time on the picket lines, the strike marches and the occupation sites, in February 2007, a month before Athanasopoulos was appointed chairman and CEO, Fotopoulos was elected head of GENOP-DEI, the powerful company union.

It was a challenging time for PPC. Its profitability had taken a real tumble in 2006. Delays in setting up the institutional framework for the opening of the market in power generation had led to extensive power cuts and fears of a blackout because of insufficient capacity. PPC itself took as long as seven months to connect new consumers to the grid.

The permanently outraged union leader did not think that the new head of the company was pushing back hard enough against the regulator on issues where he thought PPC's competitors were given unfair advantage. He was also opposed to Athanasopoulos's plans to break up the vertically integrated former monopolist, in accordance with EU directives for electricity market reform. Soon, he would have even greater cause to protest.

In the autumn of 2007 it emerged that Athanasopoulos was engaged in secret negotiations with RWE, the German energy giant, for the construction of two black–coal–powered electricity plants of a total capacity of 1600MW, equal to about one-seventh of total existing capacity in the country. The new plants would be run by a joint venture in which RWE would be the majority shareholder, with 51 per cent. 'Other than learning the technology of black coal and sharing in the profits, the primary strategic target of the venture was to open up the market by introducing real competition to PPC, which would then force it to change and become more competitive. This would have meant better services and lower prices for the consumer,' Athanasopoulos says.

Fotopoulos thought the deal with RWE was a Trojan Horse for the abdication by the state of its controlling stake in PPC. At a minimum, he knew that replacing the old lignite-fuelled plants with the new ones would mean job losses, and also that in the new joint venture, under German management, GENOP's influence would be markedly diluted.

That influence was vital in upholding the extraordinary privileges that PPC insiders enjoyed. According to figures from 2010, the average gross salary for a PPC employee was €3,280 per month, or €46,000 per year. By comparison, the average gross annual pay in DEKOs as a whole was €37,000; in the private sector it was €28,550. But the bliss of being a PPC employee – of which there still are far too many, because of cutthroat competition over three decades between PASOK and New Democracy over who would appoint the largest number of clients – did not end there. The company union had managed to extract from management thirty-seven special benefits (available to particular subgroups of employees) above and beyond the regular wage.

As a result of the periodic paroxysms of recruiting, which always tended to coincide suspiciously with the electoral cycle, one can find in the ranks of the employees whole armies of redundant administrative staff – as many as 6,000 (out of a total of 21,000), according to an internal survey undertaken by the company in 2011. One could also find on the payroll waiters making €6,000 per month, as well as nurses getting €700 per month just from overtime. None of these people could be fired.[1]

Nor were the perks limited to the working years of the lucky but not so few who got permanent contracts. PPC employees – not just the ones doing the hard work in the mines or the electricity pillars – got to retire on average about ten years earlier than private sector pensioners. The pensions they received were much higher than those of their counterparts in the private sector, and they enjoyed a number of fringe benefits, like low-cost loans from state-controlled banks and lower rates in their electricity bills.

These arrangements cost the Greek taxpayer hundreds of millions of euros annually. The PPC used to serve as its employees' insurance fund, pocketing their contributions and using them to dole out pensions but also to finance the massive infrastructure investments that extended the power grid to the whole country in the 1950s and '60s. When the time came in 1999 for PPC to be listed on the Athens stock exchange, the company was burdened by enormous pension liabilities, which it was unable to cover (no one knew exactly *how* unable, because those in charge made sure to publish no relevant records). This constituted a major disincentive for potential share buyers.

The solution devised by the government of the day, with Evangelos Venizelos as the responsible minister, followed a well-worn tradition: the liabilities were passed on to the state budget. The cost to the taxpayer of funding PPC pensions far exceeded any revenue earned from selling the state's share in the company: €4.2 billion between 2001 and 2010 alone.

Fotopoulos was not about to take threats to such an idyllic set-up lying down. The union's all-out war on the RWE deal included repeated strike action as well as invasions of GENOP shock troops into board meetings held to discuss it on three separate occasions. In the last one, on 26 February 2008, droves of grizzled union men (almost no women could be seen) entered the premises in Chalkokondyli Street in downtown Athens and took over the boardroom. Along for the ride came some prominent left-wing politicians, like SYRIZA MP Panayotis Lafazanis, who, obviously oblivious of Greece's obligations under EU law, told the cameras that PPC would remain government-controlled and vertically integrated.

Beyond the hard left, though, which can always be relied upon to block any change, especially if it carries the stench of 'foreign multinationals' and 'privatization', Fotopoulos had a more crucial pillar of political support. PASOK, the official opposition, under George Papandreou, whom the union leader had backed for the leadership of the party in 2007, was in his corner. At the 26 February free-for-all, the throngs of protesters included a number of PASOK MPs, among them the future Finance Minister, Philippos Sachinides. Papandreou, despite an international reputation as an open-minded cosmopolitan and conciliator, earned during his stint as Foreign Minister between 1999 and 2004, had decided back home to play by the tribal rules of Greek politics, whose arch-exponent had been his father, Andreas. In that vein, in particular from 2007–9, he followed a polarizing opposition strategy, lambasting even the half-hearted attempts of the Karamanlis government at pension reform and lashing out with particular vehemence at moves to privatize public sector companies.

As if all this was not enough, Athanasopoulos also faced the ire of powerful private interests which had gained a foothold in the electricity generation market and saw the entry of the German Leviathan as a mortal threat to their expansion. These companies were terrified that the direct access that RWE would get to licences for construction and operation through its connection with PPC would offer the new venture a decisive competitive advantage (such licences take ages to rise to the surface from the swampy depths of Greek bureaucracy). They also feared that, in the new environment that would be created, cosy arrangements ensuring their economic viability despite their lack of cost-competitiveness would be threatened.

Faced with overwhelming opposition, abandoned by a tired government with no stomach for a fight, PPC's chairman capitu-lated. At a press conference in April 2008, he stated that the deal was off, pointing out that it was 'unheard of for board meetings to be interrupted'.

'Mr Athanasopoulos should have discussed the deal', Fotopoulos tells me. 'And not only with us – he should have discussed it with the local communities involved.' He accepts that without his inter-vention, the deal would have gone through, justifying his actions in the name of the higher interests of the company. 'These days,' he goes on, 'the good union man, in the eyes of the system, is the mute union man. The one who pretends not to see the schemes and the swindles that take place right in front of his eyes, and only asks for higher wages now and then. Then their magazines and their newspapers will print your picture with a flattering caption, calling you responsible and serious.'

Fotopoulos sees himself as having a much more active role, and this was the real source of the conflict. Athanasopoulos, a manager with a stellar record at Toyota Greece and then as vice-president of the European division of the world's largest carmaker, was not willing to acquiesce to the traditional co-management role that GENOP had assumed through the years in the company. It was an elemental power struggle for control of one of the country's biggest companies, and it pitted the company's chief executive against all three pillars of the old order: the union, domestic big business interests and the politicians. In the lotus-eating days before the Great Crisis, it was the forces of inertia that held the upper hand.

According to a detailed report by McKinsey & Company released in 2011 ('Greece: Ten Years Ahead'), energy is one of the key sectors that can contribute to the country's return to growth. As it notes, 'energy accounts directly for 4 per cent of Greece's GVA [Gross Value Added] and plays a key role in the competitiveness of domestic industrial players. The sector in Greece has a higher contribution to the GVA of the economy compared to other countries, for example in South Europe and Germany.'

However, as it goes on to state, both the higher contribution and the recent (2000–8) growth of the GVA 'are largely driven by sector inefficiencies': 'High energy consumption, low fuel efficiency, low labour and capital productivity and an expensive energy mix characterize the Greek energy sector' in comparison with its European peers. According to the report, the sector is also characterized 'by limited "extroversion", as there is relatively limited activity of Greek energy players abroad, and narrow activity across the value chain.' The country's failure to capitalize on its potential in this vital industry is directly related to its at best halting path towards institutional reform and the introduction of competition in the energy market.

Greece's wayward route to electricity market liberalization began as far back as 1999. Prior to that, PPC was the sole supplier and retailer, as well as the owner of the transmission system and the distribution networks. With a law passed that year, Greece committed itself to opening up the supply and retail markets to competition, in accordance with EU directive 96/92.

At the beginning of 2010, two EU legislative initiatives and countless internal laws and regulations later, PPC was still pretty much the only name in the game: its share of the generation market was 91 per cent, its share of the retail market was 99.5 per cent, and the transmission and distribution networks still belonged to it, ostensibly separated by Chinese walls whose Greek public sector materials made those in the know grin with world-weary cynicism.

Fotopoulos has fought liberalization, which he refers to as 'the enslavement of PPC', every step of the way. He offers a simple narrative, with innocent victims, a terrible villain and the despicable enablers of his calumnies. 'Electricity is a social good,' he tells me. 'As such, it should be available to the poorest consumer at an affordable price. These days, where the wholesale price has climbed, tens of thousands of poor households are living in the dark. I would like to ask the gentlemen' – he repeatedly uses that phrase, with obvious contempt – 'in the government, in RAE [the energy regulator], all those who leave the door wide open for the *honourable gentlemen* of the private concerns to milk PPC: could they live without electricity for one hour, even one minute?' Private companies should not take part either in generation or in the retail market for electricity, he concludes.

The situation, of course, is more complex. PPC enjoys to this day a monopoly in the use of lignite for the generation of electric power – despite European Commission decisions and Memorandum commitments. Lignite, a type of coal that is a major contaminant but also a source of cheap energy plentifully available in Greece, gives PPC an overwhelming cost advantage over its competitors. To appease Brussels for this, successive governments have resorted to various artificial means of introducing competition, which Fotopoulos and his allies lambast as 'milking' PPC and the consumer, because they allow higher-cost electricity (from natural gas or renewables) to enter the system.

The private sector is hardly pleased with the situation. In a briefing paper issued in late 2010, the Mytilineos Group raised a number of issues blocking private investment in the energy market. It noted that the licensing procedure lasts from three to five years, due to 'the involvement of numerous authorities consecutively and not in parallel (RAE, forest authorities, town planning authorities etc.)', whose personnel often have incomplete knowledge of the regulatory framework. Things were made worse by the absence of land and forest registries, which further delay approval of new installations. Finally, 'competent authorities do not meet the foreseen maximum or even reasonable response times or are not even obliged by law to keep a specific time schedule.' The briefing paper uses the example of the delayed response by the PPC-owned transmission system operator to demands by private generators for new connections to the system.

But the chaotic nature of the system has also provided boondoggles for private generators. PPC was engaged in a long-running dispute (finally resolved after more than seven years in early 2014) about the prices at which it provides electricity – huge amounts of it – to Aluminium of Greece, a producer of aluminium and alumina (aluminium oxide) belonging to the Mytilineos Group. The former monopoly claimed that decisions by the energy regulator, RAE, forced it to sell to the company below cost. Meanwhile, the natural-gas-fired power station of Aluminium of Greece sells electricity to PPC retail (through the electricity pool) at more than double the price at which it buys from it.

There are other distortions as well. In setting up the regulatory framework for 'liberalized' power generation, policy planners faced a tricky conundrum: they had to introduce competition to a market whose incumbent enjoyed – and it was desired that it would continue to enjoy – monopoly control over the cheapest means (lignite) of producing the good in question (electricity). The solution, though far from conducive to the maximizing of social welfare, was in its way ingenious: it was decided that generators using natural gas to produce electricity would receive an annual subsidy which would cover their costs plus offer a guaranteed 'profit' of 10 per cent. This subsidy, introduced in 2010 and meant to be phased out after two years, was still going in 2013 and its size had ballooned: from €36 million in its first year to €461 million in 2012.[2]

This cost, passed on by PPC in particular to industrial consumers of energy, is one of the main reasons why Greek manufacturing faces some of the highest energy costs in the whole of the EU. As was recounted in chapter 5, in its struggle to survive the collapse in internal steel demand and the crippling nine-month strike in Aspropyrgos, Hellenic Halyvourgia turned to exports. This strategic decision was made that much more challenging by the far lower energy costs of its European competitors. Epilektos, the last large-scale textiles company in what was once a thriving industry, which exports 78 per cent of its turnover, reached the brink of bankruptcy because of out-of-control electricity costs.[3]

A separate but associated failure of the system relates to Greece's continuing dependency on coal for energy production. Figures from 2011 show that 47 per cent of Greece's total energy generation came from PPC's lignite units, while only 8 per cent came from Renewable Energy Sources (excluding PPC's big hydro-electric plants). According to projections by IOBE, an economic policy think-tank, despite increasing levels of investment in Renewable Energy Sources, on current trends the country will fall way short of its target of RES generation capacity equal to 40 per cent of the total by 2020. Fotopoulos may think that the penetration of the private sector in the RES market is another 'huge scandal' (as he told me), but from the point of view of Greece's energy strategy, that penetration is happening nowhere near fast enough and PPC has done precious little to cover the shortfall.

The delays in transferring generation away from lignite and towards cleaner sources is going to cost PPC – and by extension the Greek economy – very dearly. As of 2013 and the introduction of the new Emissions Trading Scheme (ETS), the right to emit CO_2 in the atmosphere is much costlier in the EU. At a carbon price of €10/tonne (the price level in August 2012), PPC, one of Europe's biggest emitters, would have to fork out over €500 million in 2013.[4] Given the removal of administrative controls in utility bills for industrial concerns, this cost will be immediately transferred to Greek industry, crushing what is left of it. Price deregulation hit households, too, in 2013 (until then they had enjoyed the lowest utility bills in the EU, in line with government social policy but hurting PPC's bottom line). This means that, among other things, and as if they were not burdened enough, from now on they will shoulder more of the cost of PPC's undimmed love affair with old king coal.

When the Memorandum came, as in every other sector of Greek economic life, the ground shifted in the energy market and in particular at PPC. The total wage costs of the company have been reduced from €1.7 billion in 2009 to around €1 billion in 2012. This reflects significant pay cuts which, according to the company, translated into a reduction in the average wage cost per employee of 36 per cent by the end of 2012. In addition, PPC pensioners have had their pensions repeatedly cut along with everyone else. Perhaps most important of all, one of the terms of Greece's second bailout, signed in February 2012, requires that tenure in the DEKO, including PPC, is abolished. GENOP and its political patrons have thus lost many battles; but they retreated in none without a fight, and they have so far resisted change on many crucial fronts.

The first major stand of the union in the Age of the Memorandum came at the tail end of July 2010. As politicians and journalists prepared for their August break on the islands in the aftermath of Greece's near-bankruptcy a couple of months earlier, members of the troika visited the Ministry of Environment and Energy and suggested to officials there that it was time, as per relevant EU Commission decisions of years past, for PPC to sell 40 per cent of its lignite-fuelled and large-scale hydroelectric plants to its competitors.

Fotopoulos begged to differ. In a text message that he sent to dozens of MPs from PASOK and parties of the left, he drew a line in the sand: 'We the employees of PPC will not sell any plants nor will we sell energy at cost to hot-air salesmen. Let's be clear. There are limits to everything. The struggle is not about us, it's for the consumer, so we are willing to go to extremes. We will bleed.' Fotopoulos warned the government that if it acceded to the demands of the troika, the union would strike indefinitely, potentially sinking the country into darkness.

That was only the opening round. In early 2011, as part of the privatization programme agreed by the Papandreou government and the troika, it was decided to put up for sale another 17 per cent of the government's stake in PPC by the end of 2012, bringing its share down to 34 per cent.

If this was not enough to make Fotopoulos go ballistic, as the government was revealing its plans, the redoubtable Leandros Rakintzis – investigator of government ineptitude ranging from stolen Picassos to health insurance chaos – issued his report on the financing of GENOP by PPC in the period between 1999 and 2010. Asked to look into the matter by the Ministry of Environment and Energy, the Inspector General of Public Administration found that the sums – €31.2 million – had been provided to GENOP illegally. Among other things, the money was spent on strikes and legal services which were directed against the company itself, on a study that was never carried out, on a magazine that was never distributed, on PCs whose recipients were impossible to trace, and so on. Fotopoulos blasted Rakintzis as a government tool, claimed, without much evidence, that the contributions were all legal and made much of the fact that the report came out the day after GENOP announced its decision to launch a series of strikes to protest against the further privatization of PPC. He also claimed that the order for GENOP to be cut down to size had come from the troika itself.

All this set the stage for a high-stakes showdown. On 20 June, as the new round of austerity measures and structural reforms was making its way through parliament, with large numbers of Athenians camping out for weeks in protest in Syntagma Square in front of the parliament building, GENOP began a series of consecutive forty-eight-hour strikes, which caused many parts of Greece to experience repeated power cuts. Mayors and groups of citizens filed lawsuits against the president of GENOP, and the management of PPC itself took him to court, demanding that the strike be ruled illegal. Finally, on the 29th, the union called it off, when the law incorporating the new measures – including the further privatization of PPC – was passed.

By the end of 2013, however, despite the law, the state still controlled 51 per cent of the old monopoly. A few months later, the Hellenic Republic Asset Development Fund was leaking that the sale of the 17 per cent stake would be postponed until 2016. GENOP was losing battles, but it was still far from capitulating.

A few months after the June showdown, in early September 2011, the PASOK government was once again in big trouble. A series of broken reform promises had nearly exhausted the patience of its European partners. The pressure was on for Papandreou and his new deputy prime minister and Minister of Finance, Evangelos Venizelos, to find new sources of revenue to restrain a budget deficit that was once again, in the context of an economy in freefall, spiralling out of control.

On 12 September Venizelos announced his back-of-the-envelope solution: a new extraordinary property tax on all real estate connected to the power grid, proportional to the surface area, to be levied until 2015 through the utility bill. It was the ninth supplementary tax tacked onto the PPC bill (including municipal taxes, Renewable Energy levies and TV and radio licence fees), and the most egregious one: even unemployed homeowners, whose numbers were growing fast, were not exempt. Anyone who would not, or could not, pay, faced the threat of disconnection from the power grid. The public reaction was one of universal disgust.

This groundswell of revulsion provided an opening for Fotopoulos. Venizelos's new tax, which was very quickly renamed the *charatsi* in common and even in journalistic parlance (after a tax imposed by the Ottomans on the Christian populations of the empire), allowed the head of GENOP to bolster his populist credentials. He immediately came out against it, saying that PPC should not be forced into the role of the sheriff 'putting a gun to the head of the unemployed and wage-earners'.

As always, Fotopoulos followed up on his strong words with action, again as the guardian of the higher interests of PPC, in opposition to its management and against the law. In mid-October he led a team of union officials into the company's bill-issuing centre and took it over. Before retreating with his forces, Fotopoulos, flanked by SYRIZA leader Alexis Tsipras, assorted left-wing MPs and members of the 'Can't Pay Won't Pay' movement, made sure to remind the Greek people that he would rather go to prison than cut access to power to ordinary folk.

His wish would be granted on 20 November, when GENOP occupied the IT headquarters of PPC, responsible among other things for issuing instructions for power to be cut in cases of unpaid debts to the company. The union made it clear that it had no intention of leaving, and called on citizens to join the protest outside the building on Mesogeion Avenue, one of the busiest roads in Athens. On the fifth day of the occupation, Fotopoulos was arrested. In a breathless appearance in front of the cameras before he was led away, he said that electricity 'cannot be used as a tool to blackmail Greek society'. It was hard to disagree with him.

After numerous private citizens, as well as unions, municipalities and even the Athens Bar Association, filed suit against the tax, in May 2012 the Council of State found that, though its imposition itself was constitutional, the penalty of cutting off power to those who did not pay was not. By that time, significant damage had already been done. Countless households had been brought to the edge of destitution in order to pay the tax. Others, which could not pay, lived for months with the fear of not being able to switch on the lights or the heating (very few actual disconnections took place because of the tax, especially against poorer consumers). Around 500,000 property owners did not pay the *charatsi* in 2011.

PPC itself, on paper the country's national energy champion, had been reduced to the role of a grubby tax collector, extorting money from people barely able to feed their families. This badly hurt both its reputation and its cash flow position. The appearance of the tax alongside the cost of electricity on the utility bills meant that many people who could pay for power but could not afford the tax paid neither. At the same time, the political sensitivity of cutting off power in the era of the *charatsi* meant that the company was stripped of one of its most effective means of getting its customers to pay their bills. Partially as a result, by May 2012, the sum total of unpaid bills to PPC had reached the staggering amount of €1.1 billion and the company was facing a liquidity crisis, with potentially devastating knock-on effects on the entire electricity market.

An emergency loan from a publicly owned bank agreed at the very last minute in June gave PPC some short-term breathing room. But with the rights of its shareholders and the orderly liberalization of the energy market routinely set aside to cater to the demands of Fotopoulos[5] or the needs of the government of the day, the question remains: who does PPC answer to and what role is it going to play in the future Greek energy market? Until the fog clears on these questions, it is hard to see why anyone would want to invest in the company, or to feel safe that they can compete against it on a level playing field.

As Greece entered the maelstrom of its sovereign debt crisis, and in particular after its international creditors realized that first bailout badly needed to be bailed out, an ambitious programme of privatization was put in place to shrink the state, cut the budget deficit and bring desperately needed private investment to the country. As part of the programme, a new government agency, the Hellenic Republic Asset Development Fund (HRADF), was created on 1 July 2011, with the purpose of handling all aspects of the privatization of state-owned firms and of the development of public real estate. PPC, one of Greece's ten biggest companies by market capitalization, is one of the big beasts in the HRADF portfolio.

In July 2012 Takis Athanasopoulos was appointed chairman of HRADF, tasked with directing the thankless work of overcoming legal obstacles, labour strikes, political attacks from the left and the right and thick concrete walls of investor scepticism, in order to maximize the proceeds from the sale of state assets. In an article in September 2012, Athanasopoulos predicted revenues of €19 billion by the end of 2015. This was already way below the €50 billion initially projected for that time period, but a mere month and a half later, he downgraded the target further still, to €7.7 billion.

In his efforts to achieve even that modest goal, he was likely to have further run-ins with Nikos Fotopoulos, who had made it as clear as the Aegean waters that he would fight the privatization of PPC to the bitter end. But those hoping for a rematch of the office-storming incident of July 2009 were to be disappointed. In March 2013 curiously timed felony charges were brought against

Athanasopoulos for a contract he had signed as CEO of the company in 2007 to build a new power generation unit in Aliveri, and he resigned. The curse of the DEKO was not through with him yet.

Greece's dismal privatization record during the Age of the Memorandum – no meaningful sale had taken place until the end of 2012 – is not solely the fault of the country's client-based political system, its excessively militant unions or its investment-hostile bureaucracy. After all, these problems were there before the crisis and they did not prevent the Greek state from pulling in about €19 billion in revenues from selling off shares in publicly owned enterprises between 1992 and 2009.

The handling of the privatization programme by Greece's international creditors has been a fiasco from day one. To start with, take the original target of €50 billion from privatization revenues from 2011–15. According to this target, the Greek government, in an economic environment of collapsing share prices and a shambolic public administration, would in less than five years take in almost three times the amount it had raised in the two previous decades. The Eurozone's governments knew that this was not a serious projection, but they accepted it, because it meant they could lie to themselves and to their voters for a little while longer about how much bailing out Greece would really cost.

Then, as Greece kept missing its targets and falling ever deeper into recession and debt, the Europeans slowly had to face the real bailout bill, and they balked. Around that time, in the early autumn of 2011, and especially after George Papandreou proclaimed his ill-starred referendum on Greece's second bailout on 31 October, the talk began in earnest in European circles about a possible Greek exit (soon abbreviated to 'Grexit) from the common currency. In previous months, as the initial bailout was seen not to be working, various Economics professors and analysts were coming out with suggestions in favour of a return to the drachma. But the subject remained taboo among EU government officials and policymakers. Once Papandreou let the cat of the bag with his call for a referendum, it was all Eurozone finance ministers could talk about.

The damage was incalculable. As Miranda Xafa, CEO of EF Consulting, a former member of the board of the IMF and an economist intimately involved in the stumbling first steps of privatization in Greece in the early 1990s, puts it, 'as long as Grexit was a real possibility, no investor would bring their euros to get drachmas back.' It is not just a question of potential losses from renomination (the switch to a devalued currency), but also of opportunity cost. As Xafa explains, the uncertainty about Greece's financial future meant that Greek government bonds were trading at a significant discount, creating opportunities for windfall profits: 'No real investment is likely to yield a 100 per cent return, but Greek government bonds could easily yield that if their price increased from 20 to 40 cents on the euro.'

Another factor that has badly hobbled the privatization programme is Greece's mind-boggling bureaucracy. Xafa points out that HRADF 'has struggled because there was very little preparation ahead of time. It takes time to clear titles and organize rights on land for lease or sale, which constitutes the bulk of assets under privatization. The same applies to setting up regulatory bodies for the water companies and for the ports and airports, as well as for the full liberalization of the electricity market.'

In addition to the myriad internal complications relating to assets earmarked for privatization, there are pending cases involving EU fines or investigations of Greek state companies for receiving illegal subsidies from the government. Without resolving these problems, a task hindered by the unhelpful fact that Greece is broke, the asset sales cannot move forward.

On a balmy late October day, I visited PPC's monster steam electric power plant in Agios Dimitrios, in the Kozani-Ptolemaida basin in north-west Greece. Active since 1983 and having expanded from two to five generation units, Agios Dimitrios today is PPC's biggest power station and one of five large-scale power plants in the area. It goes through 65,000–70,000 tonnes of lignite a day to produce electricity, transferred there on a narrow black conveyor belt as well as on trucks from the South Field lignite mine, the biggest one in Greece, 3.5 kilometres away. Its five massive cooling towers coughing up steam and its three blast furnaces can be seen from a great distance away. Its 'backyard', as employees call it, where up to 1.25 million tonnes of lignite can be piled up at any one time, is a series of brown-black hill-ranges, smoking at the top because of the spontaneous combustion of the coal, looking like the innards of Hades unnaturally exposed to fresh air.

An ocean of lignite lies not far beneath the surface of the Kozani-Ptolemaida basin. Greece is the second largest producer of lignite in the European Union and the sixth largest in the world. About 60 per cent of its 4.5 billion tonnes in known reserves has been found in Kozani-Ptolemaida. According to PPC, the 3.1 billion remaining reserves will last, on current projections, more than forty-five years. The vast quantities of lignite, extracted at low cost, have been used since the late 1950s by the company as fuel to produce cheap electricity that travels to every corner of the country (except for most of the islands of the Aegean, which are not connected to the continental transmission system).

But the costs of Greece's lignite dependency, in terms of the health of the local population, the environmental damage and, especially as of 2013, the financial cost of its CO_2 emissions, are heavy. Lignite is a particularly unsavoury type of coal: its low energy content means it needs far higher temperatures to be turned into electric energy, which entails more emissions. A study commissioned in 2007 by the WWF on the 'dirty thirty', the power stations in Europe that contribute most to the exacerbation of climate change, ranked Agios Dimitrios at number one. According to plant operatives, the cost in emissions rights that

PPC will have to pay for Agios Dimitrios alone as of 2013, depending on the price of carbon, may exceed €200 million.[6]

'This is something that will seriously affect PPC, as well as the national economy,' says Nikos Apostolidis, the plant manager of Agios Dimitrios. 'High growth rates in Greece have traditionally been supported by cheap power, which was made possible by cheaply available lignite.' As he admits, improved technology in existing plants can only 'marginally reduce' CO_2 emissions so, in the short term, higher generation costs will mean higher prices for customers.

More direct have been the health effects of the station's operation. The ash from the burning lignite, released into the atmosphere from the three towering blast furnaces of Agios Dimitrios or taken via another conveyor belt from the power station back to the mine to be buried, has taken a heavy toll. A report in 2007 in *Ta Nea* newspaper found that the rate of cancer deaths in the nearby village of Akrini was up to five times higher than the national average. A local lung specialist spoke of the high incidence of bronchitis, asthma and emphysema, and called for a comprehensive epidemiological study of the effects of PPC's activities.

Apostolidis claims that new electrostatic filters put in place in Agios Dimitrios between 2006 and 2008, at a cost of €142 million, have significantly reduced the emissions of ash from the plant. Conceding the sometimes tense relations with the local community, the manager of the power station points out that 'PPC used to be attacked frequently by the local people, on health issues, the environment and so on.' Now, however, with privatization being a real possibility, a local association of municipalities has been formed to resist it. It is clear why: PPC may damage the lungs of the people of Kozani, but it gives them a steady stream of paycheques, and – particularly these days – that is no small matter.

Jobs, of course, don't come as easy as they used to. Gone are the days of the pre-election recruitment bonanzas. These days, the Memorandum has imposed stringent restrictions, allowing only one person to be taken on for every ten that retire in the public sector. But even before that, Apostolidis says, the delays entailed in having to recruit through ASEP, the council responsible for all state recruitment in recent years, mean that often capable and experienced employees retire and there is no one to replace them. As he tells me, posts that PPC planned to fill in 2004 were filled only in 2010. In the ten years to 2012, regular staff at Agios Dimitrios fell from 847 to 518, according to the union officials.

To deal with the problem of a shrinking workforce, the power station has been forced to outsource a number of activities – such as maintenance or other auxiliary jobs – that it used to do in-house. This, as Apostolidis recounts, has also been a problem. 'These jobs used to be done by experienced people. Now, because PPC has to award projects according to public sector procedures, which are time-consuming and which always offer the tender to the lowest bidder, the result is often subpar. A power station like ours, which operates at the cutting edge of industrial technology, cannot work within such a system.'

Later that day, I am sitting in the South Field mine, breathing in lignite dust and being shown around E3, a German-built giant excavator, as it takes a break from devouring the earth in front of it. E3, as its operators proudly inform me, is the largest mining excavator active in the Balkans. In my best David Attenborough voice, I can inform the reader that this dinosaur piece of machinery weighs 6,000 tonnes and reaches 46 metres in height, with tracks that are 3 metres tall. It is equipped with 16 buckets, each with a capacity of 3,700 cubic metres, which, in the manner of an amusement park ride gone mad, eat up the mountain at dizzying rates, twenty-four hours a day, and direct the chewed off bits to the waiting conveyor belt below. As Triantafyllos Baltsis, the chief mechanic of this mega-tank, a man who clearly takes pride in his work, told me, it has the capacity to excavate and move up to 18,000 tonnes per hour.

Work on the E3 is hard. An old machine, bought in the 1980s, and a very complex one, plenty can – and does – go wrong. When it does, Baltsis and his team must think on their feet, often in extreme weather conditions and, if the problem is a major one, sometimes they work on it for over twenty hours straight. 'Don't forget that we hail from Odysseus', he tells me, in reference to the Homeric hero's fabled agility of mind. 'The Germans did what they did, they followed the letter of science, but when something doesn't work as planned, they call us.' Beyond the cold and the long hours, he adds, 'the work is heavy, manual. We all have herniated discs.'

Baltsis, who has been with PPC for twenty-eight years and is still active in the mines, is upset, like Apostolidis, the plant manager, at the loss of know-how and accumulated experience caused by the retirement of the old guard before they can pass on their wisdom. He also complains that critics of the company ignore the hard work that he and his colleagues put in. But he acknowledges that not all PPC employees have had to put in the hours like them. 'Vicky Stamati is also a colleague, after all,' he says, speaking of the wife of former PASOK bigwig Akis Tsochatzopoulos, who was an employee of the company and who has been incarcerated along with her husband for money laundering. 'I don't remember seeing her down in the mines, nor I imagine did the colleagues over at the power station. We don't have a spa here, you see,' Baltsis mischievously adds.

As I was driven away from PPC's industrial heartland, the afternoon rays falling gently on yellow-green acacias, the car passing by an abandoned gym that had never opened its doors and a football field overgrown with weeds, both monuments to past waste, the blue sky smudged with plumes of smoke and steam from the power station that grew still as they receded into the distance, I thought about what I had seen and heard. I remembered the conversation I had had with the plant manager, about the contradictory stance of the local community towards PPC and their opposition to its privatization. I remembered, too, that when I had asked, in response to his complaint that public sector rules made it very hard to recruit the right people or to award projects to the right contractors, whether these problems would not be solved if the firm was fully privatized, he had recoiled, speaking instead of running it more meritocratically under state control.

The glorious years of PPC, when as a natural monopoly it spread electricity to the whole of Greece, are long gone. People like Fotopoulos constantly hark back to that era to serve their own influence and privileges, often at the expense of the best interests of the company and of the Greek economy. But Fotopoulos's war cries continue to influence a political class that has not let go of the idea that state-controlled behemoths can serve as cash cows for the government and employers of choice for one's political friends and family. And they continue to resonate with a people that still harbours a secret faith that when this crisis is over, we can go back to the way things were before, with a state sector operating outside any semblance of economic logic, offering permanent jobs, high wages and generous entitlements for all.

Until these attitudes change, the liberalization of the energy market will be viewed at best as a necessary evil. PPC will trudge on, wheezing forward carrying the millstones of political interference, union histrionics and outdated production methods. Domestic private companies, leery of the murky institutional set up, will avoid large-scale investments and keep looking for ways to game the system and profit with minimum effort and risk. Foreign firms will stay away. Energy, as a potential source of Greece's recovery, will continue to be depleted.

8

Big Ships in a Perfect Storm

Hopeless at managing their own energy needs, Greeks have long proved masters at delivering those of others. Their pre-eminence as global transporters was on display again on 5 December 2012, when the *Ob River*, a monster LNG (Liquefied Natural Gas) tanker, 288 metres long, with a capacity of 84,682 deadweight tonnes (dwt) and an estimated value of over $200 million, arrived in the south-western Japanese port of Tobata. It had been hired by the Russian gas behemoth Gazprom to deliver its product to Japanese consumers. The ship belonged to Dynagas, a privately held company affiliated to the Dynacom Group of George Prokopiou, one of Greece's – and hence the world's – most powerful shipping magnates.

It was a delivery of historic significance. The *Ob River*, named after a major Siberian river, had embarked on its voyage on 7 November from Hammerfest, Norway, home to the Snoehvit LNG facility operated by Norwegian oil and gas giant Statoil, carrying 134,000 cubic metres of liquefied natural gas. From there, to get to Japan, nearly 7,000 nautical miles away, it made its way through more than 3,000 miles of the bleak, icy expanse of the Northern Sea Route, accompanied by two nuclear-powered Russian icebreakers. It was the first sea voyage of an LNG cargo through the frozen waters north of Siberia in history.

The Northern Sea Route stretches north of Russia's Siberian coast, from Murmansk on the Barents Sea in the west to the Bering Strait in the Far East. Parts of it are ice-free for only two months a year. But one of the more pronounced effects of global warming in recent years has been the accelerating pace at which the Arctic ice has been melting. In September 2012 scientists at the US National Snow and Ice Data Centre found that the area's ice cover had shrunk over the preceding summer to 3.41 million square kilometres – the lowest level since satellite records began in 1979 and around 50 per cent of the average levels recorded between 1979 and 2000.[1]

In the long term, this may prove to be an environmental catastrophe of Biblical proportions. In the short term, however, it presents those well positioned to take advantage of them with enormous opportunities. The journey between Norway and Japan via the Northern Sea Route is more than 5,000 miles shorter than the Suez Canal route. The time it takes to complete it through the glacial darkness (in parts of the trip there were no more than a couple of hours of daylight per day) is about three-fifths that of the traditional route and the fuel cost savings can exceed 40 per cent.

Sitting in his office overlooking the Saronic Gulf in the southern suburbs of Athens on an overcast, blustery early spring day, the forbidding Prokopiou, a large map of the globe lined with sea routes on the wall beside him, remembers how he got into the LNG game. 'The idea of transporting liquefied natural gas was droning around in my brain since 2003,' he tells me in his deep, gravelly voice. 'I could see that this would be the century of natural gas. Why? Because there are plentiful supplies everywhere, it is half the price of oil and it is also a quick fix for pollution and CO2 emissions. This is particularly important for the cities of China and India as they expand. If measures are not taken to limit pollution there, people will suffocate.'

In 2004, with demand for new LNG tankers practically non-existent and prices having correspondingly tumbled, Prokopiou ordered three such ships from the Hyundai shipyards in South Korea. Soon after making that decision, he amended the order, requesting that two out of three be built according to ice-class specifications. 'This thought emerged because Sakhalin Island,

Snoehvit, as well as the Shtokman and Yamal fields in Russia, which have yet to produce any gas' – all sites close to or within the Arctic circle – 'have huge reserves, and one must have a long-term perspective', the Dynacom boss notes.

The challenges were colossal: the two ice-class vessels had to be fitted with reinforced hulls capable of withstanding the Arctic ice and with equipment able to function in temperatures as low as −35 degrees Celsius. Because of the proximity to the North Pole, the usual navigation organs (compasses, GPS) did not work properly, so they had to be replaced by custom-made, Pole-compatible ones. Every step of the building process was overseen by supervisors from the classification societies, which are responsible for verifying that the extremely demanding standards required of ice-class vessels are met.

The *Ob River* was ready in 2007 and, along with the other two LNG carriers, it was placed on the spot market, without a fixed schedule or itinerary. It was an unusual move (such ships normally sign long-term contracts), which built and spread the reputation of Dynagas among LNG shippers. Meanwhile, preparation for its Arctic adventure continued. Crew training took a year-and-a-half, and for many crew members it included a spell at Russia's Makarov Academy, where they were taught the secrets of navigating through ice without freezing to death. Prior to the fully loaded passage to Tobata, the *Ob River* had been tested on shorter voyages, from Sakhalin Island to China and Japan. It had also traversed the Northern Sea Route without cargo, from South Korea to France, on a test run to make sure everything was in order.

This epic journey, in an age where few such remain on land or at sea, is a testament to the resourcefulness, the farsightedness and the global reach of Greek shipping. Greece, a small country of 11 million people, is the world's foremost shipping superpower, and has been almost without interruption for the last four decades. According to figures of the Union of Greek Shipowners from early 2013, the Greek-owned ocean-going fleet was made up of

3,428 ships, totalling 245 million dwt in capacity. This represented 15.6 per cent of the carrying capacity of the entire world fleet, including 23.6 per cent of the world tanker fleet and 17.2 per cent of dry bulk capacity.

Greece's shipping companies defy every stereotype that Greeks have been associated with by the international media during the Great Crisis: they are ultra-competitive in a truly globalized market; their family-based structures are an indispensable source of strength rather than a weakness; and, because of their flexibility and success, they are avid supporters of a completely liberalized institutional environment for the transcontinental sea trade, even while in Greece itself, most industries still struggle under the weight of over-regulation, manifold barriers to entry and other anti-competitive aspects of the legal framework.

Yet in this age of crisis, the international triumphs of Greek shipping tycoons do not necessarily translate into acclaim at home. Prokopiou is a case in point. A man who displays none of the affinity to press exposure shown by some of his contemporaries and his most famous predecessors, he got some extremely un-welcome coverage in the Greek media in May 2010.

It was a few days after Greece's government had signed the original Memorandum with its official creditors, along with the harsh austerity measures that it entailed. Elected on a platform of Keynesian expansion and forced to push through the toughest fiscal retrenchment programme the country had undergone in its modern history, George Papandreou and his Finance Minister George Papaconstantinou were desperate to shore up their socialist credentials. In this climate of panic and confusion, information was leaked that made the front pages of most newspapers about a certain 'Cypriot shipowner' who had bought up dozens of properties across Greece, had registered them to offshore companies and had not paid the taxes that he owed on them. According to the media reports, all stemming from the same leak, the 'Cypriot shipowner' – whom some named as Prokopiou – would be forced to pay €40 million in back taxes and fines, thus quenching the thirst of the masses for the rich to be brought to account.

One problem with this plotline was that Prokopiou is not a Cypriot. Some elementary fact-checking might have helped solve that one. The somewhat bigger snag, which would have required some more investigation to uncover, is that the accusation did not seem to stand up. The shipowner – who does indeed own a large number of property investments, in Greece and abroad – went himself to the ministry with a briefcase filled with documents, following which the audit into his affairs was stopped. As he reveals, he believes that the leak against him was orchestrated by people in the tax administration, in order to blackmail him into bribing them to make the story go away. Some tax officials, however, insist that the audit should have continued.

The story is emblematic of the strained relationship that has long existed between Greece's world-beating shipping community and the Greek state – a relationship that the Great Crisis has complicated further. The tax advantages long enjoyed by Greek shipping companies, in particular, have come under attack from SYRIZA and others on the left. But given the globalized nature of ocean-going shipping, and the similarly preferential treatment afforded to shipping companies in other major shipping centres in the EU and beyond, aggressive moves to tax the shipowners by a future left-wing government will lead to a mass disembarkation of ships from the Greek flag and of their owners' offices from Piraeus.

Before delving into the means of avoiding such an exodus while meeting basic demands of social justice, we need to take a quick look back – at the remarkable rise of Greek-owned shipping in the post-war period, and at the ways in which the state facilitated or obstructed it.

The Greek merchant fleet, more than that of any other country, was decimated during the Second World War. Three-quarters of Greek-owned ships were sunk by U-boats. Twenty per cent of the crew – about 2,000 men – were lost at sea and about as many were injured in ways that meant they could not continue working as sailors.[2] But Greeks had been seamen and shipowners since ancient times, and they were not about to let a hiccup like a worldwide conflagration wipe out a millennia-old tradition.

In 1946 the US government decided to sell off a large number of the 'Liberty' cargo ships it had mass-produced during the war to transport supplies across the Atlantic. With the mediation and guarantee of the Greek government, a hundred of these were bought by the big Greek shipowning families of the day – Kulukundis, Livanos, Chandris, Goulandris – at very low prices. In 1947 the Greeks also bought seven US-made T2 tankers, on similarly advantageous terms.

It was the beginning of the great *renaissance* of Greek shipping, which consisted – as it always had – of 'tramp' ships, which did not travel on predetermined routes, but instead scoured the globe for the sea-lanes that offered the most profitable opportunities. In those years of the great post-war expansion of the world economy, legendary figures like Aristotle Onassis and Stavros Niarchos led the way by investing heavily in ever-larger oil tankers, which between 1958 and 1975 made up 40–48 per cent of the whole of the Greek-owned fleet.[3] In addition, of the 1,200 'Liberty' ships sold by the US between 1946 and 1971, two-thirds would be snapped up by the Greeks, including a number of ship captains who graduated into shipowning, buying second-hand vessels with loans from their former employers. As a result, on the eve of the first oil crisis in 1973, the Greeks owned 4,126 ships with a total capacity in gross tonnage (grt) of 42.6 million, or 14.7 per cent of the total global capacity – the biggest national fleet, by the nationality of the owner, in the world.[4]

Of those ships, 2,761, more than two-thirds, flew the Greek flag (that is, they were enrolled on the Greek shipping register), paid taxes to the Greek government and employed mostly Greeks as crew members. The percentage of ships flying the Greek flag had more than doubled between 1958 and 1973.[5] This was the result of laws and decrees passed by the Greek governments in the 1950s, in particular the measure designating ships as 'foreign capital' which could be re-exported from Greece, thus easing the concerns of international lenders approving the loans for their purchase. 'Compulsory law' 465 in 1968 improved matters further, from the shipowners' point of view. It changed the taxation of ships from a gross profits-based system to a very modest tonnage tax, depending on the size and age of the ship.

As Mattheos D. Los writes in *Voyage to the Top*, the tendency to return to the Greek shipping register was also bolstered by the first collective bargaining agreement between the Union of Greek Shipowners and the Panhellenic Seamen's Union in 1951, which ended years of confrontation between workers and their employers, fomented by Communist-controlled unions. Los is the CEO of Vrontados S.A., a family shipping company from the island of Chios that has prospered for four generations by focusing on a single market (dry bulk) and abiding by a simple doctrine: 'few ships but good ones'. Vrontados continues, to this day, to fly the Greek flag on all six of its vessels – a rarity among Greek shipping companies.

Other changes in the institutional framework included Laws 89/1967 and 378/1968, which offered shipping and shipping-related companies registered in Greece the same privileges they enjoyed in major shipping hubs abroad. This triggered the repatriation of the headquarters of 'the Greeks' to Piraeus from London and New York, and opened the way for the inflow of shipping charterers, shipping law offices, representatives of ship-yards and equipment makers, all lured by the tax-free environment and the proximity to some of the biggest names in the shipping trade. Law 27/1975, one of the first to be passed after the restoration of democracy, cemented the attractive institutional environment, slightly increasing the level of the tonnage tax but retaining it as the method of taxation.

The first oil crisis initiated a long, traumatic period for global, and hence for Greek, shipping. The protracted slump of the 1980s, in particular, from 1981–7, caused both by economic recession and by the oversupply of ships on the market, caused scores of bankruptcies, as lending dried up. It led shipowners to lay up their vessels in unprecedented numbers – the Gulf of Eleusina off the coast of western Attica, congested with unemployed ships, was a stark symbol of the depressed state of the market – and to send them, in droves, to the scrapyard. It also led them, as a survival strategy, to turn en masse to 'flags of convenience', open registries like those of Liberia and Panama which offer (even more) preferential tax treatment and – crucially – the option of hiring crews from developing countries at significantly lower costs.

This 'flagging out' was exacerbated, according to Los, who was already at the time an active member of the Union of Greek Shipowners, by the rise of PASOK. As he noted in various contributions to Greek shipping magazines during that turbulent decade, the Andreas Papandreou years produced a resurgence of friction between seamen and shipowners. The unions, backed by the socialist government, became increasingly unwilling to compromise on their demands. By the end of the 1980s, owing to a combination of these reasons, only two in five Greek-owned ships remained on the Greek shipping register.

The 'deflagging' trend would continue: in 1999 marginally more than one in four Greek-owned ships flew the Greek flag; by the beginning of 2013 it was fewer than a quarter. This despite further reductions of the tax burden in the early 1990s and in the number of Greek crew members required for a ship to be classified as belonging to the Greek register.

The de-hellenization of Greek-owned ships did no harm to their global position. The shrewdest shipowners, those who had not overinvested before the 1980s crash, took advantage of it to build cheap or to buy ships at near-giveaway prices. The Greek-owned fleet emerged from the depression of that period as still the largest in the world, and retained this position, through boom and bust, until the end of the millennium.

But it was China's entry into the WTO in December 2001, with its voracious appetite for raw materials and the explosion of its exporting activity, that gave rise to unprecedented windfalls for Greece's shipping elite. It is to this China boom, and to its equally vertiginous hangover, that we now turn.

In late April 2011 George Economou, one of Greece's better known and more controversial shipping magnates, made headlines by seizing one of the eighteen ships he had chartered on long-term leases to Cosco, after China's state-owned shipping heavy-weight halted payments on some of the contracts, which had been struck in 2008, at the height of the China boom. The dry bulk sector having jumped off a cliff in the meantime, Cosco had begun, months earlier, to withhold payments on deals made at the top of the market. Economou told the press that the contracts ranged up to $80,000 a day for five-year periods for the largest vessels, and that he was prepared to seize more ships. The going daily rate for dry bulk carriers at the time was $18,000.[6]

In the end, Cosco caved in and the matter was resolved. But the episode highlighted a new phase of a relationship that had left its mark on the first years of the new millennium: that between Greek shipping and the rip-roaring, all-engorging Chinese growth engine.

The bankruptcy of Lehman Brothers in September 2008, and the worldwide recession that it caused, was a body blow to international shipping. The surge that had preceded it, caused by shifting fundamentals but also by rampant commodity speculation, had been without parallel in the modern history of the sea trade: between 2002 and 2008, the Baltic Dry Index (BDI), a principal measure of the price of the seaborne transportation of raw materials issued daily by London's Baltic Exchange, jumped from less than 1,000 points to nearly 12,000.[7] Charter rates for all types of shipping went through the roof. Dry bulk carriers reached their peak on 5 June 2008, when it cost a head-spinning \$233,988 a day on average to hire a Capesize ship, which took on the heaviest cargoes, like iron ore and coal. The daily cost of operating such a ship was about \$6,500–8,000.[8] Do the math.

Greek shipowners had the fleet capacity and the flexibility to benefit more than anyone from China's eruptive rise. Not only did they own by far the largest dry bulk fleet, but they were free from long-term contracts – unlike the second-ranked Japanese, for example, whose ships were booked by Japanese companies – and so could avail themselves of the enormous opportunities of the spot market. In 2007, at the height of the bonanza, it was estimated that Greek-owned ships delivered 60 per cent of the raw material needs of the emerging Asian superpower.[9] Shipping companies on the verge of ruin, in the aftermath of the East Asian crisis, saw their outlook transformed, almost overnight. Pretty much anyone with even a single ship to their name was making a fortune.[10]

But of course, no one wanted to own just one ship when there was so much money to be made. As chartering rates and ship values went stratospheric, and as banks tumbled over each to lend to anyone who could find north on a compass, shipowners from across the world – many of them new to the profession – embarked on an orgy of indiscriminate shipbuilding. In their quest for more capital to build more ships, many chose to list their companies on the stock exchange. Greeks were among the most enthusiastic participants: by 2012, 52 per cent of shipping companies listed on the Nasdaq and the New York Stock Exchange were Greek-owned.

Among them was Dry Ships, the flagship company of George Economou, which was riding high transporting iron ore, coal, grain and fertilizers all over the world, with China as a prime destination. Economou, a graduate of MIT, began his career in shipping in 1976. He was one of the many alumni of Thenamaris, a shipping company started by the legendary Athena Martinou, to go on to start his own company. A man given to bold — some say reckless — gambles, he had defaulted on bonds issued in New York to enlarge the fleet he owned in the late 1990s, but had managed in the end to pay 37 cents on the dollar and keep most of his ships.[11] In 2005, as the China boom was gathering steam, he took Dry Ships public, listing it on the Nasdaq and raising more than $250 million. In the months that followed, eight other Greek shipping companies, most of them in the dry bulk sector, also launched initial public offerings (IPOs).[12]

While Dry Ships was borrowing hundreds of millions to add more ships to its fleet and Economou was making the Forbes rich list, Thanassis Martinos was playing a different game. The eldest son of Athena, who had parted ways with Thenamaris in 1991 to start his own company, Eastern Mediterranean Maritime,[13] Martinos was keeping out of debt, away from the stock market and on the margins of the shipbuilding frenzy, having bought at low prices before the China boom. Long admired in industry circles for his market savvy, some were beginning to wonder if he was losing his touch, becoming overly conservative in his fifties.

'I certainly did not expect the boom to last this long,' Martinos tells me, with customary self-effacement, in his offices in Glyfada, a plush southern suburb of Athens. Despite being a shipping colossus, this is a man who is happy to call himself a 'taxi-driver', as the Greeks are referred to in global shipping circles because of their tramp routes. He also modestly says that he and his Greek colleagues were 'surprised' by the timing and speed of China's emergence, adding that the surprise was 'pleasant', in involuntarily comic understatement.

Explaining his philosophy, he has this to say: 'Shipping is generally not given to exponential growth, like new technologies, for example. The demand for shipping by sea grows on average by 3–4 per cent a year. The growth of your company must be proportional to that. Otherwise, you risk contributing to a glut of ships.' Had he been more aggressive, Martinos could have made more money when the good times were rolling. But given the cataclysm that followed, it can safely be said that there was wisdom in his wariness.

The crash, when it came, was spectacular. As trade volumes collapsed in 2008, the Baltic Dry Index caved in, dropping from 11,600 points in June to under 700 in December. Daily chartering rates for Capesizes fell by *99 per cent*, to $2,400 – way below break-even.[14] Things perked up to some extent in 2009, and although the numbers got nowhere near pre-crisis levels, the assumption was that the worst was over. But then, beginning in mid-2010, the roof fell in again. Since then, Eurozone jitters, slowing Chinese demand and budgetary brinkmanship in Washington have all played a part in the continuing woes of the shipping industry, which is facing a recession that may come to overshadow the epic slump of the 1980s.[15]

The demand-side woes are compounded, many times over, by the excess supply caused by the reckless overinvestment of the boom years. In 2010, because of orders placed prior to the crash, many of which were delayed because the shipyards had been overwhelmed with work, 3,748 new ships were delivered, with a total carrying capacity of 96.4 million grt – the largest year-on-year increase in the history of shipping. Of those new ships, 45.2 per cent were dry bulk carriers.[16]

The prudent Martinos has fared better in the days since 2008 than the overambitious Economou. The flamboyant head of Dry Ships has had to engage in difficult negotiations to restructure the company's banking debts, sell off shares in Ocean Rig, the deep-sea oil-drilling company Dry Ships acquired in 2007 (much to the consternation then of many of its shareholders), and walk away from new buildings he had ordered, in some cases paying hefty penalties.

But in the wider story of shipping's Great Recession, the Greeks are once again looking poised to emerge stronger than ever. The contrast with Germany, the world's third largest shipowning nation, is instructive. Take container shipping, which has been hit hardest of all by the global slowdown since 2008 and where the Germans have traditionally been the biggest players, controlling 40 per cent of the world market in mid-2012. The overinvestment by German shipping firms during the boom years, combined with the prolonged slump that followed, had, by the beginning of 2013, led to 150 bankruptcies of German shipping funds, with another 266 being restructured.[17] These funds often involved a multitude of small investors with little knowledge of shipping, and managers who were being paid fees for every project — e.g. every new purchase — they completed, creating obviously warped incentives.

Meanwhile, analysts spoke of 'cash-rich' Greeks swooping in and purchasing ships from distressed, over-indebted Germans. One anonymous German shipping executive, commenting on a deal by Greece's Costamare to buy a ship from an insolvent German group with 100 per cent financing from Germany's Hypovereinsbank, a privilege denied to Germans, complained to *Lloyd's List* about the bank: 'They like their Greek customers more than us.'

And well they might. As astounding as Greece's position atop the list of national merchant fleets is, what is even more impressive is the longevity of its dominance. Prokopiou, who spent the China boom preparing for the LNG era but also selling off and replacing fifty tankers and bringing the average age of his ships down to a world-beating three years, explains it thus: 'Greeks can adjust everywhere. There is an underlying philosophy which makes them thrive wherever they go — so long as the social, legal and tax framework is one that offers equal opportunity.'

A crucial element in the Greeks' advantage in the shipping trade is the structure of the average Greek shipping company. Typically, Greek shipowners (unlike the German investors in shipping funds) are directly involved in the operation of their companies. Their investment decisions, often running in the hundreds of millions, concern their own money and can often be made quickly, without the bureaucratic hassle and tussles of more complex corporate organizations. 'If you have a corporate structure, with many shareholders, and you have to announce to the newspapers that in the next semester you have to sell fifteen ships, like the Japanese do, this is certainly not helpful; everyone will be waiting for you around the corner,' Prokopiou notes.[18]

Greek shipping businesses are also often intimately linked with the owners' families, with sons, nephews and (more recently) daughters and nieces learning the ropes from early on. Conventional wisdom has it that nepotism is one of the main causes of Greece's downfall, and this is not far from the mark. Politicians and businessmen tended to give precedence to family and loyal friends over those most qualified, even in choosing key appointees and associates, often with disastrous consequences.

In shipping, however, because of its globalized, highly competitive nature, market discipline ensures that family members that don't cut it will be kept away from the levers of power. Those, on the other hand, who do display the requisite talents, are likely to contribute above and beyond the professional call of duty, because shipping is more than a job for them – it is a family affair. And Greeks take family very seriously.

Today, it is the Anglo-Saxon-educated, financially literate grandkids of the captains-turned-shipowners of the 1970s that are taking over the helm in many Greek-owned shipping firms. Some are likely to flourish further, but it is rare for business acumen to survive many generations. Martinos, whose family entered the shipping trade in the 1970s, says that 'in contrast to European families, Greek shipping families do not last beyond two or three generations. Most of the big names in Greek shipping from thirty years ago are no longer around today.'

Yet Greek shipping itself continues to thrive, as new families take the place of those that sink into the sunless depths of history. All indications are that when the post-Lehman slump is over, a new era of Greek expansion on the high seas will begin. What is less clear is how impoverished ordinary Greeks and the bankrupt Greek state will look upon a new period of healthy profits and high living for its most privileged caste. The signs on the horizon point to a coming storm.

In an editorial on 19 December 2012, entitled 'Tax-Free "National Champions"', *Avgi* newspaper, the party organ of SYRIZA, had this to say about the fourteen Greeks listed among the world's hundred biggest shipowners:

> For yet another year, Greek shipowners have expanded their activities and increased their wealth. For yet another year, they retained their privileged status beyond the reach of taxation, with the more than 50 tax exemptions that allow them to become ever richer. In other words, their presence among the hundred most powerful shipowners in the world, the increase in their wealth and the expansion of their fleets is in no way registered on the government budget. The numbers regarding their activities may indeed make them 'champions', but the revenues of the budget show that they are not so 'national'.[19]

A few days earlier, several SYRIZA MPs had submitted a parliamentary question to the coalition government in which they reminded everyone that the party had called for a drastic re-examination 'of the relations between the Greek state, shipping and the shipowning community, with the aim of repealing the 58 different tax exemptions and creating a stable tax regime, which will conform with the constitutional imperative that all Greek citizens contribute their share of the public burden'.[20]

George Stathakis, a genial, chain-smoking economist and SYRIZA moderate, was one of the party's MPs who put their name to the parliamentary question. Sitting in his small, bare office near Syntagma Square, he tells me that the issue of shipping taxation relates to the wider question of a fairer distribution of the costs of adjustment, which, he says, have fallen disproportionately on the shoulders of the least well-off since the beginning of the crisis.

It is easy to see why the tax exemptions offered to Greek shipping companies have become a rallying cry for SYRIZA: in a country where more than one in four is unemployed, where many of those without a job are forced to pay heavy taxes on property they have no income from, where pensioners have seen their pensions repeatedly cut and employees count themselves lucky if they are paid their shrivelled salaries in time, the tax privileges available to the country's wealthiest citizens have come to seem increasingly scandalous.

These privileges include: a total exemption from taxation of shipping profits, whether as corporate income or dividends distributed to shareholders; tax-free capital gains from the selling of ships; a total exemption from all levies and contributions in favour of the state or third parties for the income of shipping companies based or represented in Greece; a total exemption from the property tax imposed in 2003 on all offshore-registered real estate, equal to 3 per cent of its value, for all property leased to shipping companies and tied to their business activities;[21] tax-free fuel; and many more. Not content with these, a number of shipowners engage in aggressive tax avoidance, occasionally skirting over into evasion – especially relating to their property holdings – to further minimize what little the Greek government is able to extract from them.

The other major shipping powers, of course, offer similarly preferential treatment to ocean-going ships on their shipping register. According to a Pricewaterhouse Coopers report on shipping taxation,[22] the vast majority of the big players in shipping use a tonnage tax regime to tax shipping activity, in other words, the taxes are calculated on the basis of the tonnage of the vessels instead of the accounting profits of the firms that manage them.

The two approaches to a tonnage tax system are the Dutch model, adopted among others by Germany, the UK, France, Italy, Denmark, Japan and the US, and the Greek model, adopted by Greece, Cyprus and Malta. As the PwC report notes, 'the main advantage of tonnage tax regimes is the very low effective tax rate of on average less than 1 per cent, when the shipping business is doing well'.

The report compares how a five-year-old cargo ship of a gross tonnage of 20,000 and a net tonnage of 18,000 would be taxed in the Netherlands and in Greece and finds that the ship would pay more (€13,110 versus €10,293) if the management company was based in Piraeus. Unlike the Greek case and most Dutch model countries, some tonnage tax regimes (the United States, France, Poland) impose capital gains on the sale of vessels. But the main difference between the two approaches is that the Greek model totally exempts individual shareholders from all tax on profits.

This is where Stathakis focuses. As he puts it, 'Persons profiting from shipping will be included, like all other Greeks, in the normal system of income taxation. Shipping dividends will be taxed like dividends from any other shareholdings.' Stathakis says there are no precise projections on how much this would benefit the public purse, but his ballpark estimation is €1 billion annually – about one-tenth of the total intake from income taxation in Greece.

Yet the way profits are calculated in most versions of the Dutch model, the tax burden on owners is very low in most other shipping countries, too. Given the ease with which a shipowner can move his operations from one place to another, I ask the left-wing economist if he is not worried that taxing shipping profits will drive Greek shipping tycoons to more tax-efficient (i.e. tax-free) shores. 'Piraeus and the Greek flag retain many comparative advantages for Greek shipowners,' he tells me. 'We want to preserve these, but we also want to increase government revenue in a way that is just and consensual.'

The Great Crisis has unquestionably brought the long-dormant issue of the relations between Greek shipping and the Greek state back into the limelight. The first bad omen for shipowners was the ill-advised decision of the Papandreou government, when it took over, to incorporate the Ministry of Merchant Marine into a new mega-ministry (of the Economy, Competitiveness and Shipping), while slicing off and distributing various of its competencies (port management, port police) to other departments. The move was opposed not only by the Union of Greek Shipowners, but also by the Hellenic Seamen's Federation, the New Democracy opposition and pretty much everyone related to the shipping industry. The near-universal criticism of the decision was that it led to the fragmentation of shipping policy and that a sector so vital to the Greek economy should not be incorporated into a ministry with a wider mandate and an unwieldy set of competencies.

Prokopiou, his voice dripping with contempt, has this to say about how the Papandreou government handled Greece's shipping interests: 'When those who are clueless, who have never managed even a small kiosk, try to solve economic issues without any knowledge of the market, this is what you get.' In one meeting between the Finance Minister and the Union of Greek Shipowners, he recalls, one member, from an old shipping family, told Papaconstantinou that the policies of PASOK would drive Greek shipping once again out of Greece. 'His immediate response was: "Go! No one's keeping you here,"' the Dynacom boss tells me.

The move away from the Greek shipping register towards flags of convenience gathered pace after the 2009 election. Yet shipowners tend to overstate the relevance of supposedly hostile government policy to this development. After all, neither the PASOK government nor that of Loukas Papademos ever questioned the special tax status of Greek shipping. Indeed, the Papademos government in April 2012 re-established the Ministry of Merchant Marine.

Since May 2012, however, with the rise of SYRIZA to role of the official opposition, the tax issue has gone mainstream. The shipping-friendly New Democracy-led government passed a law in early 2013 increasing the taxes paid by Piraeus-based shipping companies on ships belonging to foreign shipping registers, to make them equal to the tax burden on Greek-flagged vessels. It also imposed extraordinary levies of 6–10 per cent, for the period between 2012–15, on the foreign exchange imported by all Piraeus-based shipping-related companies (brokers, insurance companies and so on),[23] a move which Stathakis approves as being 'in the right direction'. In July 2013 the Union of Greek Ship-owners and the government reached an agreement according to which shipping companies based in Greece would voluntarily contribute to the public purse. The participating companies would offer an additional amount equal to the tonnage tax owed by each of their ships for a period of four years, bringing in €140 million in extra revenue. The shipowners were unpleasantly surprised to find, at year's end, that the government passed a new law to make those contributions compulsory and to double their size.

The prospect of a SYRIZA victory in the June repeat elections of that year led to a number of press reports in which unnamed shipowners expressed their deep concerns and some even confessed that they were preparing to move their offices abroad. Stathakis calls the anonymous warnings issued at the time 'ill-timed' and 'completely off the mark', claiming that those who made them had no notion of the policy proposals of SYRIZA. But leading party cadres had said some incendiary things during those angst-ridden weeks between the two elections, including a call for an extraordinary tax of 4 per cent on shipping revenues, irrespective of profitability.

Since then, however, both sides have sought a more conciliatory tone. In a meeting with the Union of Greek Shipowners in December 2012, attended also by Stathakis, SYRIZA leader Alexis Tsipras voiced his support for the 'continued leading role of Greek shipping' in the international market. Speaking to me, Stathakis calls the tonnage tax system 'a long-established practice' which SYRIZA does not intend to repeal, though 'we could increase the rate by which the tax is calculated'. Even that, he explains, will be done 'by common consent'. On his account, the party has no plans to tax non-distributed corporate profits or capital gains of Greek-based shipping companies either.

Martinos, who caused a bit of a stir at the 2012 Poseidonia, the annual get-together of the world shipping community in Greece, by proposing a common EU tonnage tax, is sanguine: 'All governments, even the Andreas Papandreou government of 1981, recognized the significance of shipping, they were pragmatic and they did not change the institutional framework. I think that SYRIZA, too, understands this, and will not change the tax regime.'

Prokopiou takes a harder, less consensual line. 'Everyone is now thinking of a fall-back position – Singapore, Hong Kong, Monte Carlo, returning to London,' he says. 'Even the Turks are making amazing offers for shipping offices to move there. There are no longer any fools with millions. When it is possible with the push of a button to move your legal earnings wherever you want in the world, government policy must adjust.'

In the shipowners' eyes, they already do plenty for the Greek economy. According to IOBE, the economic policy think-tank, shipping and shipping-related activities contributed €13.3 billion to domestic value added, or 6.1 per cent of GDP in 2009. Employment in the sector and in professions related to it was calculated as ranging up to 192,000 people. Greece's trade surplus in sea transport was €12.7 billion in 2009 and €14.5 billion in 2010 – the single largest contributor to the reduction of the country's gargantuan current account deficit.[24]

Another common refrain one hears from members of the shipping community is that their ability to help Greece out of its fiscal impasse is exaggerated. Martinos says that 'shipping, too, is in crisis, and the needs are enormous.' Prokopiou agrees: 'In the early post-war period, and up to the 1970s, shipping could really come to the aid of the government, because the debt was much lower.

These days, even if the entire Greek fleet was sold off, it would barely make a dent.' Many in shipping point also to the charity work undertaken, both by the Union of Greek Shipowners and individual tycoons – in the latter case, often without publicizing the fact, they say – and to the large-scale urban development projects in Athens financed by the Niarchos and Onassis foundations.

But none of this cancels out the sense, which is bound to grow sharper as the crisis continues to wreak havoc upon Greek society, that shipowners constitute a private island of provocative privilege in an ever-expanding, constantly deepening sea of want. The stark divergence between their condition and that of everyone else has made them targets. In 2009 Perikles Panagopoulos, a respected veteran of passenger shipping, was abducted. The perpetrators asked for €30 million in ransom (the money was paid, but the police ultimately caught up with them). In 2013 Andreas Martinos, nephew of Thanassis, narrowly escaped another abduction attempt, by ramming his assailants' vehicle and making an audacious getaway.

Prokopiou is concerned about how society views the shipping elite, and blames it on the political climate that has been dominant for many years in the country. 'We want businesses to invest and to pay taxes, but we don't want the businessman. We still think of profit as sinful, we cultivate envy. If that does not change, things will not improve.'

Martinos, for his part, is more optimistic. 'The perception in public opinion and in the political class is that shipping benefits Greece. In coffee houses even in the smallest villages, people know this, and would not want to risk losing those benefits.' In the trying years to come for Greece, this proposition will be sorely tested.

Nightmares from Weimar

On the night of 12 September 2013, about twenty members of the Perama cell of the Greek Communist Party were walking the street putting up posters. Perama, home to the badly struggling local ship-repair zone, is one of the poorest municipalities in Attica. Unemployment in the town is estimated at near 50 per cent. In the zone itself, another source of perennial bitterness in the relations between the government and the shipowners, around 90 per cent of available workers cannot find work on any given day. Cheaper competition, from Eastern Europe, Turkey and beyond, is the principal cause. But shipowners also blame successive governments for leaving infrastructure in Perama untended and for allowing the PAME-controlled union of metalworkers to take over the zone, making exorbitant wage demands and constantly striking whenever employers balk at the costs.

A little before midnight on that fateful night, according to court documents, outside the Papila shipyard the group of Perama Communists was surrounded by a squad of about fifty men, carrying wooden and metal poles, some with spikes and other pieces of iron. The men wore black shirts with the insignia of the rapidly rising new element in crisis-era Greek politics: the Nazi nostalgists of Golden Dawn. Under orders from two of the men operating as squad leaders and yelling that they now ruled the streets of Perama, the horde of storm troopers attacked the Communists brutally, sending eight of them to the hospital. Meanwhile, according to sworn testimony by Sotiris Poulikogiannis, the head of the Piraeus Metal Union and one of the Communists attacked, four policemen who were positioned 50 metres away, stood idly by.[1] As Poulikogiannis told me a few weeks later, the attack had in effect been pre-announced, when Golden Dawn members visited the ship-repair zone and told workers: 'If you want to get rid of the commies, call us.'

The attack was a clear sign of the growing confidence of the neo-fascist outfit, sixteen months after the stunning electoral result that had catapulted it into parliament. That parliamentary election, the first to take place in Greece after it signed over its fiscal sovereignty to its international creditors, was extraordinary in many ways. It signalled the end of the two-party system that had dominated Greek politics since 1977, with PASOK and New Democracy succeeding each other in power and winning, between them, a minimum of three-quarters of the national vote in each electoral contest. New Democracy, which won the 6 May 2012 election, got less than 20 per cent of the vote. PASOK plummeted to 13 per cent – less than a third of its share in 2009 – and came in third. SYRIZA, on the back of its fiery anti-Memorandum rhetoric, leapt to second place.

But arguably the biggest shock of all was the rise of Golden Dawn, which surged from a mere 0.3 per cent of the vote in 2009 to 7 per cent – from less than 20,000 to 440,894 votes – and to representation, for the first time ever, in the Greek parliament, with twenty-one members. Formed as a political unit in 1987 by a small band of dedicated far-right extremists, it describes itself these days a 'people's nationalist' party, but is described by almost everyone else as the closest thing to a neo-Nazi gang to gain representation in the parliament of a European country since, well, the Nazis.

On that ominous night, liberal, cosmopolitan Greeks watched in horrified fascination as Nikos Michaloliakos, the screechy-voiced leader of Golden Dawn since its establishment, gave his histrionic, resentment-laden assessment of the electoral result.[2] The evening began with a black-clad skinhead, a bass player for a black metal band who had just been elected to parliament, barking a military command to the assembled journalists to rise ('out of respect', as he put it) when the leader entered. A few members of the press protested and were duly ejected from the room.

Addressing those journalists who remained, Michaloliakos thanked voters for 'turning their backs on the mud of the TV channels and the yellow press' – in other words, the mainstream media which reported on the dark nature of Golden Dawn. It was an apt opening for this former special forces officer who had first come to notice in December 1976, when he was arrested for a savage assault on journalists at the funeral of Evangelos Mallios, a police captain responsible for torturing countless dissidents during the junta who had been gunned down by the left-wing terror group 'November 17'. Two years after that incident, the young neo-fascist would be arrested again, and imprisoned for one year, for his participation in an ultra-right-wing terror cell. The organization was responsible for bombings causing a number of injuries in cinemas showing films produced in the USSR.[3]

His voice rising as he went on, Michaloliakos attacked the 'junta of the Memorandum' and promised to resist it 'both inside and outside parliament'. He vowed to free Greece from the 'slavery' imposed by 'international loansharks' and from the 'social jungle created by millions of illegal immigrants'. He quoted Julius Caesar ('*Veni, vidi, vici*'), ranted about porn shows on late-night TV, hailed the 'proud boys in the black shirts' – the storm troops of Golden Dawn – and ended, nearly frothing by then, with a warning: 'Those who betray the homeland, be afraid. We are coming!'

As the May elections approached, almost all the polls showed that Golden Dawn, formerly a fringe group mostly associated with violent attacks on immigrants and left-wing university students, was poised to cross the 3 per cent threshold and enter parliament. Conditions for the hatching of the serpent's egg were ideal. Greece's immigration problem – caused by a combination of the administrative disarray of its own government, European myopia and Turkey's unwillingness to do its part to stem the flows

– had been growing unmanageable already before the Great Crisis. The debilitating recession that began in earnest in 2009 made things immeasurably worse. Foreigners were now flooding into a country facing mounting hardship, which increasingly lacked the resources to take care of its own, let alone vast armies of the world's dispossessed.

The economic collapse also led to the general deligitimization of Greece's political and media elites. The two major parties were widely condemned for building a house of cards of an economy, lining their own pockets and leaving the population to pick up the pieces when the bubble of excessive borrowing inevitably burst. The country's big media were accused of colluding in this path to disaster, in order to serve the interests of the powerful businessmen who owned them. This widespread disaffection with the old politics was relentlessly exploited by the junta apologists of Golden Dawn, who were able to mask their anti-parliamentary venom with populist slogans against the existing political system. Meanwhile, the growing cynicism of public opinion towards the mainstream press meant that media attacks on Golden Dawn failed to break the group's momentum – indeed, for many of its followers, they confirmed its anti-systemic credentials.

The rise of Golden Dawn constitutes the most dangerous consequence of the breakdown of the Greek state. The failure to control immigration flows into the country, and the abdication of central parts of Athens to gangs of criminals, many of whom are foreigners, allowed the rabid followers of Michaloliakos to step in and take over the security role of the authorities. In some cases, indeed, as in the downtown Athens neighbourhood of Agios Panteleimonas where Golden Dawn first attracted widespread political support, there were strong signs of collusion between the police and the 'party'. Meanwhile, bona-fide refugees face detention, bureaucratic sclerosis, a life of squalor in cramped apartments and – more recently – a flurry of racist attacks. Often, unable to procure legal papers for months or even years, they turn to stealing, selling counterfeit goods or worse in order not to starve.

As misery spread across Greece in the Age of the Memorandum, Golden Dawn moved, in the footsteps of Hezbollah and Hamas, to replace the state in other functions as well: its members ran soup kitchens, blood drives and even a 'doctors with borders' unit that offered medical services for the needy – on the condition that they were Greek. The group had also stepped up its extra-parliamentary 'activism', which includes terrorizing, beating and killing immigrants.

The Nazis' path to power was paved by Jew-hatred and economic depression, which was brought on by externally imposed austerity and which Hitler largely blamed on the Jews. Golden Dawn was keeping closely to the original recipe. The troika's miscalculations and ideological obsessions had helped furnish the depression, and the Jews had been replaced in the propaganda by illegal immigrants. But the tale was terrifyingly familiar.

Indeed, events since that disorienting day in May had offered little succour to those who feared for the fate of Greek democracy. In the repeat election of June 2012, Golden Dawn received almost exactly the same percentage of the vote, despite – some even say partly due to – the fact that their chief spokesman attacked a female Communist MP on live television. Since then, almost all polls put them in double digits, as the third most popular party.

But eventually, the group overreached themselves. Five days after the attack in Perama, Golden Dawn thugs attacked Pavlos Fyssas, a thirty-four-year-old left-leaning rapper, in the neighbouring municipality of Nikaia. One of them stabbed him in the heart and killed him. The murder caused an uproar in the media and public opinion – both of which had reacted (with some salutary exceptions) with collective shrugs at news of attacks visited on immigrants by Hitler's eager understudies. The government and the criminal justice system, which had remained inert as the fascists spread their influence in society, finally sprang into action. Beginning on 28 September, felony charges were brought against

Michaloliakos, as well as a number of Golden Dawn MPs and local henchmen, relating to the entire history of Golden Dawn, and encompassing murder, attempted murder, extortion and much else. As this book went to press, the leader of the group and a number of his top lieutenants languished in prison, awaiting trial.

It would be a huge mistake, however, for the political establishment to believe that the threat of Golden Dawn, or of a similarly minded group, is over. This could already be seen in the first polls that came out after the arrests, in which Michaloliakos's group, despite losing support, remained the third largest party. A few months later, in particular after two of their members were murdered (an unknown left-wing terrorist group claimed responsibility, saying it was revenge for Fyssas), their support was back in double digits. It was a clear indication that the economic, social and political reasons for the rise of Golden Dawn are still there, and that it would take more than a few arrests to tackle them effectively.

Central among these reasons – and the one Greece is least able to solve on its own – was the immigration crisis. The Greek state has to regain control of its borders and of its capital, to offer refuge to those who need it and to demonstrate that it will brook no competition in the exercise of its monopoly of force. In order to achieve all this, it will require much greater support from the European Union and its member states, some of which, in a striking parallel to their incendiary response to Greece's debt troubles, have suggested solving the problem by kicking the Greeks out of the Schengen zone of passport-free travel.

How did things get so out of hand? That is a complicated story, which has its origins, like most of Greece's current woes, in the policy inertia of the prosperous years before the Great Crisis.

For most of its modern history, Greece has been an exporter rather than an importer of people. The direction of the net flows only changed at the beginning of the 1990s, when the collapse of

Communism led to mass departures of impoverished Eastern Europeans from their shattered societies and towards the more affluent countries of the European Union. For the Balkan members of the Socialist bloc, above all the Albanians, the closest such destination was Greece.

In the decade between 1991 and 2001, the official number of foreigners living in Greece (including ethnic Greeks who were citizens of foreign countries) quintupled, reaching 797,000 people, more than half of whom came from Albania. Calculations by researchers put the real number, including irregular immigrants, at about 1 million in 2001, or 9 per cent of the population.[4]

The sudden influx of mostly undocumented economic migrants led to tensions and a limited xenophobic reaction in parts of the country. Stringent laws banning immigration were powerless to stem the flow and Byzantine rules attempting to regulate it were ignored. This resulted in successive amnesty laws – three between 1997 and 2005, plus a smaller, informal one in 2007 – which officially recognized a reality they had singularly failed to shape. The immigrants who entered the country in this period were a source of cheap labour – especially in construction and farming, in jobs shunned by overeducated Greeks – which helped drive the growth of the Greek economy. Many newcomers were the victims of exploitation by their employers, being paid less than the minimum wage and receiving no health insurance. But a significant number were able to settle down and earn a legal living far exceeding what they could have made at home.

A confluence of different factors led to a rapid deterioration of the situation, starting in the mid-2000s. The most significant of these was the signing in 2003 of the Dublin II regulation by EU members of the Schengen zone of passport-free travel. The regulation, signed during the Greek presidency of the EU, stipulated that if an immigrant has entered the EU irregularly and wants to apply for asylum, he or she must do so at the first point of entry, that is, at the country where they first reached European territory.

For southern countries like Greece, where Europe began for the vast majority of African, Middle Eastern and Asian migrants, Dublin II would prove to be a disaster.

The Dublin II decision coincided with a surge in the numbers of asylum-seekers and irregular migrants entering the country, attracted by the lure of a booming economy with a new, hard currency, or seeking to escape conflict in Afghanistan, Iraq, Somalia and other dark places of the world. Asylum applications jumped from 3,083 in 2000 to 25,113 in 2007.[5] Greece's asylum processing 'system', if it can charitably be thus described, buckled under the increasing pressure. Out of 20,692 applications examined – many with years of delay – in 2007, the authorities granted asylum in the first instance to only 8 (!) individuals, or 0.04 per cent of the total.[6] The corresponding percentage that year in Sweden was 56 per cent, in the UK it was 30 per cent and in Germany 20 per cent.

The flow into Greece, from the Albanian border and, in particular, from the so-called Eastern Mediterranean route through Turkey, intensified further in the latter part of the decade. As other Mediterranean countries, like Spain and Italy, were able to reduce arrivals thanks to tougher border policies and bilateral agreements on prevention or return with sending and transit states, immigrants from the South and the East increasingly sought to enter the European Union by crossing the river Evros that constitutes Greece's land border with Turkey, or through the islands of the eastern Aegean, some of which are only a few miles from the Turkish shore.

The situation was exacerbated by the stance of the Turkish government. Peeved that its citizens – unlike those of the Western Balkans – still required visas to travel to European Union member states, even though Turkey began negotiations for admission into the EU in 2004, Ankara had signed visa-free travel agreements with countries from Morocco to Iran, allowing people from all over North Africa and the Middle East hungry for a better life to arrive with no hassle at the edge of Europe. EU and Greek officials further criticized Turkey for turning a blind eye to trafficking networks, which then helped migrants find a way in.

As a result of all this, by 2008, 50 per cent of all detected illegal border crossings into the EU occurred in Greece; in 2009 that number increased to a whopping 75 per cent.[7] Less than twelve months later, in October 2010, Frontex, the European border management agency, declared that 'Greece now accounts for 90 per cent of all detections of illegal border crossings into the EU.'[8]

Things were bad enough in the country by 2008 that Amnesty International, Human Rights Watch, the Council of Europe and the United Nations High Commission for Refugees all released reports on the systematic violation of asylum-seekers' rights in Greece. It was only the beginning: in the years that followed, the increasing flows of migrants would coincide with the onset of the Great Crisis, creating a perfect storm.

Lesvos is best known as the home of the ancient lyric poet Sappho. Visiting the north-eastern Aegean island in early April, I could see the ample sources of inspiration that it must have provided her. The olive groves sprinkled with red and violet anemones, the beds of white daisies and asphodels, the steep, tall hills, covered with oaks, pines and horse-chestnuts, the deep green-blue bays, the long stretches of sandy beach: almost three millennia after her time, the place retains its ageless enchantments.

Some, however, find it hard to revel in the charms of the Lesvian spring. The island, at the time of my visit, was well on its way once again to becoming a crossing-point of choice for migrants hoping to enter the European Union from Turkey, part of whose coast is less than four miles away. After the decision of the Greek government, against the recommendation of the EU Commission, to build a 10.5-kilometre, barbed-wire fence on the most porous strip of its land border with Turkey, supplemented by extra border guards, the migrant flows began to shift from Evros, where they had increased dramatically in 2010–11, back to the eastern coast of the Aegean. In August 2012, just after the new border guards arrived, the minor trickle of desperate people reaching the shores of Lesvos the two preceding years suddenly turned into a steady stream. Local officials and activists I spoke to the following April feared that, as the weather improved, this stream would turn into a torrent comparable to that of 2008, when more than 13,000 irregular migrants were detected on an island whose total population is 85,000.[9]

If that happens, Lesvos is ill-prepared for it. With arrivals in the first three months of 2013 averaging more than half of the 2008 numbers, the existing facilities were already overstretched. The first reception centre that was planned for the island as an initial holding and screening point was not yet up and running.[10] At the time of my visit, there was still no agreement on where it would be housed, while the mayor of Lesvos and the head of the region of the Northern Aegean were both against it. The detention centre that had existed in the area of Pagani had been shut down in late 2009, after becoming an international byword for ill-treatment and human rights abuses.

As the flows increased during the autumn of 2012, the holding cells of the police station of Mytilene (the island's main town), with a capacity of no more than forty people, could not cope. The incoming migrants, mostly Afghans and Syrians, ended up sleeping rough as they waited for the police to issue the coveted white paper of administrative expulsion. This paper, in theory, gives them thirty days to leave the country. In practice, it allows them to board ferries to Athens, from where they seek to continue their journey into Europe.

By November 2012, the numbers of the homeless and the destitute had grown so alarmingly that the mayor succumbed to public pressure and reopened an abandoned municipal camping site near the airport in order to house them. It is not the first time it has been thus employed. In the late 1990s it served as shelter for anti-Turkish Kurds and Afghanis fleeing the Taliban. Then, in 2009, when the Pagani detention centre was at its most overcrowded, housing over 1,000 people in space fit for 250, it was used briefly to ease the situation, taking in as many as 400 people, according to local activists.

This is how Zoe Livaditou, the head of the Lesvos section of the Hellenic Rescue Team NGO, who was a nurse in Pagani and who volunteers at the campsite, remembers it: 'There were rooms fit for 30 people where they put 275 women and children. There was only one toilet, and they let them out into the open air rarely, whenever the guards wanted.' Livaditou, who had served seven years in Afghanistan as a volunteer and been decorated by the President of the Republic for her work, had quit working in Pagani in mid-2009 to protest against the intolerable conditions imposed on the inmates.

These days, the camping is run entirely by volunteers, plus a contingent of Médecins du Monde that has taken over the task of basic health checks for the migrants from the island's overburdened, underfinanced public hospital. Though heavily affected by the immigration crisis, the people of Lesvos have shown consistent solidarity with the migrants over the years, organizing to provide them with better living conditions and to inform them of their rights. Their anger has been directed, instead, at local and central government, for failing to provide the proper administrative and material infrastructure to ensure dignified treatment.

It is in the campsite, under the shade of a pine tree opposite the makeshift medical office of the Médecins du Monde that I meet Ahmad, a young Afghani who has a university degree in English and who worked for UN Habitat in Herat, instructing local villagers on human rights issues. Members of the Afghan insurgency had tried to recruit him, he tells me, hoping to exploit his security clearance to launch attacks on Westerners. They had threatened his family if he did not agree to do their bidding, so he had decided to leave.

He spent one month and $800 getting from Iran to Turkey. He

stayed in Turkey even longer, until he found a smuggler in late March who would get him across for $1,500, on a small inflatable with another fifteen people. As we are talking, the other five Afghanis who made the crossing with Ahmad huddle around us. 'There was water coming into the boat,' he recalls. None of them had seen the sea before, or knew how to swim. The previous December, twenty-seven Afghanis, including two women with their babies, had drowned off the coast of Lesvos when their boat capsized. In March, nine Syrians, including a family of five, perished in the same terrible fashion.

For Ahmad and his boatmates, reaching dry land only signified the beginning of another ordeal. The dinghy left them near Molyvos, at the north of the island, where the distance from Turkey is the shortest. From there to Mytilene, it was more than 70 kilometres, which they covered on foot, walking for three days. Once they got there, they found that none of the authorities wanted to take up their case. 'We kept being sent from the port police to the police. Everyone was saying "it's not my duty". Once they even kicked us out of the police station,' he says.

After sleeping in the local park for a few nights, they ended up at the municipal camping site. Fed and housed thanks to the cease-less efforts of the activists, when I met them they were awaiting their chance to be arrested and be given the administrative expul-sion paper, so they could travel to Athens. As Ahmad tells me, he has no intention of staying in Greece. He has heard of the problems with the economy, and he hopes to make it to Holland, where he has an uncle who is a Dutch citizen.

Mohamed, a dapper twenty-two-year-old from Idlib, a major rebel stronghold in Syria, was similarly stranded. The eruption of the Syrian civil war found him in his fifth year of medical school, in a private university in Damascus. His father, also a doctor, was arrested by the regime for treating injured rebels in Aleppo. Mohamed followed in his footsteps, working in a hospital near the Turkish border for three months. Then, on New Year's Day, 2013, he drove up to the border with his mother and crossed over, on foot, to the other side.

Their first attempt to make it to Lesvos came in late February. The smuggler's rate was $2,500 per person. As Mohamed tells me, the war in Syria has sent trafficking prices off the charts. 'Before the war it was only $250,' he says. The boat, with about fifteen people on board, was spotted by the Hellenic Coast Guard before it had made it to Greek waters and was forced to turn back. Luckily for him, he had only paid the smuggler an advance of $500, instead of the entire sum.

One month later, he was better prepared. 'I did market research,' he says, smiling ruefully and explaining that he asked around the Syrian refugee camp in Izmir to see what the going rates were. On 22 March, having made an agreement to pay €2,000 for both of them, he got himself and his mother in another rickety inflatable, with another fifteen or so wretched souls. 'I was terrified,' he says, showing me a picture of the boat with its 30hp motor on his iPad, which miraculously survived the journey. 'I knew the Syrian family who had drowned a few days before.' In the end, they made it across safely, reaching Lesvos a little after midnight.

Once there, they got in touch with an Arab contact of their smuggler, who put them up and promised to get them ferry tickets to Athens, all with a hefty commission. The plan failed because his mother refused to take off her veil to help conceal her provenance, and the police found them out at the port. There followed the same game of pass-the-parcel between the police and the port police, with Mohamed and his mother finally ending up in the municipal camping site.

Because of his experience in the field hospital treating the wounded, Mohamed is thinking of becoming a surgeon after he completes his studies. But whatever he does, it will not be in Greece. The Frontex representative contacted them in the camping site and explained to them their rights regarding asylum status, he tells me. But, just like Ahmad, he wants to get to Athens and find another smuggler who will send his mother and him North – to Belgium, Sweden or Norway.

Some might argue that the problem is inadequate policing, not enough of a Fortress Europe approach, with Greece as the weakest link. The immediate effect of the construction of the Evros fence and the tougher border management policies implemented in the summer of 2012 by the Samaras government was the dramatic decrease in crossings over the land border, and the resumption of the sea routes towards Lesvos and other islands. The numbers in Evros being what they are, the overall effect was a significant fall – 23 per cent – in irregular migration into Greece in 2012 compared to 2011. On the Greek–Turkish land border, arrests went from an average of 3,994 per month in the first seven months of the year to a mere 126 in the last four.[11]

Yet some of the measures undertaken to block asylum-seekers' entry are of dubious legality. NGOs have documented numerous cases of 'push-back' by Greek security forces, both on Evros and off the coasts of the islands, where people are forced to return to Turkey without being able to submit their claim to international protection.[12] There have even been reports of Greek security forces sinking dinghies on Evros or on the Aegean, leaving people to swim for their lives.[13] This is a violation both of European law and of the Geneva Convention on Refugees.

Beyond legality and morality, there is also a question as to the long-term efficacy of tougher policies. Antonis Sofiadelis, lieutenant of the Hellenic Coast Guard and Frontex liaison for Lesvos, speaking of the shifting routes of the smugglers between Evros and the islands, likens the situation to a boat full of holes: 'You close one hole and the water comes in through the others.' The traffickers' ability to immediately redirect their activity when policy changes to new vulnerable crossing points has been a constant source of frustration on the Greek side.

But perhaps the most crucial factor is the desperate desire of the migrants themselves to get to European soil. As Sofiadelis tells me, it is often the case, once they are spotted, that they puncture the boats and fall in the water – in many instances even though they lack life jackets and they cannot swim – so that the coast guard will be obliged to rescue them. 'These people are absolutely determined,' he says. 'No amount of policing is going to deter them.'

In theory, migrants arriving in Evros or the eastern Aegean islands have the right to apply for asylum at the local police authority. With the help of Frontex personnel and NGOs like Athens-based Metadrasi, which trains and accredits interpreters in twenty-seven languages (asylum management in Greece has long been plagued by a dearth of qualified interpreters), the police and port police at the crossing points have been doing a somewhat better job of informing new arrivals of their rights and the procedures involved. But knowing that they can be detained for months – up to eighteen, according to the latest legislation – in a jail cell waiting for their application to be heard, most reject the option.

It is not only fear of detention that is a deterrent against applying. Until recently, it was still very rare to be granted asylum in Greece. According to Eurostat data for the third quarter of 2012, out of 1,525 first instance decisions on asylum applications in the country, *none* was positive.[14] The positive decisions on appeal are much higher (16 per cent in 2011),[15] but the length of time required for the process to play out – in some cases more than ten years – and the trials along the way make asylum applications an increasingly unpopular option.

These trials are best exemplified by the horrors of the Aliens' Police Directorate of Attica, on Petrou Ralli Street in downtown Athens. Those immigrants foolhardy enough to brave this administrative Mordor make their way there every Saturday – some come on Friday, or even earlier – and take their place in the long queues, hoping to be one of the very few who will be able to lodge their application and get the coveted pink card of the registered asylum-seeker (or to renew the one they already have).

According to reports by UNHCR, Amnesty International and others, as many as 300 people gather each week, with usually no more than 20 managing to see an asylum officer (except when one of the international organizations is visiting, which leads intakes to go up to 40–60 people). Scuffles often break out between asylum-seekers trying to get to the front of the queue. Gangs have set up rackets where they get paid to move applicants to the front of the line, beating up anybody who refuses to give up their place. Activists spoke of cases where people had their arms broken or were stabbed in the Petrou Ralli queues, and at least one death, of a Pakistani immigrant, seems to have been the result of such violence. The police are known usually to observe this carnage impassively.[16]

Because of all this and more, in January 2011, the European Court of Human Rights found that returning asylum-seekers from other European countries to Greece to have their application examined, in line with Dublin II, constitutes a violation of the European Convention on Human Rights. The case – *M.S.S. v. Belgium and Greece* – concerned an Afghan asylum-seeker whom Belgian authorities, in line with Dublin II, had shipped back to Greece to have his asylum application processed. The court judged his treatment in Greece to have been inhumane and degrading, and condemned both Brussels and Athens for it.

Since then, fourteen EU and Schengen countries have suspended returns of asylum-seekers to Greece. In practice, Dublin II is turning into a dead letter. But that is little comfort to the new arrivals who keep streaming in and who get caught up in the tangled, mangled webs of the Greek state.

The Papandreou government, to its credit, made a concerted effort to bring some order to the chaos of Greek immigration policy. In response to the mountainous backlog of asylum applications, which by the end of 2009 exceeded 45,000 and went on to top 55,000, it passed Presidential Decree 114/2010, to unify and speed up proceedings. P.D. 114/2010 replaced its shameful predecessor, passed in 2009, which effectively barred asylum-seekers from appealing first-instance decisions against their application. In January 2011 it passed Law 3907/2011, creating the Asylum Service and the First Reception Service, which would jointly take asylum policy out of the control of the police and into the hands of the civilian professionals.

But as with everything else in Greek public administration, particularly in such fiscally tight-fisted times, there was a great distance to travel between passing legislation in parliament and implementing it in practice. Stringent hiring rules imposed by the troika had made staffing the Asylum Service particularly challenging. It only started operating in June 2013, more than two years after the law establishing it had been passed.

Maria Stavropoulou, the Harvard graduate and veteran of two decades at UNHCR who was appointed as head of the Asylum Service in February 2012, was cautiously optimistic, when I spoke to her a few weeks earlier, about the prospects of the new agency. 'We hope to bring the time it takes for a final decision on an asylum application down to a range of twenty days to a few months,' she says. The aim is to do this by cooperating with the First Reception Service to decentralize the process, so that many more applications are handled at the entry points and not in Athens. In addition, the asylum office in the capital that will gradually replace Petrou Ralli will be open every weekday for ten hours and the target, according to Stavropoulou, is to get through eighty applications a day. Despite some kinks in its early weeks of operation, the new agency had made considerable progress towards meeting those targets by the year's end: the average time it took for a first-instance decision was down to fifty-seven days, the Athens asylum office got through forty applications a day and offices at the border (Evros and Lesvos) processed another ten to twenty daily.

But Stavropoulou does not hide the struggle that it has been to get started. As she tells me, it took political intervention from on high in September 2012 to disentangle legal and troika-related knots and allow her to hire 145 qualified people who will serve as the core staff of the service. As for employees that had to be transferred to the Asylum Service from other agencies, 'this took months, even a whole year at times. In some cases it even required the intervention of the prime minister's office,' Stavropoulou explains, her face tensing up as if she is reliving the frustration. Tellingly, she repeatedly has to interrupt our chat to discuss a thorny issue concerning the procurement of ink, which is apparently causing a severe bout of bureaucratic constipation.

The hiring difficulties faced by the Asylum Service because of rigidities in the austerity regime imposed on Greece are one aspect of the problematic relationship that exists between Athens and its EU partners on immigration. Between 2007 and 2011 the EU funnelled €198.5 million into Greece to bolster border policing and to restructure asylum policy.[17] In October 2010 it activated the Rapid Border Intervention Teams of Frontex for the first time, to help Greek police patrol the Evros border. It also reached a deal with Ankara on readmission into Turkish territory of third-party nationals who had entered the EU through Turkey, in exchange for a liberalization of the visa requirement for Turks travelling to Schengen countries.

Yet these efforts are not all that they seem. The readmission deal, which Turkey had long resisted, had not been ratified as this book went to press, because the Erdogan government only signed in December 2013, continuing to press for an easing of visa requirements before it did so. Even after ratification, there is a three-year transition period before Turkey actually has to take back any migrants who are not Turkish nationals. More generally, the Europeans – in particular certain northern member states – have been keen to forget that Greece's borders are also the EU's and have been happy to let the beleaguered country bear the brunt of what is a Europe-wide problem.

According to the European Commission, the EU is methodically working its way towards a Common European Asylum System, a project that began in the late 1990s. In reality, one of the pillars of the CEAS, Dublin II, has resulted in member states on the frontlines of immigration being saddled with disproportionately great responsibilities. For Greece, whose public administration was broken before the Great Crisis and has since more or less collapsed, the strain became unsustainable. In response, there have been calls in countries like Germany, Austria and Finland to ban Greece from the Schengen zone.[18]

The echoes of the euro crisis are unmistakable. It was no accident that Greece proved to be the weakest link in both the most ambitious feats of European integration. Its immigration and asylum policies, just like its 'no tax and spend' fiscal approach, were bound to lead to serious trouble. But the EU made things worse by ignoring the faulty institutional architecture of its common currency and passport-free area, and failing to offer European solutions to European problems.

Meanwhile, as Athens crumbled and Brussels fiddled, for many Greeks, pummelled by recession and austerity, feeling unsafe in their neighbourhoods, the ever-swelling presence of foreigners became impossible to ignore. This was the case especially in Athens, where entire districts – including parts of the historic centre – have been surrendered to lawlessness, giving Golden Dawn its first opening.

It was meant to be a great day for Manolis Kantaris. At a little before dawn, the forty-four-year-old pharmaceutical executive came down to the street from his flat on Epirou Street, near Victoria Square in downtown Athens. His wife was about to have their second child. He was also the father of two teenage daughters from a previous marriage. Equipped with a video camera to capture the special moments to come, he headed for his car to drive her to the hospital.

But 10 May 2011 was not to evolve as it should have for the

unfortunate family man. Three men attacked him a few feet from his doorstep. They were after the camera. He yelled 'thieves' and tried to get away. They stabbed him repeatedly – his arms, his neck, his back. Then, as he lay there bleeding, they went through his wallet, before making their getaway. By the time Kantaris's pregnant wife and her mother came down to see what was taking him so long, he was already dead.

The heinous murder caused outrage across the country. But though many lamented the senselessness of the crime, some were more interested in the identity of the perpetrators. It soon became clear that the three men who killed Kantaris were foreigners – two Afghanis, aged twenty-seven and twenty, who were arrested a few days later, and a Pakistani who has eluded capture. Questioning the Afghanis, the police found out they had sold the camera at the Monastiraki flea market for a paltry sum.

In response, members of Golden Dawn spoke of downtown Athens being 'overrun by people with violence in their DNA, because they come from uncivilized countries', and far-right packs attacked immigrants wherever they came across them. Immigrants' shops were smashed in the volatile district of Agios Panteleimonas, a flat inhabited by Pakistanis was set ablaze, dark-skinned men were threatened and chased throughout the city. The pogrom unleashed by the killing of Kantaris reached its horrifying climax in the early hours of 12 May, when a twenty-one-year-old Bangladeshi was stabbed to death in the downtown neighbourhood of Kato Patissia.

It was Athens that had sent out the first explicit warning about the political rise of Golden Dawn. In the elections of November 2010, Nikos Michaloliakos, heading the 'Greek Dawn for Athens' ticket, was elected to the city's municipal council. His showing was particularly strong in the fourth and sixth municipal districts,[19] encompassing boroughs like Kypseli, Patissia and Kolonos, which combined rising crime rates with a soaring immigrant population.[20]

According to a study conducted by the University of Macedonia in 2011 and 2012, 59 per cent of residents of the fourth and sixth municipal districts believe that immigrants have a negative effect on the Greek economy, versus 33 per cent who think the effect is positive. Even more tellingly, 61 per cent of the ghettoized parts of downtown Athens see immigrants as undermining Greek culture, with only 8 per cent claiming the opposite. Recent research by Anne-Marie Jeannet of Oxford University has found that out of fifteen European populations polled between 2002 and 2010, Greeks were the most negative about immigration.[21]

One obvious contributor to the strengthening of anti-immigrant feeling has been the surge in unemployment. The prolonged economic drought has made Greeks less picky about jobs they once thought beneath them and has turned the foreigners employed in those jobs, in the eyes of many, into unwanted usurpers instead of valuable helping hands.

Another crucial factor, though, is the increasing crime rate. In Athens in particular, this development is, in part at least, attributable to the ballooning population of foreigners, many of whom have no legal papers and thus turn to a wide variety of illegal activities to earn their daily bread.

According to statistics compiled by the Hellenic Police, 52 per cent of those arrested for theft and breaking-and-entering in 2010 were aliens, as were 60.5 per cent of those arrested for robbery.[22] Robberies have increased by a factor of more than six in the last two decades. Data presented in parliament by Nikos Dendias, Minister for Citizen Protection, show that the number of aliens arrested for criminal activity has more than tripled in less than fifteen years, from 6,094 in 1998 to 20,265 in 2012.[23]

'People see the drug dealers, the prostitutes, those who sell the counterfeit goods, and they are for the most part foreign. The masterminds may be Greek, but they operate behind the scenes. People are afraid to circulate in their own neighbourhoods,' says George Kaminis, the former constitutional law professor and Greek Ombudsman who was elected mayor of Athens as head of a multi-party coalition in 2010. With the invaluable assistance of hysterical media (in particular TV) coverage, certain egregious cases – like the Kantaris murder – of people killed or badly injured by foreigners for next to nothing have had a particularly chilling effect.

The fear and anger that is rampant in the neighbourhoods left at the mercy of criminality was ably exploited by Golden Dawn. Taking advantage of the absence of the police, the group made its presence felt, its members posing as people's militias come to protect Greeks from the ravages of bloodthirsty foreigners. For Mayor Kaminis, however, it was not just the crisis that created fertile ground for Golden Dawn's message of hate: 'We remain a xenophobic society,' he argues. 'Our culture has little tolerance for those who are different.'

The exodus from the polluted, congested city centre had already begun in the 1980s, as the Athenian middle classes headed en masse for the greener pastures of the northern suburbs. In the 1990s, parts of the neighbourhoods they had left behind began filling up with the first wave of Eastern European and Balkan immigrants. Since many of these newcomers had no legal status, some among them became involved with criminal networks to earn a living.

But it was not until the next decade that that the decline and fall of downtown Athens gathered pace. Konstantinos Zouganelis had a front row seat to the breakdown. He was the owner of Guru Bar, a gem of Athenian nightlife with gourmet Thai food and avant-garde jazz music, that was always filled to overflowing, its denizens spilling out into the streets on Theatrou Square, in the fashionable borough of Psyrri. It was the early 2000s: the country had joined the euro, the Olympics were approaching, there was excitement in the air and money in people's wallets, which the young and eclectic were spending freely in hotspots like Guru.

But with the arrival of the Olympics, and especially after the global circus had left town, things deteriorated rapidly in Psyrri.

African sex workers, especially Nigerians, flooded the streets below Athena Street and the Varvakeios market. The transfer to the area of OKANA, the government's anti-drug agency, just after the Games, attracted hordes of the addicted. Initially, they went to receive their dose of government-approved methadone. But soon the streets around the building became the epicentre of the heroin trade. 'It was surreal,' Zouganelis recalls. 'You had like a hundred dealers standing around outside. Some of the junkies would go in, get the methadone pills, sell them to someone else in the line and use the money to buy heroin.'

Soon the neighbourhood had been transformed. Buildings that used to house artisans and craftsmen – activities banned according to the latest zoning laws – were rented by immigrants, who then proceeded to sublet them to their compatriots, often to far more of them per apartment than was consistent with human dignity or basic hygiene. As the owner of Guru remembers it, the Nigerian prostitutes became ubiquitous and were soon joined by Somali heroin pushers, Afghanis selling hash, Pakistanis selling stolen mobile phones, North Africans smashing car windows for petty loot. 'Each ethnic group had a very specific area of activity and they were careful about getting on each other's turf,' he notes. When they did overstep their bounds, there was violence between them. When they didn't, the victims of violence were those rash enough to pass through the lower part of Sofokleous Street, many of whom were dragged out of their vehicles, robbed and beaten in broad daylight. Then there were the addicts, many of whom were immigrants, sprawled all over the streets, shooting up, shitting and pissing in plain view.

By 2007, when things had got well and truly out of hand, Zouganelis joined with a few other citizens living or working in Psyrri and the surrounding neighbourhoods to form an association dedicated to the salvation of the historic centre. Two years earlier, he had sued the Ministry of Finance for the lost profits his business had suffered because of the collapse of law and order in the area.

It was to no avail. The authorities, unable or unwilling to co-ordinate with each other, failed to reverse the situation. To the prodding of Zouganelis and his fellow activists, they responded with statistics about their own area of responsibility and threw the *ballaki efthinon* (the little ball of blame) to the other agencies involved. The abdication of control was highlighted by the fact that Athens city hall was no more than a hundred metres from the main drug market. 'In front of city hall, if you slowed down your moped, a policeman would come and tell you off. But on the steps behind the building, drug users were sniffing junk', Zouganelis observes with wry bitterness.

This was the dire state of affairs that faced George Kaminis when he became mayor in 2010. His office made him the public figure most associated in people's minds with the problems of downtown Athens. The trouble was that, unlike his counterparts in cities like London or New York, his authority did not extend to any of the crucial agencies whose coordination would be necessary to begin reversing the situation.

'There is nothing that the city can start and finish on its own,' he tells me. 'You have to go through the Regional Authority, the Ministry of Culture, the Ministry for Citizen Protection, the metropolitan planning organization, the agency responsible for the integration of archaeological spaces.' As he explains, this makes it nearly impossible to achieve the kind of coordination necessary to make the city centre liveable again. 'The only solution is for the whole – or the greater part – of the Attic basin to become a unified, metropolitan municipality, with its own government,' he says, echoing some of his predecessors. The reaction of central government to this is hardly auspicious, however. As Kaminis laments, 'They won't hear of it.' It is not just because of the innate reluctance of centralized authority to give away powers it has amassed; ministers like to showcase big initiatives in the capital, where they will get the most coverage, and are loath to give up such a privileged field of self-promotion.

Meanwhile, the historic centre continues to haemorrhage residents and small businesses. Zouganelis himself reached his breaking point in 2009 when, with lethargic addicts often blocking entry to his establishment, with Theatrou Square strewn with shit and piss and broken needles, he decided to shut up shop. His lawsuit against the government had yet to be heard in late 2013. He still lives in Psyrri, and says things are occasionally better in the neighbourhood these days, in part because of a stronger police presence. He points out, though, that this is usually at the expense of other nearby districts, and safety remains a concern.

As he pointedly asks: 'The city offered at some point to cut municipal taxes for people who returned here to live. But what good are tax incentives if you fear for your life?'

In the first days of August 2012, Greece's month-old government initiated Operation Xenios Zeus. The hideously mislabelled operation − 'Xenios' means 'hospitable' − was, in the overblown words of minister Nikos Dendias, a response to the 'greatest invasion ever' of Hellenic soil, which he compared to the descent of the Dorians some 3,000 years ago. 'We will not allow our towns, or our country, to be occupied and become a migrant ghetto,' he vowed. In the interests of this aggressively expressed aim, other than the 1,800 border guards sent to Evros to 'seal' it, 4,500 police-men were deployed in Athens, to round up those illegally present.

Xenios Zeus was still ongoing at the time of writing. By February 2013, when the police stopped publishing the numbers of detainees, it had detained more than 80,000 foreign nationals in Athens. Only 4,538 of them had been arrested, however.[24] The rest could produce the necessary legal papers, and had only been brought in because − for want of a less crude explanation − they looked foreign. With government-sanctioned racial profiling the order of the day, and with numerous reports in the press and by human rights organizations about police brutality towards immigrants and close links between some officers and Golden

Dawn, it was no surprise that the operation led to excesses.

Some foreign nationals were held even though they produced the appropriate paperwork. A number of those detained complained of being beaten by their captors. Among them, as revealed in a BBC Magazine article in January 2013, were a South Korean and an African-American tourist, both of whom produced passports when asked but were still handcuffed and physically assaulted by the police. The African-American, Christian Ukwuorji, was hospitalized with a concussion. After the incident, the American State Department posted a notice on Greece on its website warning US citizens of the possibility of 'unprovoked harassment and violent attacks' by the Greek police 'against persons who, because of their complexion, are perceived to be foreign migrants'.[25]

But even in cases of individuals caught without papers, Xenios Zeus leads to gross infractions of Greece's obligations under European and international law. For one thing, EU law stipulates that undocumented immigrants may be detained only when it can be shown that it is necessary and that less restrictive measures will not be sufficient. In addition, given the well-documented Odyssey that was involved in merely registering a claim of asylum in Athens, especially before the new Asylum Service began to operate, it was highly likely that those arrested and shipped off to police holding cells or detention centres would be sent home to places where their lives would be in danger, in violation of the principle of non-refoulement (not to mention all sense of decency). Alternatively, if they cannot be sent home, they face the possibility of long spells of captivity.

Then there is the question of the detention facilities themselves, or in government Newspeak, 'closed hospitality centres' (the Samaras government seems to have a particularly warped conception of hospitality). Rights groups have repeatedly criticized Greece for the conditions in such facilities. The European Court of Human Rights has on more than one occasion ruled that the treatment of immigrants held there violates the prohibition against inhuman and degrading treatment. In November 2012, conditions at the detention centre in Komotini, a few kilometres from Evros, led to clashes between inmates and the police. In April 2013, migrants held in the detention centre in Amygdaleza, in the north-east of Attica, went on a hunger strike, with activists accusing the police of responding by clubbing them and referring to them as 'filth'.

The spectre haunting Greece's conservative-led government, and determining the harsh stance of Samaras and Dendias, was the growing popularity and assertiveness of Golden Dawn. After the June elections, staying true to their leader's vow to fight both inside and outside parliament, Golden Dawn members and their fellow travellers took their cause, with mounting ferocity, onto the streets. They have attacked foreigners selling counterfeit goods, smashing their stalls. They have visited public hospitals as self-appointed labour inspectors, looking for immigrant nurses to kick out. Despite their well-established links with paganism and hostility to the Jewish origins of Christianity, they have also lately rediscovered their Orthodox Christian conscience. Driven by its dictates, in October 2012 they came together with religious fanatics outside a small theatre in downtown Athens showing *Corpus Christi*, a play calling the sexuality of Jesus into question. They threatened to burn alive the theatregoers as well as the cast and director. Subsequently, instead of coming down hard on members of the obscurantist mob, the public prosecutor charged everyone involved in putting on the play with blasphemy. On 25 March 2013, to celebrate the anniversary of the start of the Greek war of independence against Turkey, a Golden Dawn contingent went to the offices of Mega channel, one of the main private television networks, and pelted it with eggs and yoghurt, to protest against the Turkish soap-operas it was showing. One member of the protest delegation, the party's parliamentary whip and age-old fascist Christos Pappas, even urinated on the doors.[26] Golden Dawn members of parliament have in fact been present at all these 'initiatives', even if most of them have managed to keep their trousers on. They have learned well, it seems, the lessons of Goebbels about using the weapons of democracy – like the immunity of parliamentary deputies – against it.

Then, of course, there was the violence. In a report released in October 2012, UNHCR spoke of an alarming rise in racially motivated attacks in Greece, and an inadequate response by the authorities. According to the refugee agency, rights groups had recorded eighty-seven racial attacks in the first nine months of the year; it speculated that the real number was much higher, as many foreigners were too scared to go the police or were turned away when they went to press charges. A similar picture emerges from the April 2013 report by the Greek Ombudsman's office, a constitutionally sanctioned independent watchdog, which recorded 253 racial attacks reported as such in 2012, 222 of which took place from May to December, after Golden Dawn became a parliamentary party. As the report noted, these numbers are 'only the tip of the iceberg', given that many racially motivated attacks go either unreported or unrecorded. 'The failure to deal adequately with such behaviour by the proper state authorities sustains the false impression that these can be tolerated,' it added.[27]

Xenios Zeus was part of Samaras's response strategy towards Golden Dawn. He bet that by getting tough on immigration and turning a blind eye to police excesses, he could arrest the rise of Michaloliakos and his gang of Holocaust-denying hooligans. They, for their part, understood this, and reacted by accusing the government of half-measures and by attempting to violently block the transfer of immigrants to detention centres, demanding at every opportunity that the '3 million illegals' (a figure they have plucked out of the clear blue sky) be deported immediately.

The prime minister had shown himself reluctant to crack down on the group, possibly fearing that an aggressive stance towards them would alienate the right-wing voters who had been lured by their anti-system message and whom he was trying to attract

back to New Democray. Perama and the murder of Pavlos Fyssas
– where the victims were Greeks – changed the political calculus.
But it should be noted that before they occurred, some New
Democracy parliamentarians as well as officials and commentators
on the right, had begun whispering the idea of a possible future
coalition with Golden Dawn, if all else failed.

The government, in short, was playing with fire. Despite the
significant early success of Dendias's policies in reducing the
number of new entries into the country, Golden Dawn had seen
its support continue to grow. So long as the game is 'who will be
tougher on foreigners?', the extremists – Golden Dawn themselves
or whoever succeeds them – will be playing with home advantage,
and government policy will be led into ever murkier moral and
legal territory. Meanwhile, economic stagnation and absence of
political reform will continue to eat away at the legitimacy of the
system and offer sustenance to anti-system forces, however virulent
their rhetoric.

Nowhere is this loss of legitimacy more evident, and a greater
cause of concern, than among Greece's younger generation. Exit
polls in the May election put Golden Dawn in fourth place in the
preferences of 18–34-year-olds. According to some opinion polls
conducted after it was entrenched in parliament, it had become
the second most popular party in that age group. It is another
symptom of the manifold crisis engulfing Greek youth, which will
be the subject of the final chapter.

10

Out with the Old

It was a normal Saturday night in the centre of Athens, the prosperous capital city of a confident, developed Western country which, after decades of turbulence – dictatorships, wars, occupation, civil strife – had placed itself firmly at the heart of Europe. That was the fairy tale, at least. That night – 6 December 2008 – a bullet would smash that decaying façade, and offer an ominous warning: there was something rotten in the former kingdom of Greece, the damage it had caused went deep and the consequences were only just beginning to be felt.

Alexis Grigoropoulos, a fifteen-year-old high-school student from the affluent northern suburbs of Athens, had made his way with a small group of friends to Exarcheia, the downtown neighbourhood well known for its alternative bars and cheap eateries but also as a hotbed of anarchist activism, often directed against the police. It was St Nicholas Day, and he was visiting a close friend who was celebrating his nameday.

On patrol in Exarcheia that night was thirty-seven-year-old police officer Epaminondas Korkoneas along with his partner, Vasilis Saraliotis. At some point, as they were riding around, they ran into a group of four or five youths and there was a stand-off. Bottles showered down on the squad car. A flash grenade was thrown in return. After they drove off, Korkoneas, who had been serving in the unruly district since 2001 and who was known among his colleagues as a hothead, insisted to his partner that they leave their vehicle and go back to find 'those fucking kids' on foot – something explicitly forbidden to officers in Exarcheia.

A little while later, around nine o'clock, on the corner of

Tzavela and Mesologgiou streets, the two policemen ran into Alexis Grigoropoulos and his group – also no more than four or five in number. They began swearing at them, provoking them. Alexis, who was sitting having a sandwich, got up and demanded to know the reason for the cops' aggressive behaviour. At this, Korkoneas took out his revolver and fired twice. One of the bullets went though the boy's heart. He died instantly.

Within minutes, a crowd gathered at the scene. As its size kept swelling and shock was giving way to rage, a platoon of riot policemen appeared. The response from the crowd was furious. The rage grew. By midnight, Athens was in flames. All across the city centre, protesters were clashing with police, smashing shop windows, torching cars, chanting 'This night belongs to Alexis' and the old favourite, its force now renewed: 'Cops, pigs, murderers.'

The rage spread: that same night, there were demonstrations in more than twenty other cities, from Alexandroupoli in the northeast to Heraklion and Chania in Crete. The weeks that followed were without precedent in the history of the post-junta Greek Republic. High-school students throughout Greece walked out of their schools and marched to police stations to protest, often throwing eggs or paintbombs. University students occupied their campuses and administration buildings. Groups of protesters took over radio stations and, on one occasion, the studio of the state broadcaster, where they unfurled a banner urging generalized unrest. 'Stop watching, everybody out into the streets', it read. In Athens, the anarchists, who for decades had hijacked peaceful protests by throwing rocks and Molotov cocktails and attacking the police, now seemed to have grown into an army, as angry youths joined their hooded ranks to smash and torch everything in sight. Police stations, banks, shops, cars, historic public buildings, even the humongous Christmas tree towering over Syntagma Square, opposite parliament, were consumed by fire. Looting was widespread.

By the end of the first week of the riots – which some commentators were by then calling an 'uprising' – the riot police were running low on supplies of teargas. Despite its prolific use, there were times when the police, restrained to some extent by a conservative government terrified at the prospect of another fatality, had completely lost control of the capital. It later emerged that some members of the cabinet had proposed the imposition of martial law. Demonstrations of solidarity with Greece's youth, some of which also turned violent, occurred in most European cities, and as far away as Melbourne and Buenos Aires.

It was only after Christmas Day that the *Dekemvriana* ('the December Events', as they were dubbed, in reference to the first phase of the Greek civil war in December 1944) began to peter out. In hindsight, it is clear that this was only the end of the beginning, that the riots were the first rumblings of the coming cataclysm. The murder of a teenager by a policeman's bullet was widely viewed as tragically symbolic of a system that was killing its young. There was a lot of talk about youth unemployment, low wages for young workers ('the 700 euro generation'), a spreading anxiety that they would be the first generation to be worse off than their parents. Many on the left laid the blame at the door of the purported 'neoliberalism' of the New Democracy government, which saw the young as cheap labour to be exploited and which valued profits over people.

A few months later, the crisis over the mountainous debt owed by the Greek state would creep to the centre of the world's attention. This crisis sent youth unemployment skyrocketing to levels that back in 2008 would have been laughed off as the products of a diseased imagination. It made wages of 700 euros a relic of the good old days and it guaranteed that Greece's youth – those not taking the increasingly popular option of emigration – would suffer a long, cold winter before they could return to the standard of living enjoyed by their parents' generation.

In so doing, the Great Crisis revealed the true cause of the plight of Greece's young, one ignored by the dominant narrative.

It was not an excess of neoliberalism that was the problem, but – if anything – not enough neoliberalism; in the peculiarly Greek form of statist crony capitalism, the old ruled and the new – young entrepreneurs looking to start a business, graduates looking for work, upstart companies looking to enter a protected market – were kept down. Even worse: as the bill for the follies of the client-based political system was coming due, it became abundantly clear that priority number one for the outgoing *Polytechneio* generation, who had come of age around the time of the fall of the colonels, was to transfer as much of the burden of adjustment as they could onto their kids.

This great betrayal, and its ideological suppression, lies at the heart of the tragedy of Greece's young. The history of this tragedy is intimately linked with the history of Greek higher education after the junta. It is in Greece's universities that successive waves of young Greeks learned the twisted terms of the political trade, and where the failure of the system to prepare them for the challenges of tomorrow had the most disastrous consequences.

In late August 2011, just as Greeks were returning home from their summer break to face the toughest autumn of the post-junta era, a rare thing occurred in the Greek parliament: the PASOK government and the New Democracy opposition came together and voted for a major bill. The bill, for the reform of the higher education system, was the first one of any consequence on which the two parties had reached consensus since the 2009 elections. It was also the first time in Greece's post-junta history that PASOK and ND had voted together on a bill related to the restructuring of higher education. With the additional support of LAOS, a minor populist right-wing party, the bill, spearheaded by Education Minister and former European Commissioner for Social Affairs Anna Diamantopoulou, garnered 255 votes in the 300-seat house.

Though flawed in parts, the law was in many ways a break-through. It revoked the right of students to take part in the election of university administrators, which had been the wellspring of the system's corruption, and set an upper time limit of six years for earning four-year degrees (the average at the time was nearly eight years). It called for the establishment of new governing councils, whose members would include professors from outside the institutions as well as prominent non-academics. It allowed private donors to directly fund research for the first time. Most important of all, on a symbolic level, it repealed the asylum clause of the 1982 higher education law passed by the PASOK government of Andreas Papandreou. The asylum clause explicitly guaranteed the protection of academic spaces from police incursions, an oddity in a state governed by the rule of law in which academic freedom was enshrined in the Constitution. In practice, the clause had developed from a curiosity to a monstrosity. It allowed anarchist hooligans and criminals to use university grounds to avoid arrest and it gave free rein to leftist thugs to terrorize professors who did not conform to their preferred version of revolutionary politics.

But if the George Papandreou government expected these salutary reforms, and the widespread support they commanded in parliament, to translate into smooth implementation, they had another think coming. Student organizations opposed to the law began a mass occupation campaign, the umpteenth in recent times, which already by the first week of September had spread to the vast majority of Greek universities, disrupting the autumn exam period.

Questioned on the occupations, Theodosis Pelegrinis, rector of the University of Athens, said that 'It is for the students to decide whether the exam period will be moved. Neither the rectors nor the senate can decide the timing, because it is the students that decide whether they will take part.'[1] The congress of rectors appealed to the Council of State to have the law thrown out as unconstitutional. Though they officially opposed the occupations, they did little to avert them and some actively encouraged them, for example by suspending the exam period so that students coming back from the beaches would have the time to organize the 'resistance'.

Meanwhile, the vanguard of the revolution once again took matters into their own hands. In many institutions, far-left groups violently blocked the election of the new governing councils. In some cases, they did this by stealing the ballot box. Professors who were members of the election board or who had spoken out in favour of the reform were verbally abused, their faces were plastered on posters declaring them enemies of the people, their classes disrupted, their offices ransacked and redecorated with spray-painted slogans. Some were even slapped around. These activities went on sporadically for more than a year without any arrests being made. The asylum provision had been abolished on paper, but in practice the assailants still enjoyed immunity.[2]

The unholy alliance between student party politicians and university administrators had been created by the 1982 reform promulgated by Andreas Papandreou, which his son was now attempting to undo. In the decades since then, unperturbed by a political system that had other priorities, it had turned universities into a bastion of mediocrity, nepotism and corruption, where the exchange of political favours and the right of a militant minority to play at revolution always took precedence – often enforced through intimidation or violence – over the demands of academic excellence and the need to prepare graduates for an ever-shifting jobs market.

That had not been the plan. The 1982 law was meant to democratize the university. It would open it up to younger, more progressive academics, ending the dominance of the conservative old guard, and increase students' participation in university affairs, on the model that had already been implemented by Western European countries at a time when Greece was still languishing in the grip of dictatorship.

How this did these noble intentions go so horribly wrong? How was the democratic progressivism coursing through Greek universities in the early 1980s reduced to the stale conservatism of 2011, often defending its privileges through authoritarian thuggery?

The 1982 asylum clause was probably unique for a liberal democracy, but its inception is not hard to explain. It was passed by the first left-wing government in Greece's history, as a political homage to the *Polytechneio* events of November 1973. During four days between 14 and 17 November of that year, students had occupied the grounds of the National Technical University of Athens (the *Polytechneio*), transmitting through a radio signal messages of protest against the junta of the colonels. On the 17th a tank stormed the gates of the university and the students came under police fire. Dozens were killed (the precise number is still debated today). In its aftermath, what little public support the regime still retained after six years in power evaporated. The junta fell eight months later.

Even though the students' uprising did not directly cause the downfall of the dictators, their heroic stand became the foundation myth of the *Metapoliteusi*, the era of the post-junta Republic. Students were considered the avatars of progressive change. Student radicalism was widely tolerated, even when it broke the law, notably through the widespread practice of campus occupations. November 17 became a national holiday and even the Marxist terror group named after it was little criticized for the first two assassinations it carried out – of the CIA station chief in Athens in 1975 and of Evangelos Mallios, the arch-torturer of the police during the junta.

Society feared its rebellious youth much less than it feared the remnants of the dictatorship, which many suspected of plotting to retake power. The conservative New Democracy governments which had been in power since 1974 were criticized for not having done enough to cleanse the state apparatus of these remnants, and there was concern about whether the dark forces of

Greek politics would allow Andreas Papandreou, with his anti-Western, quasi-communistic rhetoric, to become prime minister.

Yannis Panousis, an MP for the reformist Democratic Left since May 2012, was a young left-wing academic when PASOK came to power in 1981. After studying Law in the University of Athens, he had been forced, as a known leftist, to spend thirty months as a conscript in the army during the dictatorship. Soon after the fall of the colonels, he left for France and a post-graduate degree in Criminology. When he returned home in 1978, he joined PASOK; in 1982 he was one of the architects of the framework law on higher education.

'The law was the legislative imprint of the demands of the *Metapoliteusi*, of the student movement and what was then called the "progressive academic caucus",' Panousis recalls, sitting in his office in parliament, his intelligent eyes sparkling behind the traditional grey beard of the ageing intellectual of the left. Aside from the asylum clause, its significance highlighted by the fact that it was the second article of the bill, the law upended the status quo by repealing the university Chair positions and the lifetime autocratic privileges of the professors who held them. Academic decisions − on tenure, PhD committees and so on − would henceforth be made democratically, by the entire teaching staff. Student participation was also introduced for the first time, in a radical form. It was determined that students would take part in the general assemblies of the departments and in the elections of department heads, deans and rectors, with a quantitative influence without precedent in the post-May '68 reforms that swept through Western universities.

This worked well enough at first. Progressive (read: centre-left and communist) professors and students voted on ideological grounds and the fusty old order was replaced by a younger, more open-minded generation of academics. Pre-eminent among them was Michael Stathopoulos, a professor of Law who was elected to the prestigious post of rector of the University of Athens in 1983.

Stathopoulos, a leftist but never a party man, won the support of the three left-wing parties (PASOK and the two factions of the Communist Party that existed then) and was called upon to harmonize the demands of the revolution with the need for continuity and order at Greece's leading university.

This delicate balancing act was sorely tested on the twelfth anniversary of the *Polytechneio* uprising, on 17 November 1985. On that day, as was already the established tradition, skirmishes broke out between police and anarchist elements in Exarcheia. A police truck went up in flames from a petrol bomb and, in the ensuing confusion, a policeman shot dead a fifteen-year-old boy. During the violent protests that followed, a group of anarchist students and their fellow-travellers occupied the old chemical laboratory belonging to the University of Athens and refused to leave. After much haggling and agonized reflection, Stathopoulos and the institution's asylum committee, which included a student, gave the green light for the police to enter the laboratory building and remove the occupiers. It was the first time asylum had been lifted after the passage of the 1982 law.[3] It would be ten years before it was lifted again, at the National Technical University of Athens, again on 17 November. On that occasion the rector would relent to government pressure, and only after the 600-plus occupiers had vandalized the administrators' offices, the building of the School of Fine Art, laboratories, classrooms and anything else that came across their path.

Stathopoulos was widely condemned for his decision to allow the police onto university grounds. The PASOK government, he recalls, though privately supportive, washed its hands of him in public. Almost thirty years later, he is adamant that he made the right choice. 'The gravest disease of our universities is the occupations,' he says, 'and we are all – professors, politicians, journalists – to blame for fostering an ideological climate in which they were an acceptable practice.' An old friend of the SYRIZA-bashing Theodoros Pangalos – they were schoolmates in the 1950s –

Stathopoulos, who served as Justice Minister under Simitis in 2000 and who is today a member of the exalted ranks of the Academy of Athens, is another prominent left-winger who is repelled by what the Greek left has turned into.

The toleration of lawlessness in universities was one aspect of the fall of the left. The other was the acceptance, if not the embrace, of corruption, starting in the second half of the 1980s. By this time, the revolutionaries were becoming the new establishment. Student participation fell, allowing the heads of the youth wings of the political parties to take over proceedings and to develop personal power relationships with rectors over whose election they held sway. 'There was a new sense of arrogance among student leaders; they thought they owned the university,' Stathopoulos recalls. The professors, for their part, overcame their ideological differences over the framework law and sought to milk the opportunities afforded by the new situation for all they were worth.

Countless members of the teaching staff, though listed (and paid) as full-time academics, spent almost all their time in their much more lucrative private practices, as lawyers, doctors, civil engineers and so on. Students, who might have been expected to protest against this, did not. Their silence was bought with passing grades awarded irrespective of academic performance. The practice had begun in the immediate aftermath of the junta, when professors tainted by their association with the regime sought to curry favour with their charges by passing them even when they turned in blank sheets of paper. As time went by, it became so widespread it got its own name: the 'democratic five' (with ten as full marks). Laxity of standards in the name of progress and democracy became the rule everywhere. Exams could be retaken *ad infinitum*. Students who had failed Economics 101 could sign-up for the more specialized second-year course, hoping eventually to be granted the 'democratic five'. There was no deadline for finishing one's studies. 'Student participation became student complicity. Everyone was in on it,' Panousis, the MP, says.

But that was nothing compared to what happened in the 1990s, when EU money started flowing into Greek universities. Professors able to attract such funding acquired undue influence in university affairs and were able to hire friends and relatives without anyone objecting. Corruption flourished. Research grant applications were inflated and only a small fraction of the funds went towards research, the rest lining the pockets of professors. Student leaders and their comrades became 'research assistants', paid by the Greek taxpayer. Many of them were promised PhDs and some even got them. The special treatment they demanded to deliver their electoral support to a candidate grew increasingly outrageous. When the decisions of the Ministry of Education displeased them, they voted to occupy their university, in general assemblies of the students which were anything but general and in which they used any number of anti-democratic stunts to get the decision they wanted.

The politicians not only failed to tackle the problem at its roots, but made things worse. Ministers signed off on institutions' budgets, ignoring blatant signs of drunken-sailor-style spending. Parliamentarians' main contribution to the development of higher education was their constant push for the creation of new academic departments. These were often set up in the middle of nowhere, far removed from the seat of the university to which they nominally belonged. That mattered little to the politicians extolling their merits; what was crucial to them was that the new department be built in their electoral constituencies, the grateful *souvlaki* shop owners and bar proprietors of which would never be allowed to forget who had brought them all these hungry, thirsty, outgoing new customers. Influential pols also exploited the broken system to transfer their kids to whichever university they preferred, if they were unhappy with the one where they had found a place. Marieta Giannakou, one of the braver of Greece's recent Education Ministers, said in 2004 that if the names of those who had benefited from transfers up to that time were made public, 'parliament itself won't be able to withstand it'.[4]

As the ideals of the progressive university were sinking into this moral morass, the extreme leftist students stuck firm to their own, rigidly embraced ideology. Protected by the asylum provision of the 1982 law, coddled by rectors who didn't have the guts or the inclination to stand up to them, they came to exercise a form of ideological terror over academic life. In one indicative case that Panousis recounts, from the mid-2000s, about a hundred students invaded a meeting of the senate of the University of Athens, protesting against legislation passed by the government. The rector, a famous Greek academic who went on to serve briefly and without distinction as Minister of Education, vowed to the wild bunch that had taken over his senate meeting that he would not implement the new law. The kids were not satisfied. They demanded that each member of the senate make a personal commitment to oppose the law in practice. Panousis says he was the only one to refuse.

Sometimes, things went further even than this. In February 2009, a few weeks after the Grigoropoulos riots had died down, Panousis was delivering a speech on social care for released prisoners in a cultural centre belonging to the University of Athens when a group of masked thugs barged in, shouting slogans in support of individuals arrested during the riots and against the government and the police. They attacked and beat the professor with a crowbar. It was neither the first nor the last such incident to take place.

'The new equilibrium in the university today is fear,' Panousis asserts. 'Professors are terrified of speaking out, they are afraid their office walls will be spray-painted, their cars burned.' Stathopoulos, for his part, appeared before the Council of State in 2012 to oppose the appeal of the congress of rectors against the Diamantopoulou reform. 'I had become outraged with the bad implementation of the old law, the exchange of favours,' he says.

Such is life in Greece's temples of higher learning in the Age of the Memorandum: radical change, in the context of reduced funding, has angered the established interests – professors as well as student politicians. Salutary developments, like the beginnings of rigorous evaluation of staff and the restriction of the influence of party politics, compete with the stalling tactics of recalcitrant rectors and the disruptive raids on administrative meetings by 'politicized' students. Meanwhile, those members of the student body less interested in politics and more focused on the desperate search for gainful employment are left, more than ever before, to their own devices.

Spyros Lambrinidis thought it was a straightforward idea. An above average product of the Greek school system, he had bypassed the mind-altering trip of Greek university life to study Computer Science at Edinburgh, thus becoming immune to the heavy 'can't do' attitude that infects many inmates of Greek higher education institutions, even among those who excel academically. Having then worked as a software engineer in London for three years, he had come home in 2005 to undergo military service – like university, another drug-like experience that teaches young Greeks a lot about how to make it in contemporary Greek society. Afterwards, untypically for someone with his experiences and professional ambitions, he had decided to stay.

In early 2011, aged thirty-two and having landed a job as head of engineering at People Per Hour, a promising Greek web start-up, Lambrinidis wanted to fish around in the best Computer Science departments of Greek universities, to find agile young minds ready for a challenge. He remembered how in Edinburgh, companies would organize presentations on campus where they showcased the career opportunities they had to offer and tried to entice the best students to join them, for a summer job or full-time after graduation. He thought he could do something similar in Greece. Silly him.

He phoned around to the career offices of the three top Greek institutions in the field of software or computer engineering. He told them People Per Hour wanted to organize a presentation on campus, to talk about what it does and what kind of people it was looking for. At the time, the starting take-home pay the company offered was €1,300 a month – something of a small miracle in an economy sliding in those days into its fourth consecutive year of recession, where the vast majority of young people were either unemployed, grossly underpaid or working dead-end jobs un-related to their studies.

The response, he tells me, ranged from tepid to hostile. The people he spoke to in the two Athenian universities in particular – the University of Athens and the National Technical University – kept giving him the bureaucratic runaround. They told him it would be difficult for the university authorities themselves to organize an event and urged him to act unilaterally: go to the main notice board on campus and pin up an announcement. When he pressed one professor to tell him why the university administration was so hesitant about bringing their students together with private companies keen to offer them jobs, everything was illuminated. 'There's this anarchist group of students here,' he was told. 'If you come to do a presentation, they're likely to beat you up.'

The story highlights some of the many ways in which Greek higher education, despite the excellent theoretical grounding offered in its best institutions, fails to prepare students for the job market. It begins with the manner of a student's entry into a particular department of a particular university, through a gruel-ling system of national entrance exams requiring the exact memorization of entire textbooks. Based on the grades they get in these exams, students are distributed to institutions in quotas fixed by ministerial diktat, in a way that often overrides their own preferences and without any assessment of the entrants' qualities by the institution itself. Once in, students have to contend with the chaos of classes interrupted by political groups reading out communiqués, exam periods suspended because of occupation and courses taught by PhD students because the professors are away on their day jobs. Meanwhile, both students and academic staff at the TEIs (institutes of technological education) are constantly pushing for a blurring of the distinction between the institute and the universities, resulting in the danger that 'TEIs will drift further way from the core mission of meeting the country's needs in skilled technicians', as the OECD put it in a 2011 report.[5] The hostility of the Marxist and anarchist students to private enterprise is only the pointy tip of an enormous iceberg.

The consequences of this were already evident before the Great Crisis, but since 2010, things have gone from worrying to devastating. At the halfway mark of 2013, youth unemployment (ages 15–24) in Greece had reached a stomach-churning 59.2 per cent, compared to 22.9 per cent at the end of 2008, before the Great Crisis had erupted.[6] At the end of 2010, only a few months into the Age of the Memorandum, Greece had the fourth lowest employment rate for graduates among the EU-27. In data from 2006–10, out of forty-eight countries belonging to the European Higher Education Area, Greece is one of only three countries (the others are Turkey and Georgia) where graduate unemployment was actually *higher* than the unemployment of individuals with lower education credentials. It was also, according to data for 2009 – that is, before the collapse – by far in the lead in the average time it took for the transition from a university degree to a job (12.2 months, with the runners-up, Italy, clocking in at 9.8 months).[7]

These facts explain the high levels of Greek brain drain reached already before the crisis hit. A 2010 study by the University of Macedonia, which sampled 2,734 Greek graduates of higher education who had worked for at least one year abroad, found that 61 per cent never even tried to find work at home, including 47 per cent of those who had completed the whole of their university studies in Greece. Of those who did look for a Greek job before they left, the majority made the effort for less than six months.[8] Since then, anecdotal evidence, plus some far from comprehensive hard data, indicate that the flow of Greek doctors, academics and engineers out of the country has been gathering pace.[9] Unlike past emigration waves, which involved mostly unskilled workers, this one is made up of Greece's best and brightest. That is terrible news not only for the prospects of economic recovery, but also for the wider project of social and political rebirth that Greece so urgently needs.

And yet, amidst the doom and gloom of the crisis, there are signs of hope for Greece's young. Nowhere is this more evident than in the country's emerging start-up scene.

In February 2013 I accompanied Spyros Lambrinidis to the Athens Start-Up Weekend, the Greek version of an event held in more than a hundred cities around the world, which aims to bring people with bright ideas together for fifty-four hours in the hopes of launching new start-up companies.

Lambrinidis participated in the event as a mentor – one of a number of successful members of the start-up tribe who, along with executives of bigger companies interested in the field of technology, marketing experts, lawyers and others, come to offer advice to the hundred or so participants, as they seek, in the space of a weekend, to transform the lightbulb above their heads into a workable business proposition. But it's not just altruism that drives people like Lambrinidis to these events. 'The Start-Up Weekend is a great place to find new talent,' he says.[10]

One of the organizers of the event is Stavros Messinis, a hyperactive devotee of the network economy who in 2009, in his mid-thirties, co-founded the CoLab working space in downtown Athens, as a place for start-uppers to work and collaborate. CoLab was the outcome of an idea that someone threw out at the second Athens Start-Up Weekend, and has since evolved into one of the main hubs of start-up activity in the capital. 'The concept was to gather like-minded people in the same space and offer them what they need in terms of connectivity and interesting content – presentations, tech meet-ups and so on,' he explains.

When I ask why he hopes the start-up community can offer Greece a leg-up on the hard climb of recovery, given the dire situation the country is in, he surprises me. 'I don't see a dire situation,' he tells me. I stare at him, trying to make out if I am in the presence of a particularly dry ironist. But he's deadly serious. 'I see a very highly educated population, with good family values and support networks behind them.' But do they not lack the necessary schooling in the skills required to become a business success? 'They do, but they are fast learners.'

Messinis's optimism is not groundless. Greece is already home to three of the world's ten biggest mobile marketing companies. More recently, making use of developments like cloud servers, new web development tools and social media marketing that have dramatically reduced the cost of starting up a start-up, new Greek success stories have surfaced and are beginning to make an impact. Taxi Beat, the company behind a brilliant application that allows people to choose their taxi driver according to the amenities provided and the ratings of other users, has already spread from Athens to Paris, Rio de Janeiro, São Paulo and Mexico City. In December 2013 it announced a $4 million funding agreement led by London-based Hummingbird Ventures. BugSense, which is a diagnostics service for developers of mobile apps, is used by over 5,000 developers and companies around the world, and was taken over in September 2013 by US-based Splunk, a pioneer in the field of operational intelligence. Persado, a spin-off of Upstream, a world-leading Greek digital marketing firm, which specializes in mathematically complex 'persuasion marketing', secured a $15 million funding round in early 2013, led by Bain Capital.

Even the domestic capital drought that has afflicted most sectors of the Greek economy is no longer an issue for Greek techies. In late November 2012, in an Opencoffee meeting (another industry institution) in the Benaki museum, it was announced that four new venture capital funds would be set up, financed in part through the Jeremie programme of the European Investment

Fund. Their combined financial firepower exceeds €40 million and may reach up to €80 million, all of which would go into funding innovative Greek tech companies.

This sense of potential is what led Nikos Moraitakis back to Greece at the most unlikely time – April 2012, on the eve of the 6 May elections that would usher in six horrendous weeks of Grexit-mania across the globe. A widely intelligent, restless graduate of Imperial College London, Moraitakis was a key figure in the rise of Athens-based Upstream into a global mobile marketing powerhouse, as vice-president in charge of business development since 2005. As he tells me, to join Upstream he had to quit a management consultant position at Ernst & Young, a move that many close to him thought he was mad to make.

It was a winning gamble: by 2012, working out of Dubai for Upstream, he was taking in an annual salary well into six figures at the tender age of thirty-four. On the side, he had invested in and was acting as an adviser to Taxi Beat. It was at this point that he decided to come home and start his own business, along with another Upstream alumnus, Spyros Magiatis. Compared to this, the move to Upstream from Ernst & Young was downright sensible.

'This is a time of great opportunity for Greece,' Moraitakis says. 'There are funds willing to spend money; the competition for that money is not too great; the costs of starting up are a fraction of what they used to be; an ecosystem is being created, through common working spaces, founders' meetings and so on; there is a sense of solidarity, with companies helping each other any way they can; and there is a large pool of talented, unemployed young people out there.'

We are chatting in the new, barely furnished offices of Workable, the company he has co-founded, in a modern, open-spaced office complex in Gerakas, a north-eastern suburb of Athens. The company offers clever, user-friendly software to facilitate recruitment at small and medium-sized firms, using online profiles instead of CVs. Upstream, which is housed in the same complex, was one of the original investors in Workable. 'Imagine that!' Moraitakis marvels: 'A Greek businessman who finds out an employee is resigning to start his own firm and offers to fund his effort, instead of trying to undermine it.'

What comes out unmistakably in our discussion, as it did in my talk with Messinis and Lambrinidis, is a business ethos, seemingly pervasive within the Greek start-up community, which is the polar opposite of the approach of your average Greek businessman. That traditional approach mandated a ruthless stance towards one's competitors in a given sector. This either led to anti-competitive practices to block the entry of other players, if the firm in question was an incumbent, or to illegal methods to gain market share at the expense of more law-abiding firms. With the tech start-ups, the mentality is very different, at least in these early, idealistic days. They share information, they offer each other free use of their applications (Workable, for example, offered its software to all Greek start-ups for six months to help them streamline their recruitment); the more established ones, like Upstream, even fund their successors.

The start-up approach is also different when it comes to labour relations. Greek employers in non-unionized companies, meaning most of the private sector, are infamous for offering low wages, no benefits and a generally disagreeable working environment, in which the employee more often than not feels like an exploited appendage rather than a meaningful contributor to a common project. By contrast, Greek start-ups, attempting to channel the practices of the giants of Silicon Valley, emphasize the need to make work fun and to treat employees as partners, not instruments. The office complex that is home to Workable and Upstream even includes yoga classes and massage services for over-stressed employees.

'Our view is that you must exhaust your creativity on your product. As regards the rest of it, just do what smart Americans do: give employees good salaries and benefits, give them beautiful offices to work in, offer them equity in the company,' Moraitakis tells me. 'If you treat people well, people who are used to employers who are trying to cheat them, then they will give you their best, and then some. Greeks have this quality of going the extra mile for a project they feel they own.'

None of this is to ignore the plethora of roadblocks and potential pitfalls facing Greece's web entrepreneurs. The ecosystem is still in its infancy, as is the pool of investors with the knowledge to back the right projects. Dealing with the bureaucracy on labour and tax issues remains a pain, just as it is for all of Greek businesses. Another problem that will be faced down the line is that of scaling up. As Moraitakis points out, Greece suffers from a major shortage of people who have the necessary experience to take a successful new business from 10 to 100 (let alone to 500) employees.[11]

Time will tell how the sector will evolve. But the fundamentals are promising. At the end of my conversation with Moraitakis, we talked about the potential for Greece's most successful business community, the shipowners, to spend some of their wealth on local tech start-ups, something which has already begun, albeit in tiny increments. The CEO of Workable made an illuminating analogy: 'Shipping is a level playing field. The sea is stateless, under one law. It's just like the internet.' Without the deadweight tonnage of the state dragging them down, Greece's web entrepreneurs could in time develop into an international success story, over-turning negative stereotypes about the country and fuelling the recovery from its crushing recession.

On 1 February 2013 two groups of masked individuals, eight in total, armed with Kalashnikov rifles among other weaponry, robbed an ATE Bank branch and the local post office in the northern town of Velvedo. Four of the perpetrators were arrested the next day by the police, despite taking a local dentist hostage in their attempt to escape. The case caused a national uproar because the captured individuals appeared badly beaten in photos and TV images and it emerged that their mugshots had been Photoshopped to cover the scars. The police, rather unconvincingly, claimed they used force only during the arrests.

But the four young men also attracted attention because of their background and age. All of them came from middle-class families and were born in the comfort of the northern suburbs of Athens. The oldest was twenty-four years old. Along with his twenty-one-year-old associate, they were wanted as members of the 'Conspiracy of the Cells of Fire', a terrorist group formed after the 2008 riots that followed the murder of Alexis Grigoropoulos.[12] The youngest of them, twenty-year-old Nikos Romanos, was one of Alexis's closest friends, the one whose nameday the ill-fated teenager had gone to Exarcheia to celebrate on the night he was killed.[13]

Romanos quit school soon after the tragic events of 6 December. He was scheduled to appear as a witness in the trial of Korkoneas and Saraliotis, the officers charged with Grigoropoulos's murder, but he had refused to do so (Korkoneas, in the end, was convicted of first degree murder and sentenced to life in prison; Saraliotis got ten years). He explained his reasons in a message to a Greek news website in April 2010: 'I had no intention of appearing at the trial, because I am not in the least interested in its outcome,' he wrote. Responding to claims made by Alexis Kougias, the controversial, publicity-courting defence attorney for Korkoneas, that he was a member of far-left organizations, he referred to them as 'conspiracy-minded plots of a conceited shyster'.[14]

But tests carried out by the police after his arrest showed that his DNA matched that found on the scene of an arson attack in which five city buses were burnt on 27 June 2009. The attack was one of several executed in the first half of 2009 by 'Shadows of Fire', another anarchist group that had sprung up after Grigoropoulos's murder. In a proclamation sent out after an attack in March of that year, the group made a direct reference to the teenager's killing as an inspiration for their activities.[15]

The extremist moment sparked by the December riots was intensified further as the Great Crisis began sweeping through the country, leaving livelihoods in ruins and angry young men without jobs or prospects. In a country that had long suffered from terrorism but thought it was done with it, especially after the police captured the members of '17 November' in the summer of 2002, 'revolutionary' political violence has made a forceful comeback. The increasingly frequent attacks range from petrol bombs in car dealerships to robberies and murder. The tone of the political tracts they put out is more nihilistic than the Marxist manifestos of '17N', they are thought to have more connections with organized crime and their membership appears to be constantly replenished by young people with no faith in the future, irrevocably alienated from society and the state. As one commentator puts it, referring to the shadowy elders of these self-styled 'urban-guerrillas': 'every incident of police violence, rioting and popular indignation is used as an opportunity to recruit new members.'[16]

In statements written in prison after his arrest, Romanos refers to himself as a 'prisoner of war' and a partisan of the 'anarchist struggle'. He calls for 'the levels of violence to be multiplied' and states that he does not recognize the authority of the law or of the 'judicial mafia'.

His case, and others like it, constitute the mirror image of the skinheaded twenty-year-olds who find meaning by marching in the black shirts of Golden Dawn, swearing allegiance to the nation and the Leader with the screeching voice and beating immigrants senseless or worse. The greater the number of young people that stray towards these opposite extremes, the more they talk about bringing down the state or 'cleaning up the filth' instead of business plans and funding opportunities, the likelier it becomes that the social fabric will be torn to shreds. If that happens, December 2008 will look like a walk in the park by comparison.

Epilogue
Staring into the Abyss

It had been a disorienting, tumultuous weekend. A little past midnight as Friday turned into Saturday, 27 June 2015, Alexis Tsipras, the left-wing firebrand who had been elected prime minister in January on a platform of reversing austerity while keeping Greece in the Eurozone, had called a referendum on the latest set of budget-tightening and reform measures proposed by Greece's creditors. He had urged Greek voters to reject the proposal.

The referendum announcement had sent shockwaves across Europe. Many Greeks had driven after midnight to the nearest ATM, as well as to petrol stations to fill up. The referendum was called for 5 July, but before that, on 30 June, the four-month extension of Greece's second bailout programme would expire. On the same day, Greece was due to repay approximately 1.6 billion euros to the International Monetary Fund (IMF). That deadline was now only three days away, and the money to make the payment was not there.

The decision to hold the referendum while negotiations on the final version of an agreement to succeed the second bailout were still taking place in Brussels severed whatever bonds of trust remained between Tsipras and Greece's creditors. The end of the bailout programme also meant the suspension of emergency liquidity support from the European Central Bank (ECB) to Greek banks. It was clear to everyone involved that if banks opened on Monday, there would be total mayhem – a violent death of the banking system, via a massive haemorrhage of cash by terror-stricken depositors. The least horrific option available to prevent

Greece from sliding out of the euro even before the vote was held, as well as to maintain public safety in the country, was the imposition of a bank holiday and capital controls.

So it was baffling that Yanis Varoufakis, Greece's flamboyant finance minister and the man many, both within Greece and throughout the Eurozone, thought chiefly responsible for the unfolding disaster, tweeted the following Olympian assessment at 2.59 p.m. Greek time on Sunday, 28 June:

> Capital controls within a monetary union are a contradiction in terms. The Greek government opposes the very concept.

A few hours earlier, Yannis Stournaras, the governor of the Bank of Greece, who had served as Finance Minister under the previous conservative-led government of Antonis Samaras, had participated in a conference call with his fellow members of the governing council of the ECB. Stournaras had been in Basel on Friday attending the annual conference of the Bank of International Settlements when he got a call from Yannis Dragasakis, the deputy prime minister and a leading figure in the moderate camp within the cabinet. Dragasakis stunned the governor with news of the referendum. 'You are taking a terrible risk,' Stournaras said. Dragasakis, who, it would emerge, shared his interlocutor's qualms about the decision, emphasized the need to push for an increase in ELA (emergency liquidity assistance) from the Bank of Greece to the Greek banking system. Without a massive increase in ELA, which could not happen without the consent of the governing council of the ECB, capital controls would be unavoidable.[1]

In the conference call on Sunday morning, Stournaras asked for a 6-billion-euro increase in the level of ELA. The request was unceremoniously denied. Instead, the discussion turned to proposals that would effectively have shut the door on Greece's membership of the Eurozone. One involved the revocation of the licences of the banks by the Single Supervisory Mechanism, the regulator of the Eurozone's systemically significant credit institutions. Another envisaged Greece's disconnection from the Eurozone's Target2 system of payments – cutting off Greek banks from the rest of the continent. The call ended with the council freezing ELA at current levels and Stournaras being given a strict deadline – midnight – for the imposition of capital controls. If the deadline was not met, it was made clear that the ECB would resort to one of the more drastic options discussed.

That afternoon there was a meeting of the Greek Council for Systemic Stability to discuss the legislative decree to close the banks. The participants, including Stournaras and Varoufakis, argued over key aspects such as daily withdrawal limits from ATMs and the process for transferring funds abroad. One participant, oblivious to the bleak reality of the very limited amounts of actual cash in bank branches, proposed a daily withdrawal limit of 200 euros. Stournaras proposed that it be set as low as 40 euros. In the end, the amount was fixed at 60 euros. Varoufakis seemed to those present to be in a buoyant mood, even touting the benefits of capital controls, such as the increase in the use of cards and electronic transactions. A top banker noted with alarm the utter lack of contingency planning by the ministry, as well as the claim by Deputy Finance Minister Nadia Valavani that it would be 'unfair' to allow people access to their possessions stored in safe-deposit boxes when others could only withdraw so little money from their accounts.

The meeting was over by 8 o'clock, but the night's drama was far from over. At the Maximos Mansion, the prime minister's office, Tsipras was waiting for Varoufakis to come so that they could finalize the legislative decree in time for Stournaras's midnight conference call. But the Finance Minister arrived at Maximos much delayed, no more than half an hour before midnight.

What followed was an explosion of months of pent-up anger at

Varoufakis. His cabinet colleagues lashed out at him for his late arrival, his lax attitude in the face of potential catastrophe and the gaping holes in the draft decree. Tsipras was particularly incensed that there were no provisions for pensioners who did not have credit or debit cards and could therefore not withdraw their pensions from ATMs. Tensions rose further when Varoufakis proposed his strategy of retaliation against the creditors to those present – not in a proper cabinet meeting, but on the fly. The Finance Minister, as he later disclosed, spoke in favour of setting up a parallel payment system to alleviate the liquidity crunch asphyxiating the economy, announcing the intention to default on bond payments owed to the ECB on 20 July and to 'renationalize' the Bank of Greece – to bring it back under the control of the government in Athens. He had made similar suggestions in previous months. They were once again summarily rejected and, after a brief shouting match and frantic last-minute revisions, Stournaras got the call at five minutes to midnight with the Government Gazette Issue number under which the decree would be published. Total annihilation had – temporarily – been averted, at the price of cryogenically freezing the banking system and hoping that conditions in the coming days and weeks would allow it to be slowly and painfully revived.

How had things descended to this point? How had Greece, after the cliffhanger of its repeat election in June 2012, once again found itself so close to a euro exit, and a true humanitarian crisis?

SYRIZA had been a minor force on the Marxist hard left of Greek parliamentary politics before the eruption of the Great Crisis. It had been led since February 2008 by Alexis Tsipras, a student activist since his teens with a solidly middle-class background (his father owned a construction company) and little experience of the world beyond the narrow confines of the Greek far left. Tsipras, then aged only 33, won the leadership contest held by Synaspismos, the core constituent of the SYRIZA coalition, as the candidate of the leftist faction, promising to reconstruct the electoral majority forged by PASOK under Andreas Papandreou in 1981.

At the time, those ambitions seemed to betray delusions of grandeur. In the elections of September 2007, SYRIZA had polled just above 5%. After briefly shooting up into double digits in the polls following Tsipras's election, the disparate coalition, plagued by infighting between moderates and radicals, was in danger of not crossing the 3% threshold required for parliamentary representation. In the October 2009 election, in which PASOK triumphed with nearly 44% of the vote, SYRIZA received an unimpressive 4.6%. Tsipras had made it into parliament, but there was little sign of his spectacular rise to come.

The group's electoral lift-off was fuelled by the public's rage at an ever-deepening recession, and by the humiliation of externally imposed austerity, in the period leading to the May 2012 election. SYRIZA tapped both these elements of popular anger. It told voters that it was the creditors that were to blame for Greece's woes, along with their stooges in Greek ministries. It hammered home the message that all that was required for the country to recover was to reject the bailout recipe of cuts and structural reforms and take back control of Greece's economic destiny. At the same time, it claimed that its aggressive approach would not endanger the country's position in the Eurozone.

It was a manifesto rife with contradiction, offered by a loose alliance ranging from the social democratic left to Maoist elements that was still not a unified party (it would – at least in form – become one in late 2013). Its leading figures had next to no experience of government and few contacts in the seats of European power or in the markets. But Tsipras, with his winning smile and idealistic words, and with no connections to the political dynasties that had brought the country low, seemed like the embodiment of change, of the new chapter that Greek politics so desperately needed.

The May election, which propelled SYRIZA into second place, did not produce a governing coalition and a second one was called for 17 June. In the intervening period, the fear of 'Grexit' – a Greek exit from the euro – which had exploded onto the scene as an issue when George Papandreou had called a referendum on the terms of Greece's second bailout at the end of October 2011, reached fever pitch. Greek share prices collapsed and one eighth of the remaining deposits in Greek banks were withdrawn. The Bank of Greece had to engage in high-stakes logistical and legal acrobatics to make sure no bank branch in the country was left without cash, and that ELA kept flowing to the banks despite the fact that Greece's debt had rendered them insolvent.[2]

At the end of it all, New Democracy, presenting itself as the only party that could guarantee the country's euro membership, pulled off a narrow victory, with 29.6% of the vote. But SYRIZA gained another 10 percentage points compared with May to reach a voting share of 26.7% and established itself as the new major party in place of PASOK.

Following a protracted negotiation, the new government, a three-party coalition led by New Democracy under Antonis Samaras, came to a crucial agreement with its creditors, ratified by the Eurogroup of November 2012.[3] In return for achieving a primary surplus, and faithfully implementing agreed-upon structural reforms, Eurozone members, pressed by the IMF, committed to offer Greece further debt relief. The deal led to the release of more than 40 billion euros in loans to Greece. It looked like a real turning point, the moment when the ghost of Grexit, which had dominated headlines on and off for over a year, could finally be laid to rest.

Over the next year-and-a-half, things seemed to be moving in the right direction. The programme remained on track in terms of the fiscal targets – in fact, in large part thanks to the dogged efforts of Finance Minister Stournaras, Greece achieved a primary surplus a year earlier than expected in 2013.[4] The Greek government was able to tap the capital markets in April 2014 for the first time in four years,[5] unemployment began to edge downward from its staggeringly high levels and growth was projected year-on-year for 2014, after six years of recession.

Yet at that crucial juncture, a series of moves by the key players – Samaras, the German chancellor Angela Merkel and the IMF – combined to push the Greek recovery off the rails.[6] Samaras had paid the political price for reneging on his pre-election rhetoric concerning a renegotiation of the second bailout in favour of disciplined implementation, at least on the fiscal side. He now hoped that the Europeans would move on further debt relief, as they had promised to in November 2012, and as the IMF was pushing them to.

But Merkel, the most powerful leader in the Eurozone, kept putting off the discussion on debt. Meanwhile, the IMF, unheeded in its calls for further restructuring and deeply suspicious of the Greek political system and public administration, insisted on ever more demanding austerity and reform measures. Unwilling to accede to the Fund's line on Greek debt and mindful of the significance that her party's MPs placed on strict IMF oversight of Greece if they were to continue supporting the bailout, the German chancellor had little inclination to press the troika's toughest member to be more lenient on Samaras.

Feeling that he had done more than enough on the fiscal front and loath to do more on structural reform (slippages in the implementation of which were the key reason behind the IMF's unforgiving micromanagement), Samaras was backed into a corner. He had little to show Greek voters in terms of a reward from the creditors for his fiscal discipline. The pressure from Tsipras, on substance (he was anti-austerity) and process (he was pushing for reclamation of sovereignty), was growing. In May 2014, SYRIZA won the European elections, beating New Democracy by close to four percentage points.

The prime minister's reaction to that defeat sealed his fate. In early June he forced the resignation of Haris Theocharis as head of public revenue (see chapter 2), in a decision that infuriated the creditors, and that was discussed as high up as the Eurogroup – a forum which rarely involves itself in personnel decisions in the ministries of member states. Shortly thereafter there was a government reshuffle in which committed reformers who had angered vested interests were let go, to be replaced by a motley crew of unabashed populists and unserious TV personalities.

Samaras was trying to beat Tsipras at his own game – attempting to tear up the hated *mnimonio* (the bailout agreement) before the leader of the opposition got a chance to. In a visit to Merkel in September, he tried to enlist her support in his quest to end Greece's programme early, at the end of 2014 (when the European loans were set to end), instead of in March 2016 (the date of the last IMF tranche). The idea was to replace it with a looser form of surveillance, based on renewed access to the bond markets for Greece and without the IMF's involvement. In effect, he bet that the fear of SYRIZA would convince Berlin to support him in his quest for easier terms from the troika.

The chancellor was apprehensive and hinted strongly that Wolfgang Schäuble, Germany's redoubtable Finance Minister, also needed to be convinced. Since at least 2011, when he had presented his Greek counterpart Evangelos Venizelos with the outline of a German plan to ease Greece out of the euro,[7] Schäuble had become the arch-exponent of the 'infected-limb' theory: he believed that, in the best interests of the Eurozone, Greece had to leave it. Predictably, he showed little interest in being flexible.

Neither did the IMF. The Fund's official line, as the fifth and final review of the second bailout sank ever deeper into a quagmire of mutual recrimination, was that the government was woefully behind in the implementation of structural reforms – a result of constantly putting off the toughest measures for the next review.

But it cannot have escaped its attention that there had to be a vote in the Greek parliament by March 2015 at the latest on a new president of the Republic. The government's candidate needed an increased majority of 180 to be elected, in the absence of which parliament would have to be dissolved and there would be an early election. Tsipras had made it clear that he would use the parliamentary vote to achieve precisely that. Frustrated with Samaras, especially with what they viewed as his reluctance to go after large-scale tax evasion and to attack vested business interests, many key figures – in Berlin, Washington and even Frankfurt (the seat of the ECB) – came to view the prospect of a SYRIZA government as a welcome development for the prospect of needed reforms. Others, seeing things more clearly, knew that a showdown between the new government and the creditors was inevitable, and were loath to offer Tsipras the advantage of a completed bailout programme and more than 7 billion euros in bailout money, which would strengthen his hand significantly in whatever renegotiation he sought.

Seeing that a deal was effectively out of reach, Samaras brought the presidential vote forward to December, after securing a two-month extension of the programme to the end of February. The candidate he put forward, Stavros Dimas, a former New Democracy minister and EU Commissioner, failed to amass the necessary number of votes. Elections were called for 25 January, in which SYRIZA won with a 7.5-point margin, promising an end to bailout conditionality and humiliating reviews, a repeal of a hated property tax instituted by Samaras, increases in pensions for the least well-off, an all-but-complete halt to privatization, and a lot more besides. All of which – Tsipras promised at every turn – would happen without jeopardizing Greece's position in the Eurozone.

To those in Europe who had chosen to ignore his domestic rhetoric and to focus on the conciliatory words he spoke in international forums, his speech on the night of that fateful election victory was a rude awakening: 'The sovereign Greek people today have given a clear, strong, indisputable mandate,' he said. 'Greece has turned a page. Greece is leaving behind destructive austerity, fear and authoritarianism... The verdict of the Greek people renders the troika a thing of the past for our common European framework.'

It would, of course, prove rather more complicated than that.

'I call on you to decide – with sovereignty and pride as Greek history demands – whether we should accept the extortionate ultimatum that calls for strict and humiliating austerity without end, and without the prospect of ever standing on our own two feet, socially and financially. We should respond to authoritarianism and harsh austerity with democracy – calmly and decisively.'

Standing in front of the Maximos fireplace, a few minutes after midnight on 27 June 2015, Alexis Tsipras was back where he felt most comfortable: in campaigning mode. With the referendum, he was once again asking the people to make good what he had claimed had already been achieved on that hope-filled night of 25 January: the end of austerity and the reclamation of economic sovereignty. In the five gruelling months since his election victory, he had realized what he should have known all along – that he had promised impossible things, and that he was facing a stark choice, either to submit to another bailout programme, or to let his country slide out of the common currency. Unable to shoulder the burden of that choice, he passed it on to the voters.

The cabinet was divided over the referendum proposal, but those who were in favour were jubilant. Temporarily at least, they had been freed from the drudgery of convincing their parliamentary group to support the onerous set of measures that the prime minister himself had proposed a few days earlier, in a last-ditch effort at compromise.

As they exited Maximos, one after another made statements of strong support for the referendum. Nikos Pappas, the Minister of State, Tsipras's closest associate and the main proponent of going to the people, spoke of 'a beautiful night which will be followed by a beautiful day'. Panagiotis Lafazanis, the hard-line Minister for Energy and Productive Reconstruction, expressed his certainty that Greeks would vote 'No' against the 'barbaric policies of the creditors'. In the meeting of the inner cabinet where Tsipras had revealed his intentions a few hours earlier, Lafazanis had enthusiastically backed his ideas, though he had been taken aback by the silence in response to his insistent questions about what the government would do if it won but the Europeans refused to budge. Zoe Konstantopoulou, the radical speaker of parliament who had been a thorn in Tsipras's side from day one of his ascension to power, prodding him to take a more confrontational stance, now made an emotive declaration of fealty to the prime minister, while blasting the creditors for their attempt to blackmail Greece.

The next day, Saturday, as the rush to petrol stations and ATMs intensified, and as Varoufakis faced his angry colleagues in a hastily convened Eurogroup in Brussels, parliament sat to vote on the government's proposal. It was an explosive session that lasted more than twelve hours. The opposition parties challenged the constitutionality of the proposal, both because the Greek Constitution forbids referenda on fiscal issues and because of the very short deliberation period (a mere week). Their criticism was echoed a few days later by the Council of Europe, which stated that the Greek referendum did not meet international standards – the first time the Council of Europe had questioned the credentials of a referendum held in an EU member state.[8] Opposition deputies spoke of an attempt at a neo-communist takeover, of a 'conspiracy of the drachma' which had finally revealed itself.

Ministers retorted that the opposition was on the side of the creditors. Lafazanis went as far as to attack the pro-European, anti-government protesters who had taken to the streets in recent weeks in Athens, as the threat of a breakdown in the negotiations loomed ever larger. He said they were a front for 'reactionary interests'. Panos Kammenos, the Minister of Defence and head of the coalition partners the Independent Greeks (ANEL), in a semi-unhinged address, said that if the creditors' demands on defence cuts were accepted, it would be 'tantamount to disarming Greece'. He then went on to bemoan the rise of a nebulous new order which opposes nation-states and the Christian Orthodox religion, and promotes 'only globalization'. SYRIZA MPs queued in front of the ATM inside the parliament building, which was repeatedly restocked, to withdraw their euros. New Democracy at some point left the hall in protest against house speaker Konstantopoulou, who was never good at remaining above the fray, and who was particularly partisan that day in her handling of the proceedings.

Meanwhile, news came from Brussels that the second part of the Eurogroup had taken place without Varoufakis. He was effectively shut out. The Greek minister said that an improvement in the creditors' proposal by the 30th – when the programme ended – would lead the government to support a 'Yes' vote. There were reporters in tears. The break-up of the euro seemed to be turning into reality.

In Athens, the government got its way. With 178 votes (from SYRIZA, ANEL and Golden Dawn), the referendum proposal was approved, at nearly three in morning. The next day, the Greek government bowed to the inevitable and imposed capital controls. The stage was set for the week from hell.

A limited number of bank branches opened during the week (about 1,000 across the country by Wednesday), in order to serve pensioners without bank cards – who could only withdraw 120 euros per week – and to allow people to apply for cards and e-banking services. There was a sizeable police presence around the branches that had opened, and by and large the crowds were calm.[9]

Still, these were scenes of a country sliding away from the developed world into a darker, more turbulent condition. Old people had to queue for hours to receive only a small part of their pension. Some came before dawn, only to be told later on that, because of rationing rules, the particular branch would not be serving them on that day because their family name did not begin with the right letter.

A special committee was formed to approve requests by businesses to transfer money abroad. Banks also dealt in-house with demands to transfer money outside Greece for students or those receiving medical treatment outside the country. Bank executives dealt with calls from the provinces for new branches to be opened because in some remote areas old people had to travel tens of miles to get their 120 euros. I spoke to one top banker who joked that her phone had become like a 1-800 number, with people calling from all over the country with all sorts of requests and queries. The special committee on overseas transactions gave priority to payments for food and drug imports, which meant that many applications from manufacturers dependent on imported raw materials were not even sent on by the banks.

Many employers shut up shop. Others put their employees on leave until further notice. Despite the fact that internet banking within the country was not restricted, some companies paid their employees in cash, mindful of the fact that no one wanted to increase the level of their deposits in Greek banks.

The fear of losing these deposits, either through a haircut or through the dramatic devaluation that would follow a return to a national currency, also led to an orgy of spending. Using e-banking, many rushed to pay down debt or taxes, to buy luxury items, or to settle accounts with service providers or suppliers. It was a preemptive strike against expropriation – you cannot lose what you have already spent. People also stocked up on food – raiding supermarket shelves for beans, pasta and rice products.[10]

At the same time, a number of developments strengthened the feeling of isolation and the foretaste of the consequences of an exit from the euro. Imports declined dramatically and the first shortages appeared, especially in pharmacies. Tourist reservations temporarily fell by an average of 50,000 per day, as foreign governments issued travel directives about the complications caused by capital controls.[11] As many as forty-five airlines stopped accepting bookings via Greek travel agencies. Greeks were also cut off from globalized consumption.[12] Greek digital consumers could no longer pay for Gmail accounts, Facebook ads or iTunes music.

On the question of who was to blame for the slow descent of the country into the Third World, public opinion was divided. One lady I talked to in the ATM queues, whose pension had been cut from 1100 to 720 euros, directed her anger at Wolfgang Schäuble. All across downtown Athens, the pro-government camp had put up posters of Schäuble, looking particularly ghoulish, with the not-too-subtle caption: 'He has been sucking your blood for five years. Time to tell him "No".' For others, like a thirty-five-year-old accountant I met at a pro-Europe rally three days before the referendum was announced, the EU was the only safeguard for Greek democracy and against the power of local special interests.

On Monday night, there was a 20,000-strong rally in front of parliament in support of 'OXI' (Greek for 'No'). The next day, on the date on which the Greek programme expired and Greece became the first developed country to default on the IMF, there was an equally large demonstration by the 'Yes' campaign in the same place, despite the pouring rain.

Tensions between the two sides, separated to a significant extent along class lines, had already begun to flare in the heated final days before the breakdown of the talks. On 23 June, a group of extreme leftists gathered in the square prior to the arrival of the pro-Europe demonstrators, and greeted them with ferocious slogans that harked back to the Greek civil war. On Tuesday 30 June, the police blocked a contingent of far-left protesters from reaching Syntagma Square and attacking the 'Yes' campaigners. The slogans from the pro-Europe crowd had grown fiercer, too (one lumped Tsipras and Kammenos in with the Nazis of Golden Dawn, branding them as 'traitors who want the drachma').

Under the influence of a government bent on dividing Greeks into 'the people' and 'the fifth columnists of the troika', Athens became a seething cauldron of acrimonious debate. The 'Yes' men railed about rumours of pressure by the government on civil servants to vote 'No', while the naysayers complained about the anti-government bias of the private TV networks. In ATM queues, in bars and on street corners, in discussions with cab drivers and between colleagues at work, by email, on the phone and on social media, people with set ideologies and people who had never been political before argued about the meaning of the referendum. Was the choice as simple as 'No' to austerity or 'Yes' to the euro and Europe? Would a 'No' strengthen Greece's negotiating position, or bring it to the brink of Grexit? Was the country being hijacked by neo-communist radicals trying to turn it into a socialist dystopia or were those supporting the 'Yes' campaign the stooges or, worse still, the collaborators of the Germans and the oligarchs?

The division of the country between the pro- and anti-bailout camps, that had already caused so much damage, had morphed into 'Yes' v. 'No', and had become deeper still. As the crisis reached its awful peak, so did the estrangement of Greeks from Greeks.

In the end, despite uncertainty and fear, as the fog of bankruptcy spread across everyday life, the prime minister turned the tide of the campaign. In repeated interviews and TV addresses, culminating in his masterful performance at the final 'No' rally in Syntagma Square on the Friday before the vote, he imposed his interpretation on the referendum. Beyond ending austerity, it was about restoring democracy, national pride and dignity, he kept saying. A lot of what he said was not only divisive but deceptive in the extreme (that a 'No' vote would strengthen Greece's negotiating position vis-à-vis its creditors, that Greece's position in the euro was safe, that people's deposits were not in danger). But Greeks love to see themselves as heroically fighting for lost causes, and Tsipras – especially on that Friday night – moved them in a way that they hadn't felt since the heyday of Greece's foremost post-junta populist, Andreas Papandreou.

In the early afternoon on Sunday 5 July, a moderately hot and dry summer day, I drove about an hour outside Athens to the hills of Voetia, to speak to voters about the decision at hand – whether to accept or reject the latest terms offered by Greece's creditors. In the village of Pyli, sitting in the shade at the edge of the courtyard in the school that served as a polling station, a middle-aged civil servant explained to me the reasons why he was going to vote 'No'.

The EU 'has strayed' from its founding principles, the man said. It used to be about peace, but also about solidarity and equality between the bigger and smaller member states. This is no longer the case, he argued. He got down to specifics: 'Even back in 2010, they [Greece's Eurozone partners and the IMF] knew that the debt could not be repaid, given the lack of growth. So why did we embark on that programme?'

Another man, a thirty-year-old unemployed teacher, said of Tsipras: 'He is the only one who said "No".' Describing the past five years of strict external reviews in return for cash to keep the country going, he said: 'We were like junkies, begging for the next fix. He is putting a stop to that. That's why we support him – and we will support him all the way.'

Early in the week, the polls gave the 'Yes' campaign a slight advantage. By the end of it, the consensus forecast was that it was going to be neck and neck. But the mix of anti-European feeling, revolutionary zeal and sheer desperation at endless fiscal belt-tightening, combined with Tsipras's charisma, proved too strong. On 5 July, 61.3% of Greeks voted 'No' in the referendum (including 67.4% in the prefecture of Voetia).

Having once again proved his superior skills as a campaigner, the prime minister now faced a tougher audience.

Yanis Varoufakis had been an unexpected choice to lead SYRIZA's effort to renegotiate Greece's bailout. He had no policymaking experience and he was not a member of the party – in fact, in a blog post in June 2012, in the run-up to the crucial repeat election, he had written the following about SYRIZA: 'I recommend that (even those who have Greek amongst their languages) you do not read their manifesto. It is not worth the paper it is written on. While replete with good intentions, it is short on detail, full of promises that cannot, and will not be fulfilled (the greatest one is that austerity will be cancelled), a hotchpotch of policies that are neither here nor there. Just ignore it.'[13]

An indistinguished academic economist, with a contrarian approach to the subject and expertise in game theory, Varoufakis grew up in Greece and attended Moraitis, an elite private school. He had taught abroad – in the UK and Australia – for most of his professional life.

In the year 2000, he returned to Greece and became a professor at the University of Athens. He served briefly, between 2004 and 2006, as an adviser to George Papandreou when the latter was leader of the opposition. But he remained unknown until the outbreak of the world financial crisis in 2008 and, in particular, until its sovereign debt phase, of which Greece was the first victim.

Stournaras had played a key role in Varoufakis's successful bid for tenure at the University of Athens. Yet Varoufakis built his profile in Greece as an anti-system economist at Stournaras's expense, railing against the austerity policies that the latter was implementing as Finance Minister between 2012 and 2014.

His interpretation of the euro crisis – that the Eurozone leadership was forcing Greece and other troubled economies to pretend they were solvent and to undergo crushing austerity so that Europe's banks didn't have to realize massive losses – made him very popular in left-wing circles. Alexis Tsipras, who had never read economics and knew little English, was wowed by this cosmopolitan, articulate, self-assured economist. He admired his brashness and thought he could be his secret weapon in his bid to change the terms of Greece's bailout. In November 2014, before the January election had even been called, he asked Varoufakis to be his Finance Minister if SYRIZA won.[14] In the early days of the election campaign, a little after the new year, Varoufakis was already informing foreign ambassadors in Athens that he was going to have the job.

In SYRIZA's 25 January triumph, Varoufakis got more votes than any other parliamentary candidate. Two seats short of a full majority, Tsipras chose to ally himself with ANEL, a right-wing nationalist party formed in 2012 to oppose Greece's second bailout programme. A party made up of cranks, anti-Semites, homophobes and other loudmouths, it gained support by attacking Germany and by calling pro-bailout MPs and ministers collaborators of the 'occupiers'. Tsipras could have chosen either of two pro-European centre-left parties – the new-fangled Potami or the diminished PASOK. That he chose Kammenos (head of ANEL) instead was a clear sign of his confrontational intentions.

The appointment of Varoufakis was an even stronger signal. The new Finance Minister quickly showed that he had no interest in switching gear from iconoclastic analyst to chief economic diplomat. Revealing his appointment on his blog before the government had made the official announcement, he vowed to keep on blogging, making up for the diminished frequency and length 'with juicier views, comments and insights'.[15] In an interview in early February with *Der Spiegel*, when asked about his past description of the Greek bailout programmes as 'fiscal waterboarding', he doubled down on it, comparing troika technocrats to CIA torturers.[16]

On 29 January, in the first meeting of the new cabinet, Tsipras set the tone for the coming showdown. 'We do not intend to go towards rupture, but neither will we continue the catastrophe [of the existing programme],' he said. A couple of days later, Jeroen Dijsselbloem, chairman of the Eurogroup and Dutch Finance Minister, visited Athens to find out the bearings of the new government. In a press conference at the Finance Ministry,

Dijsselbloem heard Varoufakis declare the new government's unwillingness to cooperate with the troika of the EU, the ECB and the IMF, quoting a European Parliament report calling it a construct based on 'rotten foundations'.[17] That same day, Varoufakis told the *New York Times* that Greece did not want the 7.2 billion euros that made up the final tranche of the second bailout and that 'we have to… rethink the whole programme'.[18]

On 4 February, just after Varoufakis visited the ECB leadership in Frankfurt, the Bank revoked the waiver allowing Greek banks to use Greek government bonds as collateral to borrow from it. The waiver, first put in place in early 2010, allowed Greek banks to retain access to cheap ECB funding despite the collapse in the credit rating of Greek government paper. Now they would have to rely exclusively on ELA, at a much higher interest rate.

That decision by the ECB played a key role in undermining trust between the two sides early on. As a key adviser to Tsipras told me, 'it allowed the hardliners within the cabinet to tell the moderate camp "we told you so", and the moderates had to accept it'. Yet Varoufakis played a significant part in forcing the central bank's hand. According to persons privy to his meeting with Mario Draghi that day, the Greek Finance Minister insisted that Greece was bankrupt. This statement, along with all the public assertions by Varoufakis and Tsipras about the election signifying the end of the programme, made it all but inevitable that the ECB would conclude that it was 'currently not possible to assume a successful conclusion of the programme review'[19] – a necessary condition for the waiver.

In this crucial early period, there was a lot of support, in Europe and the United States, for SYRIZA's position on the need for further debt restructuring that would permit a lowering of the targets for future primary surpluses and thus a less restrictive fiscal policy. Influential voices, like that of Reza Moghadam, who had recently retired from his position as head of the European Department at the IMF and was at Morgan Stanley, and that of

Mathieu Pigasse of Lazard, the investment bankers, were calling for a substantial easing of Greece's debt burden.[20]

On the other hand, the hawks among the creditors, above all Germany (especially its Finance Ministry) and its Eurozone satellites, were determined to resist any modifications of the existing programme. Varoufakis has claimed that in that early meeting in Athens, Dijsselbloem told him that either Athens would accept the terms of the bailout programme or Europe would impose capital controls.[21]

In those early days, during his visit to London on 2 February, as well as high-profile meetings with George Osborne and with dozens of City investors, Varoufakis was invited to a private dinner at the Greek ambassador's residence. The guests included Moghadam and the famous American economist Jeffrey Sachs. Moghadam, who had attended Eurogroup meetings as an IMF official, counselled Varoufakis to avoid confrontation and try to build alliances. Sachs, meeting him for the first time, advised him to eschew wider European issues and focus exclusively on Greece and immediate debt relief – on which he urged him not to give an inch. Sachs became a key outside adviser to the Greek minister.

With Greece's programme set to end on 28 February, the pressure was on for a new understanding to be reached. The Athens government – or at least the moderates within in – sought a compromise between its radical manifesto and the commitments undertaken by Greece in the second bailout. It was mindful that it could not go too far in compromising, as Lafazanis and his faction, the Left Platform, controlled nearly 40% of the votes in the central committee, and had made no secret of the fact that their priority was to make good on the party's anti-austerity promises, even if it meant a return to the drachma.

It took three Eurogroup meetings in ten days, one European Council meeting and a critical phone call between Tsipras and Angela Merkel for a deal to be reached on 20 February for a four-month extension of the second bailout. At that point, the rate of deposit withdrawals was getting out of hand. Greek bankers warned the government that without an agreement, there would have to be capital controls. The government, too, was running out of cash.

The extension offered a respite, but only a temporary one. Varoufakis at the time described the text of the agreement as making use of 'creative ambiguity' to verbally bridge the differences between the two sides.[22] He later claimed that the troika betrayed the spirit of the deal by insisting that any reform proposals coming from the Greek side could not replace the prior commitments of the second bailout, which were still in place.[23]

The text of the 20 February agreement does not bear out Varoufakis's charge.[24] It offers leeway on the level of the primary surplus for 2015, and speaks of 'the successful completion of the review on the basis of the conditions in the current arrangement, making best use of the given flexibility which will be considered jointly with the Greek authorities and the institutions'. The essential requirement for the creditors was that the numbers had to add up.

If there were different ways to read the Eurogroup statement, what was unambiguous was that Greece, already facing a severe liquidity crunch, would get no bailout money until the review was completed (this was one of the reasons why SYRIZA radicals viewed the agreement with such trepidation). The clarity of this, combined with the ambiguity on the required reforms and the review process, set the stage for more crises in the negotiation, until the nearly terminal one of 26 June.

March was a month of stalemate. Meetings between troika representatives and Varoufakis's team in Brussels got nowhere. The Greek side claimed the troika was not interested in their proposals. One of Varoufakis's closest associates told me the creditors would leak stories about the lack of preparation of Greek negotiators before meetings even took place. The creditors were openly derisive of some of the proposals, like the one about wiring tourists and housewives to uncover tax cheating by shops and restaurants. They were also taken aback at the replacement of the chief technical negotiator George Houliarakis, an aide to Varoufakis and later alternate Finance Minister. Houliarakis had established a good working relationship with the other side, and it was thought that his sidelining in favour of someone personally closer to Varoufakis was not unrelated.

Meanwhile, in Athens, the creditors' technical teams faced a brick wall of non-cooperation: officials would stand them up or refuse to impart any meaningful information at meetings. They were blocked from accessing the ministries (something Varoufakis was particularly proud of) and hounded outside their hotel. As the liquidity situation of the banks and the government got increasingly desperate, hardliners on both sides kept raising the spectre of Grexit as a way out if a deal proved impossible.

It was a time of mounting tension. Kammenos, the Defence Minister, threatened that if the EU pushed Greece too far, the Greek government would allow undocumented migrants, including IS terrorists, to make their way to Berlin.[25] The lax attitude to the rising tide of immigrants and refugees would come back to haunt Athens a few months later. The Tsipras government, and especially Speaker Konstantopoulou, brought the issue of German reparations for the Nazi occupation of Greece back to the table. All this annoyed the German government, but enthused the public at home.[26]

Tsipras's first meeting with Merkel in Berlin, on 23 March, had a calming effect. The two leaders got along on a personal level. After a five-hour meeting that lasted deep into the night, the Greek delegation came away with the sense that Merkel would back Tsipras over the heads of the troika and help loosen the terms of the review.

It was the same mistake Samaras had made six months earlier. The chancellor, pressed by the hawkish Schäuble and an increasingly restive parliamentary group, was in no mood to overrule the troika (which essentially meant the IMF). Weeks passed, with little progress. With the liquidity situation becoming critical (the ECB in late March forbade Greek banks from buying more treasury bills, even though their portfolios were way below the 15-billion-euro ceiling),[27] discussions began in earnest within the cabinet about alternative sources of funding.[28]

Varoufakis's idea of an IOU-type parallel currency was shot down because it was thought that pensioners, in particular, would revolt at receiving a piece of paper instead of their pension – or worse yet, an electronic tax credit. A secret group set up by Tsipras – unbeknownst to Varoufakis – intensified its efforts to open up a credit line from Russia (Lafazanis was a particularly strong proponent of 'a deep strategic relationship' between the two countries). High-level efforts were also made to secure commitments by China to buy Greek debt. There were secret trips to Latin American countries to secure emergency imports of fuel, medicine and beef in case the need arose, and two visits to foreign-currency-printing companies to find out how long it would take to have a new currency in circulation.

The idea was even floated to use the banknotes in the National Mint – amounting to some 17 billion euros – to pay wages and pensions. The main problem with this idea was that the notes had not been approved for circulation by the ECB, and if they were appropriated without its permission, it would declare them counterfeit, leading to complete financial chaos.[29]

For Greece's Finance Minister, April was the cruellest month. He visited Washington twice – the first time to be told by Christine Lagarde that there could be no flexibility in the repayment schedule to the IMF, the second time to receive a thinly veiled public dressing-down by Treasury Secretary Jack Lew.[30] Then, on 24 April, at the Eurogroup meeting in Riga, frustration at Varoufakis boiled over. As he himself has admitted, there was fierce criticism of the Greek government in the meeting, and demands for a slew of new austerity measures to bring the teetering public finances back under control.[31] Though he denies it, it is likely that the altercation got personal as well (a couple of months earlier, in one of the meetings, he had nearly come to blows with Dijsselbloem).[32] Varoufakis did not attend the official dinner, and tweeted afterwards, in typically modest fashion:

> FDR, 1936: 'They are unanimous in their hate for me; and I welcome their hatred.' A quotation close to my heart (& reality) these days

On the day he posted that tweet, Tsipras, having spoken to Dijsselbloem beforehand and been apprised of the extent of the bad blood between his minister and his European colleagues, reshuffled his negotiating team, sidelining Varoufakis.[33] But he did not ask for his resignation, and Varoufakis's presence continued to serve as an obstacle to a deal.

As April gave way to May, the temptation to default on the IMF grew ever stronger (Tsipras had seriously considered doing so as early as 9 April).[34] On 12 May, a payment of approximately 750 million euros was scheduled, and the government decided to miss it. A letter was written and sent by the prime minister explaining why. In the meantime though, Stournaras, by this time central bank governor, had acted on his own and used the reserves in the country's IMF holding account, kept at the Bank of Greece, to make the payment.[35] Meanwhile, Varoufakis prepared his own version of a reform programme, with the help of Jeffrey Sachs and the British Conservative Eurosceptic former Chancellor of the Exchequer Norman Lamont.[36] Tsipras rejected the plan as too risky and accepted an ambitious medium-term primary surplus target of 3.5% of GDP without consulting his Finance Minister in the hope of securing a deal. Yet Varoufakis still would not resign, though he had written a resignation letter as early as 27 April.

The countdown to 'the accident' – as the possibility of a dead end in the negotiations and a Greek default was widely referred to at the time – began in earnest on 1 June. That night, Angela Merkel hosted French President François Hollande, European Commission President Jean-Claude Juncker, Mario Draghi and Christine Lagarde – but not Alexis Tsipras. The product of their meeting was what came misleadingly to be known as the Juncker proposal. It was five pages long, and represented the worst of all possible worlds for Greece. The Commission had caved in to the IMF's more stringent approach to structural reforms and fiscal targets. The Fund, in turn, had once again agreed to put off any discussion of debt relief, at the insistence of Berlin.[37]

The creditors insisted that this was not an ultimatum, but it was close enough. The offer was rejected out of hand by Athens. At the last minute, despite assurances by the prime minister a day earlier to the contrary, Greece made it known that it would not be paying the 300 million euros or so that it owed the IMF the next day. Instead it got permission to bundle all of its June payments – about 1.6 billion euros – into a single one, at the end of the month,[38] and 30 June – also the date at which the four-month extension of the bailout would expire – became even more of a day of reckoning.

Over the next three weeks, negotiations continued, but in an increasingly hostile climate. Juncker accused Tsipras of not offering credible proposals and of lying to the Greek parliament about the negotiations.[39] Tsipras spoke of the 'criminal responsibility' of the IMF for the Greek crisis.[40] As the two sides were moving closer on the substance of the negotiations, they were moving further apart in tone and feeling.

On Monday 22 June, the Greek side made a last-ditch attempt at securing a deal. It offered a ten-page proposal which included 7.9 billion euros in new austerity measures (almost exclusively taxes) for 2015–16 alone.[41] The initial reaction to this – from the Commission – was positive, and Tsipras thought he was on the home straight. Then, on Wednesday, the troika returned the Greek offer having crossed out almost everything that diverged from the five-page proposal they had submitted three weeks earlier. The creditors' proposal only offered funding for six months, by the end of which the two sides would need to reach a long-term agreement on further lending and its terms.

It was the last straw for Tsipras.[42] His proposal had caused a great deal of turbulence inside his parliamentary group and SYRIZA at large. Those of his associates – chief among them Nikos Pappas – who had been urging him to call a referendum at earlier moments of crisis in the negotiations now redoubled their appeals. The prime minister was suddenly more receptive. On Thursday, at the European summit in Brussels, he was harshly criticized by the Dutch prime minister Mark Rutte, who told him that there had to be an agreement with the troika immediately, otherwise the next summit would focus on managing Greece's exit from the euro. The next morning he met with Merkel and Hollande, where it became clear to him that they would do nothing to meaningfully alter the terms on offer. Already before that meeting, Tsipras had assembled his retinue in a Brussels hotel room and told them that he was seriously considering calling a referendum on the creditors' latest proposal.

That night, after marathon sessions of the inner and then the full cabinet, he called the German and French leaders. In their conference call, he spoke for about ten minutes about the political difficulties he faced without getting to the point. When he finally did, Merkel and Hollande asked whether he would support a 'Yes' vote, and he would not commit to do so. They both made it clear to him that not doing so would be tantamount to not supporting Greece's euro membership.

A little after midnight Greek time, with the two sides still negotiating in Brussels, Tsipras gave his televised address calling the referendum, and urging Greeks to vote 'No'. The accident had happened.

As the size of Tsipras's victory on 5 July became clear, there was an explosion of euphoria in the country. Syntagma Square, the focal point of so many angry confrontations between police and demonstrators throughout the bailout period, was flooded with joyous crowds, waving Greek flags and 'OXI' signs, dancing traditional Greek dances, some laughing ecstatically, some crying. After five years of economic pain and humiliation at the hands of Greece's creditors, after so many instances of making their voices heard only to be ignored by their government, many Greeks now felt they had a leader who was standing firmly with them, and would not bow to outside pressure and betray them. They didn't know what would happen next, but they felt hope, after a long period of mounting despair.

But others feared the worst. In the febrile climate of those days, some became convinced that the Greek government had already decided to take the country out of the common currency. They thought that in the week after the referendum the prime minister would play at negotiating, then pin the blame on the Europeans for the inevitable breakdown and urge Greeks to support a return to the drachma as the only option consistent with national pride and dignity.

There was a shocking sense of dislocation and confinement among the people who had taken part in the 'Yes' rallies – the lawyers and students, the shipping executives and housewives from the leafy northern suburbs of Athens. They had taken part in unusually well-behaved demonstrations, the older among them recalling that they had last taken part in one in the 1970s. For them, Europe was not just a cash cow; it was a version – however garbled, especially in recent years – of what they wanted Greece to become, as it rose out of Balkan provincialism and instability. That is what drew them towards the 'Yes' campaign – not the Stockholm Syndrome or a bizarre attachment to a failed bailout recipe.

As companies and families made plans to escape abroad, 'Yes' voters talked about Greece being led into a perfect storm of deeper depression, currency instability and political authoritarianism. There were dark forebodings about the country turning into

Venezuela on the Med, falling into the Russian orbit, of tanks on the streets to quell civil unrest and of a shadow economy in euros where Greeks would seek refuge from the collapsing new national currency. Congratulatory messages to Tsipras on the night of the referendum from Nicolas Maduro, Christina Kirchner and even Fidel Castro didn't help allay these concerns. "'That's it," I thought. "We will turn into Cambodia,'" one top banker remembers thinking, as he sat in his office that night taking in the results.

After the resounding, desperate 'No' of the Greek people, it did seem as if the way was open to extremists on both sides – the Schäuble contingent in the European North and East and the Lafazanistas in Athens – who, for very different reasons, wanted Greece out of the Eurozone. After the results became clear, every leader of consequence in Europe signalled that there was very little room for manoeuvre. The statement by Sigmar Gabriel, the vice-chancellor of Germany and leader of the centre-left SPD, was indicative. Speaking to the *Bild* newspaper in an emotional state, he said that Tsipras had 'torn down the last bridges across which Europe and Greece could move toward a compromise'. With liquidity on the verge of completely drying up, the enthusiasm of the anti-austerity brigades rising to fever pitch and incandescent rage at the Greek government in the seats of European power, it seemed the only way for Tsipras to keep the country in the Eurozone would be to ignore the people's verdict – a verdict he himself had passionately urged. Even if he was willing to do that, which many (including Lafazanis) thought impossible, there was no guarantee that the creditors would be open to further talks. Greece was hanging by a thread.

As early as Sunday night, as the extremists at home and abroad geared their energies towards cutting the country loose from the common currency, there began a frantic final push towards a deal. Tsipras himself, it quickly became clear, was not preparing to leave. Despite the flirtation with Russia, despite Varoufakis's wild ideas and the visits to currency-printing companies, the prime minister had never authorized the kind of detailed contingency planning that would have made Grexit a viable option. He was also haunted by fears that the moderates in the cabinet would abandon him if he moved in that direction, leading to the fall of the government and his replacement as prime minister.[43] Unable to choose between a third bailout and the chaos of a euro exit, he had delayed his decision for months, then thrown it to the voters. He had wanted to show that, unlike his predecessors, he was willing to fight to the end for a better deal. Perhaps he had also hoped for a narrow 'Yes', which would facilitate the tyre-screeching U-turn he was called upon to make. Whatever the truth, he now found himself having to make it against the deafening roar of the voters' verdict – the one he had called upon them so eloquently to deliver.

He got to it immediately. In his appearance on TV on Sunday night after the results were in, he struck a unifying note and made it clear that he had no mandate to break with Europe. The next morning, Varoufakis resigned – another necessary condition for a deal to be struck.

Varoufakis's removal from the picture, aside from mollifying the Europeans, was also a relief for Yannis Stournaras.[44] Concerned about the prospect that the Finance Ministry would unilaterally put forward a legislative decree introducing a parallel currency, violating the ECB's monopoly on such matters, the governor of the Bank of Greece had already contacted the President of the Republic, Prokopis Pavlopoulos, on 26 June, a few hours before Tsipras announced his decision to call a referendum. Stournaras told Pavlopoulos that he might be asked to sign a 'highly illegal' and 'extremely dangerous' decree that would make Grexit inevitable. Pavlopoulos, a centre-right politician who had served as a minister under New Democracy between 2004 and 2009, assured the governor that he would not sign anything without consulting him.

But Stournaras had further cause for concern. He had been informed that there were plans by a militant faction within the ruling party to raid the National Mint and seize its euro banknotes. His chief of security, a hard-nosed former deputy head of the Greek Police who specialized in drugs enforcement and had a penchant for taking no prisoners, increased the protection measures at the Mint and reinforced the governor's personal guard. He also contacted key personnel at the headquarters of the Greek Police, warning them to be on high alert in case the threat materialized.

Meanwhile, the Grexit scenario gathered momentum in Europe. On Monday night, 6 July, François Hollande hosted Chancellor Merkel at the Elysée. During the discussion Merkel floated the idea of a temporary Greek exit from the Eurozone. Hollande, not known for his confrontational stance vis-à-vis the chancellor, this time put his foot down: France would oppose this all the way, he said, adding that there was no such thing as a 'temporary' exit.[45]

The next day, Tsipras went to Brussels for a Euro summit, without any concrete proposal for the resumption of negotiations. He also spoke at the European Parliament in Strasbourg. Both were brutal affairs for him. He was attacked from almost all wings of the parliament, and made to speak from the second row instead of the first, which is traditionally reserved for visiting heads of government. Perhaps worst of all for a leftist like him was the fact that the only vocal support he received was from the luminaries of the anti-European far right – xenophobic populists like Marine Le Pen and Nigel Farage.

That night, at a joint press conference, Jean-Claude Juncker and EU Council president Donald Tusk set a Sunday deadline for an agreement and spoke in ominous terms. We 'can't exclude the black scenario' of non-agreement, said Tusk, mentioning that Greece may need humanitarian aid. Juncker added that 'the Commission was prepared for everything' and that it had compiled a 'detailed' Grexit plan. The next day, in a meeting of the MEPs belonging to the European People's Party, EPP president Joseph

Daul spoke of Grexit as a foregone conclusion and said the consequences would be devastating.

That same day, 8 July, his third Wednesday as Finance Minister, Euclid Tsakalotos, a soft-spoken Marxist educated at St Paul's and Oxford, made an official request for a third bailout. The request was accompanied by a programme of exacting fiscal measures and ambitious structural reforms.

Speaking on Friday to his parliamentary group, many members of which had deep-seated objections to the proposed measures, Tsipras adopted a dramatic tone. He said that what was on the line was not just Grexit, but the survival of the state.[46] The long debates that followed in the SYRIZA parliamentary group and then, after midnight, in the plenary session were a watershed moment in Greek politics. The myths of the anti-bailout camp were vanishing into thin air. The angry rhetoric of those who attacked previous pro-bailout governments as 'collaborators' and 'traitors' was gone. In its place, among the vast majority of MPs, there was an acceptance, however grudging, that euro membership is in Greece's vital interest, too critical to be endangered by ideological flights of fancy or reckless negotiating strategies. In the vote – held once again way past midnight – to authorize the prime minister to negotiate a third bailout agreement, 251 MPs (more than five out of six) voted 'Yes'. They did not include Panagiotis Lafazanis or the absent Yanis Varoufakis, who was on holiday on the island of Aegina.

On the same day, three New Democracy MEPs visited Juncker to plead with him to prevent disaster.[47] Having initially given them only fifteen minutes, the president of the Commission ended up lecturing them for three quarters of an hour. He attacked Tsipras and his predecessors, all the way back to Karamanlis, and said the rich don't pay taxes in Greece. He mockingly called them 'great patriots' – which was a bit rich from the long-time prime minister of the tax avoidance capital of the EU. Despite this – and calling himself 'a friend of Greece' – he vowed to do his best to keep Greece in the Eurozone. He said that France would support him in his efforts, but then asked his visitors the critical rhetorical question: how would he handle Merkel, Schäuble and their allies?

A few hours later, a day ahead of the crucial Saturday Eurogroup, Juncker, along with a few other top officials, would receive an email from the German Ministry of Finance with a chilling proposal: to offer Greece a 'time-out' from euro membership of at least five years. The proposal stated unequivocally that a haircut of Greece's debt within the Eurozone could not be legally allowed, but if it left the common currency area, there could be generous debt relief. Schäuble had worked out the content of the proposal with the chancellor, and had also informed Gabriel.

The German proposal set the stage for a weekend of Hitchcockian suspense. At the Saturday Eurogroup, Tsakalotos was the victim of sustained aggression, and found support only from the French, the Italians, the Cypriots and the president of the ECB, Mario Draghi. The Finnish Finance Minister insisted that he had no authority to discuss another bailout and that talk should move to discussing the logistics of Grexit. The way in which Schäuble pushed his proposal went beyond his understanding with the chancellor. She had seen it as a way to put the fear of God into the Greeks so that they would finally come to terms and sign a new bailout. He did his utmost to turn Grexit into reality.

The Saturday meeting broke up in rancour. A second meeting on Sunday morning also failed to produce full agreement. The statement issued after its conclusion included the 'time-out' proposal. It was in brackets, to signify that it had not been agreed on by all. But it was there.

It was now time for the heads of state and government of the Eurozone, and for the nail-biting endgame. The chief actors were Tsipras and Merkel, with supporting roles for Tusk and Hollande. The meeting began at 4 p.m. on Sunday 12 July and concluded seventeen hours later, a little before nine on Monday morning. It had nearly broken up in failure at around four in the morning.

The Greek delegation had left and headed for the offices of Greece's Permanent Representation, believing a deal to be impossible. Hollande had followed Tsipras there and convinced him to come back to the table.

The final session, which had begun around five in the morning and lasted for three hours, concerned the German demand – widely viewed as humiliating – that the Greeks set up a 50-billion-euro privatization trust fund, to be incorporated in Luxembourg. In the end, Merkel bowed to Tsipras's insistence that the trust fund be based in Athens, and a compromise figure was reached on the percentage of its revenues that would go towards investment, instead of paying off debt.

It was a minor concession, in the context of the total surrender of the Greek side. The three-day torture session in Brussels, and the harsh terms imposed on Athens by its European partners in order merely to begin talks on a third bailout, marked the end of an era in Greek politics. It was made clear that the populism of a painless alternative path leads to a bitter dead end.

Their prime minister's treatment at the hands of the creditors, and in particular the Germans, however, will do little to change the minds of Greek voters convinced that the EU has strayed from the noble path. The new bailout, approved by the Greek parliament in yet another late-night session on 14 August, is based on the same failed recipe of fiscal strangulation that undermined the previous two programmes. It is an orphan programme – believed in by neither the government that has to implement it nor its most important creditors (Germany and the IMF).

The Greek government had proposed a different policy, and had been elected on that basis. However foolish Tsipras had been to promise all things to all people, however clumsily – even recklessly – he handled the negotiation, he was right that Greece needed less austerity and more debt relief. Moderate members of the Greek government, like Deputy Prime Minister Yannis Dragasakis, told me, after the deal on the third bailout, of their belief that the overriding concern of the fiscal hawks in Europe was to make an example of SYRIZA, so that no one else in the European South would be tempted by a radical-left, anti-austerity message. This is no mere conspiracy theory. SYRIZA's inexperience and ideological sclerosis should not serve to whitewash a policy that has brought untold damage to the weaker economies of the Eurozone, especially given that it has to be forced down the throat of electorates.

Tsipras called a snap election right after securing passage of the third bailout through parliament. He won, with a margin almost as high as that of January. Meanwhile, Popular Unity, the party formed by Lafazanis and other former SYRIZA-ites who broke with the prime minister over the 13 July agreement, failed to reach the 3% threshold and was left out of parliament. It was a testament to the unpopularity of the idea of a return to the drachma.

But political stability remains elusive. It took only a few months for the new Tsipras government to become engulfed in the twin crises of mass protests against the bailout terms and the ceaseless flow of refugees. As 2015 gave way to 2016, there were persistent delays in the bailout negotiations and – with its northern borders sealed off – Greece was called upon to implement a European deal with Turkey on the refugee crisis which stretched its meagre capabilities beyond breaking point. Talk was rife of yet another early election. Six years of failed rescue programmes had left Greeks poorer and angrier at Europe than ever, and many Europeans convinced that Greece can never be reformed.

The Greek Question remains unresolved, festering, ripe for another relapse into chaos.

Acknowledgements

There are probably too many people who deserve thanks for contributing to the contents of this book or helping it materialize in other ways. George Kyrtsos, my boss at *City Press* and *Free Sunday*, gave me opportunities and responsibilities other Greek newspaper publishers never give to people under thirty, as well as the benefit of his biting, self-deprecating insights on the last three decades of Greek politics. Alexis Papahelas, the managing editor of *Kathimerini*, gave me space to dig deep into the stories that make up the book and then offered me a free-ranging reporting job at the paper that has kept widening my understanding of all aspects of Greece's drawn-out drama. Matina Stevis, my best friend in journalism, has been a constant fount of advice and support (as well as great *Wall Street Journal* stories). Theodore Pelagidis, an economist with a rare grasp of the political roots of economic dysfunction, has been a discerning guide through the dark maze of Greek political economy. Dimitris A. Sotiropoulos at the University of Athens was kind enough to read through the manuscript and offer helpful advice.

In my quest to export myself beyond Greece's borders, Kit Rachlis, the editor of *The American Prospect*, was the catalyst. He gave me the chance to contribute regularly to the website of the fine magazine he runs. He also published a 3,500-word essay of mine on Greece in December 2011 that prefigures some of the key themes in the book. Being edited by Kit was a great learning experience, one I will always be grateful for. Bruce Clark of *The Economist*, a great writer and true philhellene, has been a mentor to me from my earliest efforts to express myself in what is still – if only by a whisker – my second language. Bill Antholis at Brookings has grown from an interview subject, during the US presidential primaries of 2008, to a close friend, who has helped me at various points in the last few years to take the crucial next step in my career.

My desire to write a book in English about Greece began as something improbable – I was, after all, too unknown, not to mention too Greek, for the anglophone world. It would probably have remained wishful thinking if it hadn't been for my agent, Natasha Fairweather at United Agents (it was still AP Watt when we first spoke), who believed in the project and helped me shape it when I began researching it. In Bella Lacey at Granta, I have been blessed with an editor who is as enthusiastic and committed as any writer could hope for. I also owe a debt of gratitude to everyone who generously offered me their time and thoughts on Greece, its past and its prospects for the purposes of the book.

Above all, I have benefited from the love, affection and conversation of my friends, in Athens and abroad, my parents, my sisters, Eleni and Elli (both London-dwellers), my brother-in-law George and my wife Aliki, with whom I engaged in low-intensity warfare over desk space in our flat, her laptop against mine, her drawings against my copies of troika assessments.

Most Greeks who have experienced the world beyond their country's confining borders have long been faced with a dilemma: live and work abroad, eschewing the beguiling charms of Greek life in order to make the most of themselves, or stay at home, sacrificing greater ambitions for the easy comfort of family and community. As the Great Crisis has made life considerably harder for the vast majority of us, the temptation to flee has increased. Writing this book was, among other things, a way for me to examine where I stood on this question. After completing it, I remain agnostic. As the battle between an introverted, narrow-minded Greece and an open, cosmopolitan one continues, one thing is certain: if talented Greeks abroad do not bring their talents home, Greece's perspective will narrow further, and the crisis will have gone to waste.

Notes

Chapter One: The Keratea Troubles

1. Don De Lillo, *Underworld*, London: Picador, 1999, p. 302.
2. BiPRO, 'Screening of Waste Management Performance of EU member-states', report prepared for the European Commission, July 2012.
3. Eurostat landfill statistics: http://europa.eu/rapid/press-release_STAT-12-48_en.htm
4. According to a report that year by the Ministry of the Interior.
5. www.ekathimerini.com, 'Greece faces more than 70,000 euro daily fine for illegal dumps', 21 February 2013 (http://www.ekathimerini.com/4dcgi/_w_articles_wsite1_1_21/02/2013_484017).
6. See Can't Pay Won't Pay in Public Transport initiative, 'Open Call on Transport', 20 January 2011 (http://denplirwnwmmm.blogspot.gr/, in Greek).
7. See 'Koufodinas dreams of a new type of urban guerilla warfare' (http://www.tovima.gr/society/article/?aid=459648, in Greek).
8. On Mandra, see Pangalos's speech in parliament on 11 June 2003 (http://www.hellenicparliament.gr/Praktika/Synedriaseis-Olomeleias?sessionRecord=9a83f9f2-78f6-48ed-96e4-9c618dcf726e, in Greek); the tanks comment was made on 12 March 2003, on Skai radio.
9. Region of Attica, 9th meeting of EDSNA: 'The way is open for integrated waste management in Attica', 27.8.2012 (http://www.patt.gov.gr/main/index.php?option=com_content&view=article&id=5299:9--------------&catid=3:2008-09-06-21-42-59&Itemid=31&lang=el, in Greek).
10. On 6 September 2012, during a meeting of the regional council.

Chapter Two: A Taxing Issue

1. National Bank of Greece, *Monthly Macroeconomic Outlook*, May 2010.

2.   Nikolaos Artavanis, Adair Morse and Margarita Tsoutsoura, 'Tax Evasion Across Industries: Soft credit evidence from Greece', Fama-Miller Center for Research in Finance, University of Chicago Booth School of Business (2012).

3.   See Notis Paraskevopoulos, 'Opengov and meritocracy', column in *Kathimerini* newspaper, 30 November 2012 (http://news.kathimerini. gr/4dcgi/_w_articles_columns_1_30/11/2012_503371, in Greek).

4.   It became so during 2013. It is now no longer possible to carry out an audit without registering it with Elenxis, a development which considerably curtails the leeway for arbitrary practices.

5.   For example, on Skai TV's popular *Folders* journalism show on 30.1.2012 (http://folders.skai.gr/main/theme?id=288&locale=en, in Greek).

6.   See 'New outstanding debts of 9.2 billion in 2013', *Naftemporiki*, 3 February 2014 (http://www.naftemporiki.gr/finance/story/760793, in Greek) and 'Outstanding Debts reach 44 billion euros', Skai website, 17 December 2012 (http://www.skai.gr/news/finance/article/219706/se-44-disekatommuria-euro-anerhodai-oi-lixiprothesmes-ofeiles/, in Greek).

7.   Drymiotis appeared on the same *Folders* show as Spinellis, in January 2012.

8.   'Fines on Fuel Smugglers Frozen', *Kathimerini*, 18 October 2011 (http://news.kathimerini.gr/4dcgi/_w_articles_ell_100022_18/10/2011_459719, in Greek).

9.   'Little gain from the equalization of fuel tax rates', capital.gr website (http://www.capital.gr/tax/News_tax.asp?id=1763552, in Greek).

10.   See 'A step backward on the autonomy of the Secretariat for Revenue', *Kathimerini*, 1 March 2013 (http://news.kathimerini. gr/4dcgi/_w_articles_politics_1_01/03/2013_512828, in Greek); for a penetrating comment on the government's unwillingness to unhook its talons from the new office, see the column by K. Kallitsis, 'The "spoils" and the Secretariat for Revenue', *Kathimerini*, 10 March 2013 (http://www.kathimerini.gr/4dcgi/_w_articles_kathpolitics_1_10/03/2013_486646, in Greek).

Chapter Three: The Torn Safety Net

1.   Eurostat government finance statistics (http://epp.eurostat.ec.eur opa.eu/portal/page/portal/government_finance_statistics/data/

main_tables) and Taxation Trends in the European Union statistical books.

2. IMF Fiscal Monitor, 'Taking Stock: A Progress Report on Fiscal Adjustment', October 2012.

3. Michael Mitsopoulos and Theodore Pelagidis, 'Vikings in Greece: Kleptocratic interest-groups in closed, rent-seeking economy', *Cato Journal* 29 (Fall 2009), pp. 399–416 (http://www.cato.org/sites/cato.org/files/serials/files/cato-journal/2009/11/cj29n3-3.pdf).

4. Rent-seeking is the attempt to earn income by applying social and political pressure to affect the distribution of existing wealth instead of through producing new value.

5. It was Dimitris Kontos, the head of EOPYY, in a speech to the 'Healthworld' conference in September 2013.

6. OECD System of Health Accounts for Greece, OECD Health Database 2012.

7. See Olga Siskou, 'An Estimation of Private Health Expenditure in Greece', PhD dissertation, University of Athens (2006, in Greek); Olga Siskou et al., 'Private Health Expenditure in the Greek Health Care System', *Health Policy* 88 (2008), pp. 282–93.

8. OECD System of Health Accounts for Greece, 2003–2011.

9. Figures from EOPYY accounts and from a Finance Ministry report on the new insurance fund.

10. See Hellenic Statistical Authority, 'Survey of Income and Living Conditions of Greek Households 2012', press releases on 'Poverty Risk', 29 November 2013, and 'Economic Inequality', 9 December 2013 (in Greek).

11. The threshold of poverty is defined as an annual income of €5,708, or €11,986 for a family of four.

12. According to the Hellenic Statistical Authority, in the third quarter of 2013, 955,500 Greeks belonged to the ranks of the long-term unemployed – 71 per cent of the total.

13. Pointed out by Manos Matsaganis in his paper 'The Welfare State and the Crisis: The Case of Greece', *Journal of European Social Policy* 21 (5), 2011.

14. See data released by the employment agency of the Ministry of Labour: http://www.oaed.gr/images/STOIXMAKROX RANERGl.pdf

15. Michael Mitsopoulos and Theodore Pelagidis, *Understanding the Crisis in Greece*, Basingstoke: Palgrave Macmillan, 2012.

Chapter Four: Pensions, Retired

1. See Kevin Featherstone, 'The Politics of Pension Reform in Greece: Modernisation Defeated by Gridlock', papers presented at the Conference of the Modern Greek Studies Association, Toronto, 16–18 October 2003.

2. World Bank, 'Averting the Old Age Crisis', September 1994.

3. Statement to the press by Christos Polyzogopoulos, 16 October 1997.

4. On 25 October 1997 (see http://www.iospress.gr/mikro1997/ mikro19971025.htm, in Greek).

5. See *Rizospastis* newspaper, 15 October 1997 (http://www. rizospastis.gr/story.do?id=3701400&publDate=, in Greek).

6. Published on 23 November 1997, entitled 'Expositions and those who Expose themselves'. It can be found at http://manosmat saganis.blogspot.gr/1997/11/blog-post.html (in Greek).

7. See IMF, 'Greece: First Review after the Stand-by Arrangement', September 2010.

8. In a column for *Kathimerini* newspaper, 7 July 2010.

9. See European Commission, '2009 Ageing Report: Economic & Budgetary Projections for the EU-27 Member-States (2008–2060)' (http://ec.europa.eu/economy_finance/publications/public ation14992_en.pdf).

10. For example, Stefanos Manos of 'Drassi' (see https://www.youtube. com/watch?v=M6W5Pp0CGTg, in Greek).

11. The *Polytechneio* is the National Technical University of Athens, scene of the student uprising that shook the junta to its foundations in 1973 and precipitated its fall a few months later.

12. Many of them, however, had their pensions cut in subsequent rounds of austerity.

13. Eurostat, 'People at Risk of Poverty & Social Exclusion', data from January 2013 (http://epp.eurostat.ec.europa.eu/statistics_explained/ index.php/People_at_risk_of_poverty_or_social_exclusion).

Chapter Five: The Return of Class War

1. Figures from ELSTAT, the Hellenic Steelmakers' Union (ENXE) and from a study of the Greek steel industry by the ICAP Group.

2. The new building code was passed in 2000, the year after the earthquake.

3. Figures from ELSTAT and ENXE.

4. See a video of the speech, at https://www.youtube.com/watch?v=SwjtZGsbOQM (in Greek).

5. See the video, uploaded by Golden Dawn itself (http://www.youtube.com/watch?v=5b8TBnbNoUo, in Greek).

6. See 'A Hard Line, on Samaras's Orders', *Kathimerini*, 21 July 2012 (http://news.kathimerini.gr/4dcgi/_w_articles_ell_100005_21/07/2012_489762, in Greek).

7. See Matsaganis, 'The Welfare State and the Crisis', op. cit.

8. IMF, 'Advice on Labor Issues', 8 February 2013 (http://www.imf.org/external/np/exr/facts/labor.htm).

9. See EU AMECO database figures for real unit labour costs per employee (http://ec.europa.eu/economy_finance/ameco/user/serie/ResultSerie.cfm).

10. Figures from the AMECO database and from INE–GSEE Institute, 'Annual Report on the Greek Economy & Employment', 2012.

11. See http://www.imf.org/external/pubs/ft/scr/2010/cr10110.pdf

12. 'Greek Oil Refiners Draw IMF Rebuke', September 2012 (http://online.wsj.com/news/articles/SB10000872396390444620104578010360773875202).

13. See the OECD's Competition Assessment Review of Greece (November 2013), p. 46. The report, focusing on four core sectors of the Greek economy (food processing, retail trade, building materials, tourism), identified 555 regulations and 329 provisions harmful to competition. Tackling them, according to the OECD, could increase Greek GDP by €5.2 billion annually.

14. The second approval, including the entire, surreal history of the planned investment, can be found online: http://et.diavgeia.gov.gr/f/ypeka/ada/%CE%92%CE%9F%CE%96%CE%A60-65%CE%A4 (in Greek).

Chapter Six: Investment and the Deep Blue Sea

1. See *To Vima*, '3,000 Signatures for the Tourism Project in Messinia', 9 August 2009 (http://www.tovima.gr/finance/finance-business/article/?aid=282731, in Greek).

2. See *Kathimerini*, 'A Positive Role Model of Creativity Far Removed from Mean-Spiritedness', 26 January 2011 (http://news.kathimerini.gr/4Dcgi/4Dcgi/_w_articles_columns_2_26/01/2011_430105, in Greek).

3.   In the *Journal of Modern Greek Studies* 17 (1), May 1999.

4.   See *Kathimerini*, 'Why Does the State not Demolish Illegal Homes?', 14 October 2007 (http://news.kathimerini.gr/4dcgi/_w_articles_ ell_2_14/10/2007_244791, in Greek).

5.   See for example the references in a speech entitled 'The Contemporary Culture of the Consumer Society' by Yannis Michail of the Hellenic Society for the Environment and Culture, available online at http://www.nomosphysis.org.gr/articles. php?artid=3099&lang=1&catpid=1 (in Greek).

6.   See for example his interview in *Rizospastis* on 30 January 2001 (http://www.rizospastis.gr/story.do?id=639582&publDate= 30/1/2001, in Greek).

7.   In more recent years, for obvious reasons, Northern Europeans have reworked this Zorba stereotype, in darker hues. Greeks began to be described as lazy instead of laid-back, corrupt instead of freewheeling. German tabloids like *Bild*, which led this base campaign, forgot to mention that Greeks worked much longer hours than Germans and that in all the major corruption scandals in Greece, the companies doing the bribing were German.

8.   See McKinsey report, 'Greece: Ten Years Ahead', p. 39 (http:// www.mckinsey.com/locations/athens/GreeceExecutive Summary_new/pdfs/Executive_summary_English.pdf).

9.   With Law 3550/2007, passed in March 2007.

10. See my piece in *Kathimerini*, 'When the courts "block" investment', 9 June 2013 (http://news.kathimerini.gr/4Dcgi/4Dcgi/_w_ articles_columns_2_09/06/2013_523228, in Greek).

11. UNCTAD, *Investment Country Profiles: Greece*, February 2012 (http://unctad.org/en/PublicationsLibrary/webdiaeia2012d9_ en.pdf).

Chapter Seven: Power Struggle

1.   See 'Possibility of Redundancies at PPC', *Kathimerini*, 15 January 2012 (http://news.kathimerini.gr/4dcgi/_w_articles_ economy_2_15/01/2012_469235, in Greek).

2.   See my 'One year on, they're still waiting for special billing from PPC', *Kathimerini*, 7/7/2013 (http://news.kathimerini.gr/4dcgi/_w_ articles_economyepix_100002_07/07/2013_525914, in Greek).

At the time, the assistant Minister for Energy told me that the extra 10 per cent was going to be phased out.

3. Indicatively, in 2008 labour costs constituted 63 per cent of total cost for Epilektos, versus 27 per cent for energy costs. In 2012, energy costs had risen to 45 per cent, a higher share than labour costs (39 per cent).

4. In subsequent months, the EU carbon price collapsed to less than a third of this amount, which was good news for PPC, though not for Europe's hopes of transitioning to a clean-energy economy.

5. The militant union man faced a new set of challenges in 2013 in his quest for continued influence in the running of PPC. In April, he was charged with breach of trust for the spending excess in GENOP revealed by the Inspector General of Public Administration. Two months later, he resigned as head of the union. It is still too early to write him off, though, as he is now a member of the board of directors – as the 'workers' representative' – of PPC, and not likely to be a silent one.

6. This amount was revised downward drastically, due to the aforementioned collapse of the European price of carbon in 2013.

Chapter Eight: Big Ships in a Perfect Storm

1. See the press release of the US National Snow and Ice Data Center on 19 September 2012 (http://nsidc.org/news/press/2012_seaiceminimum.html).

2. Mattheos D. Los, *Voyage to the Top: Post-War Greek Shipping 1945–2000*, Kallithea: Akritas Publications, 2000 (in Greek), p. 15.

3. See Ioannis Theotokas and Gelina Harlaftis, *Leadership in World Shipping: Greek Family Firms in International Business*, Basingstoke: Palgrave Macmillan, 2009, p. 21.

4. Los, op. cit., p. 38.

5. Ibid.

6. See *Financial Times*, 'Cosco faces threat of worldwide ship seizures', 23 August 2011 (http://www.ft.com/intl/cms/s/0/93983096-cd8f-11e0-b267-00144feabdc0.html).

7. See the relevant Baltic Dry Index charts (http://www.bloomberg.com/quote/BDIY:IND).

8. See *Financial Times*, 'Bigger fleets cut cost of transport on seas', 28 September 2009 (http://www.ft.com/intl/cms/s/0/6dfda3d8-ac54-11de-a754-00144feabdc0.html#axzz2habsgdao).

9. See *The Economist*, 'The Greeks and the Chinese: Doing business for aeons', 21 August 2008 (http://www.economist.com/node/11977024).

10. During this period, the maritime links between Greece and China deepened in other ways as well. More and more Greek shipowners began turning to China, instead of South Korea and Japan, for their shipbuilding needs. This trend has gathered pace of late: Greek orders with Chinese shipyards, which were less than half those placed with Korean ones in 2008, had nearly reached parity with South Korea in the year through September in 2013, and had far outstripped Japanese yards, according to Athens-based XRTC Business Consultants. Meanwhile, in a 2008 deal, Cosco leased half of the port of Piraeus, Greece's biggest, and proceeded to ramp up activity in the formerly state-run cargo terminals.

11. See Forbes' listing of the world's billionaires in 2008 (http://www.forbes.com/lists/2008/10/billionaires08_George-Economou_ISLV.html).

12. *Financial Times*, 'Greek Fleet Operators Find IPO Odyssey far from Plain Sailing', 16 November 2005 (http://www.ft.com/intl/cms/s/0/fdb738f4-5645-11da-b04f-00000e25118c.html#axzz2habsgdao).

13. Thenamaris, run by Dinos Martinos, is one of the largest Greek-owned shipping companies today. Together with Eastern Mediterranean and Minerva Shipping, operated by the younger brother, Andreas Martinos, they make up a formidable family triumvirate.

14. See *Financial Times*, 'Bigger fleets', op. cit.

15. Analysts predicted the recovery to begin in 2014–15.

16. See International Maritime Organization, 'Shipping Facts and Figures', 2012 edition, p. 10 (http://www.imo.org/KnowledgeCentre/ShipsAndShippingFactsAndFigures/TheRoleandImportanceofInternationalShipping/Documents/International%20Shipping%20-%20Facts%20and%20Figures.pdf).

17. *Lloyd's List*, 'Germany crosses fingers on avoiding KG apocalypse', 4 March 2013 (http://www.lloydslist.com/ll/sector/finance/article417800.ece).

18. In late 2013, however, the Dynacom owner took Dynagas, the

company managing the *Ob River*, public, on the Nasdaq exchange. Dynacom remains privately held.

19. *Avgi* editorial, 'Tax-Free "National Champions"', 19 December 2012 (http://archive.avgi.gr/ArticleActionshow.action?articleID =737932, in Greek).

20. The full question can be read (in Greek) at the party website (http://www.syriza.gr).

21. The exemption was revoked in 2010, with Law 3842, which increased the offshore property tax to 15 per cent for owners who did not wish to reveal their identities.

22. PricewaterhouseCoopers, 'Choosing a Profitable Course around the Globe', 2009 (http://www.pwc.com/en_GX/gx/transportation-logistics/assets/choosing-profitable-course.pdf).

23. See *Imerisia* newspaper, 'Extraordinary levies for shipbrokers', 14 January 2013 (http://www.imerisia.gr/article.asp?catid=26526& subid=2&pubid=112977630, in Greek). However, the law, 4111/2013, was amended two months later, reducing the contributions to a range of 3–5 per cent for the same period.

24. IOBE, 'The Contribution of Ocean-Going Shipping to the Greek Economy', January 2013, in Greek.

Chapter Nine: Nightmares from Weimar

1. See *Kathimerini*, 'The revealing court documents about Perama that "tie up" Golden Dawn', 4 October 2013 (http://www. kathimerini.gr/4dcgi/_w_articles_kathremote_1_04/10/2013 _521558, in Greek).

2. You can see it here in all its gruesome glory: http://www.youtube. com/watch?v=vZxpzLIaEaY

3. For the preceding, and most other historical information about Golden Dawn in the text, I am grateful to Dimitris Psarras, *The Black Book of Golden Dawn*, Athens: Polis, 2012.

4. See the Greek Census of 2001, and Anna Triantafyllidou, 'Greek Immigration Policy: Problems and Prospects', ELIAMEP, December 2005, pp. 9–10 (in Greek).

5. Hellenic Police immigration statistics, as compiled by UNHCR Greece (http://www.unhcr.gr/genikes-plirofories/statistika.html).

6. Ibid.

7. Christal Morehouse and Michael Blomfield, 'Irregular Migration

in Europe', *Migration Policy Institute*, December 2011, p. 11 (http://www.migrationpolicy.org/pubs/tcmirregularmigration.pdf).

8. See Frontex press release in October 2010 (http://www.frontex.europa.eu/news/frontex-deploys-rapid-border-intervention-teams-to-greece-PWDQKZ).

9. Statistics from Hellenic Police, Lesvos Port Police. The number of arrivals in Lesvos in 2013 ended up exceeding 4,000.

10. It started operation a few months later, in September 2013.

11. Hellenic Police illegal immigration statistics: http://www.astynomia.gr/index.php?option=ozo_content&perform=view&id=12080&Itemid=429&lang=, in Greek.

12. Among the more recent critical reports is by Amnesty International ('Frontier Europe: Human Rights Abuses on Greece's Border with Turkey'), published in the summer of 2013. See pp. 11–14 (the entire report can be found at http://www.amnesty.org/en/library/asset/EUR25/008/2013/en/d93b63ac-6c5d-4d0d-bd9f-ce2774c84ce7/eur250082013en.pdf).

13. Ibid.

14. Eurostat, 'Asylum applicants and first instance decisions on asylum applications: third quarter 2012'.

15. Figures by the Greek section of UNHCR.

16. For (a lot) more shocking information on the iniquities of Petrou Ralli, see the UNHCR's campaign and the blog accompanying it: http://asylum-campaign.blogspot.gr/2012/06/campaign-for-access-to-asylum-in-attica.html

17. Specifically, from the External Borders Fund, the Return Fund, the European Integration Fund and the European Refugee Fund.

18. See *Wall Street Journal*, 'Immigration Emerges as another Crisis for Greece – and EU', 15 September 2012 (http://online.wsj.com/news/articles/SB10000872396390444506004577617383132000476).

19. See figures in the official election results page of the Ministry of the Interior: http://ekloges-prev.singularlogic.eu/dn2010/public/index.html#{%22page%22:%22level%22,%22params%22:{%22level%22:{%22dhm_d%22,%22id%22:9186}}}, in Greek.

20. These neighbourhoods were the source of the 'founding myth' of Golden Dawn's entry into the mainstream. According to an oft-told story, which came in multiple versions, desperate shopkeepers and homeowners tried to get the police in these areas to protect

them against criminal immigrant elements (thieves, drug peddlers, counterfeit goods hawkers). The police failing to respond, they turned to Golden Dawn, which 'cleaned up the streets' in the brutish manner it is accustomed to. A different take on that story – that the police actually colluded with the neo-Nazis by directing concerned citizens to them for help – turned out to be significantly true: a number of police officers arrested in the wake of the Fyssas murder as accomplices of Golden Dawn are charged with doing just that, and also of refusing to hear complaints of racial attacks by immigrants.

21. For an account of the University of Macedonia research, see *To Vima* newspaper, 27 May 2012 (http://www.tovima.gr/society/article/?aid=459656, in Greek); for Anne-Marie Jeannet's findings, see *Daily Telegraph*, 4 April 2013 (http://www.telegraph.co.uk/news/uknews/immigration/9970122/Britons-have-become-more-tolerant-of-immigration-as-numbers-increase.html).

22. Recoverable at: http://www.astynomia.gr/index.php?option=ozo_content&lang=%27..%27&perform=view&id=24766&Itemid=1058&lang=, in Greek.

23. See *Kathimerini*, 'Statistics on aliens' criminal behaviour by nationality', 14 February 2013 (http://portal.kathimerini.gr/4dcgi/_w_articles_kathbreak_1_14/02/2013_483092, in Greek).

24. Figures are from the Hellenic Police.

25. *BBC Magazine*, 'The Tourists held by Greek Police as Illegal Migrants', 10 January 2013 (http://www.bbc.co.uk/news/magazine-20958353).

26. Pappas, a particularly nasty specimen, was also arrested and placed in custody after the Fyssas murder, as second-in-command of the paramilitary wing of Golden Dawn. Police found a shrine to Nazism and Fascism in his home in Ioannina. Old photographs also surfaced of him giving the Nazi salute, a swastika flag in the background.

27. The press release on the UNHCR report can be found on their website (http://www.unhcr.gr/nea/deltia-typoy/artikel/49b49c9c379d5e504203738ab6416134/paroysiasi-apotele.html?L=atsdqryhvohsech, in Greek); the Greek Ombudsman's report can be found at: http://www.synigoros.gr/resources/docs/eidikiekthesiratsistikivia.pdf (in Greek).

Chapter Ten: Out with the Old

1. On Vima FM radio, on 30 August.

2. More recently, however, the climate had begun to change: university authorities were less hesitant about inviting the police to enter their grounds in cases where criminal activity was taking place. In July 2013 the police was even called in to break up yet another effort by 'revolutionary' students to break up a meeting of the new governing council, which had been created by the Diamantopoulou reform. Rector Pelegrinis and the left voiced their dismay at the implementation of the rule of law.

3. See the episode of *The Folders* current affairs show for an instructive look back on the events of 1985 (in Greek): http://www.youtube.com/watch?v=oxmmho8Q18E

4. See *Kathimerini*, 'Giannakou statement on transfers stirs reactions', 15 October 2004 (http://news.kathimerini.gr/4dcgi/_w_articles_politics_1_15/10/2004_120023, in Greek).

5. OECD, 'Education Policy Advice for Greece', p. 76 (2011).

6. See Eurostat unemployment statistics at: http://appsso.eurostat.ec.europa.eu/nui/submitViewTableAction.do

7. Data on graduate unemployment are from 'The European Higher Education Area in 2012: The Bologna Process Implementation Report', chapter 5.

8. The main findings of the University of Macedonia survey, plus links to relevant commentary in the Greek press, can be found at: http://rdpru.uom.gr/?q=el/node/198 (in Greek).

9. See for example this report in the *FT*'s financial blog Alphaville: http://ftalphaville.ft.com/2012/09/19/1166421/benefiting-from-greeces-brain-drain/?; or this, from Bloomberg Businessweek: http://www.businessweek.com/articles/2012-05-24/greeces-brain-drain-has-begun

10. The winners of Athens Start-Up Weekend that year were a bunch university students from the National Polytechnic University who thought up a web app that would improve the efficiency of Greece's notoriously unreconstructed road freight transport market, characterized by a very high percentage of lorries making empty trips. See my 'Bright Minds, Pioneering Ideas' in *Kathimerini*, 24 March 2013 (http://news.kathimerini.gr/4dcgi/_w_articles_economy_1_24/03/2013_515165, in Greek).

11. Workable made an impressive step in the direction of scaling up

when it reached a $1.5 million funding deal, announced in March 2014, led by Greylock IL, the European affiliate of Greylock Partners, one of the top venture capital firms in the world.

12. See 'The Four Arrested for the Robbery in Velvedo', *Imerisia* newspaper, 2 February 2013 (http://www.imerisia.gr/article. asp?catid=26510&subid=2&pubid=112988033, in Greek).

13. See, for example, 'Alexis's Friend who Became a Terrorist', *To Ethnos* newspaper, 4 February 2013 (http://www.ethnos.gr/article. asp?catid=22768&subid=2&pubid=63777114, in Greek).

14. The letter can be read at: http://www.zougla.gr/greece/article/ giati-den-kata8eto-sti-diki-tou-aleksi (in Greek).

15. See 'The "fiery shadows" of 16-year-old Nikos Romanos', *To Vima*, 14 February 2013 (http://www.tovima.gr/society/article/ ?aid=498282, in Greek).

15. See Romanos Gerodimos, 'Post-Modern Terrorism', *Ta Nea* newspaper, 9 February 2013 (http://www.tanea.gr/opinions/all-opinions/article/4789670/?iid=2, in Greek)

Epilogue: Staring into the Abyss

1. For the background story of how capital controls were imposed, see *Kathimerini*, 'The path from "No" to the new harsh set of measures', 12.7.2015 (http://www.kathimerini.gr/823270/article/ epikairothta/politikh/pws-ftasame-apo-to-oxi-sto-neo-sklhro-paketo, in Greek), as well as subsequent interviews given by some of the protagonists to the author.

2. For the tense period between the two elections of 2012, see *Kathimerini*, 'Six Weeks from Hell', 1.12.2013 (http://news.kathimerini. gr/4dcgi/_w_articles_politics_2_01/12/2013_541754, http://news.kathimerini.gr/4dcgi/_w_articles_ politics_100002_01/12/2013_541753, http://news.kathimerini. gr/4dcgi/_w_articles_politics_100003_01/12/2013_541752, http://news.kathimerini.gr/4dcgi/_w_articles_ politics_100004_01/12/2013_541751)

3. The Eurogroup statement can be found here: http://www. consilium.europa.eu/uedocs/cms_Data/docs/pressdata/en/ ecofin/133857.pdf

4. The primary surplus, of 0.8% of GDP, was confirmed in April 2014 by the European Commission: http://www.reuters.com/article/

greece-primary-idUSB5N0N100B20140423

5. See *Reuters*, 'Greece Returns to Bond Markets, Says End to Bailout Near', 10.4.2014 (http://www.reuters.com/article/greece-bonds-idUSL6N0N21X220140410).

6. On the mechanics of the fall of the Samaras government, see *Kathimerini*, 'The review that was never completed', 7.6.2015 (http://www.kathimerini.gr/818336/article/epikairothta/ereynes/h-a3iologhsh-poy-den-ekleise-pote, in Greek); *Kathimerini*, 'The Greek-German Breakthrough that wasn't', 10.5.2015 (http://www.kathimerini.gr/814707/article/epikairothta/politikh/h-ellhnogermanikh-ypervash-poy-den-egine, in Greek); *Wall Street Journal*, 'How Greece and Germany brought Europe's Long-Simmering Crisis Back to a Boil', 21.1.2015 (http://www.wsj.com/articles/how-greece-and-germany-brought-europes-long-simmering-crisis-back-to-a-boil-1421890324).

7. On Schäuble's proposal to Venizelos, see *Kathimerini*, 'When Schäuble analysed Grexit for 90 minutes', 7.2.2016 (http://www.kathimerini.gr/848563/article/epikairothta/politikh/otan-o-soimple-anelye-epi-90-lepta-to-grexit, in Greek).

8. See the *Wall Street Journal*, 'Greek Referendum Not in Line with European Standards, Watchdog Says', 1.7.2015 (http://www.wsj.com/articles/greek-referendum-not-in-line-with-european-standards-says-watchdog-1435761444).

9. See my 'Letter From Athens' for *Politico* ('Will Greece's government fall?') on 2.7.2015 (http://www.politico.com/magazine/story/2015/07/will-greeces-government-fall-119710); the newspapers at the time published the list of open branches – for example, http://www.naftemporiki.gr/finance/story/972531/ta-katastimata-ton-trapezon-pou-tha-anoiksoun-gia-tin-pliromi-ton-suntaksiouxon

10. For indicative stories from those days, see *Kathimerini*, 'The fear of a deposit haircut led luxury purchases to shoot up', 8.7.2015 (http://www.kathimerini.gr/822678/article/oikonomia/ellhnikh-oikonomia/o-fovos-gia-koyrema-kata8esewn-ektina3e-tis-agores-eidwn-polyteleias, in Greek); *Kathimerini*, 'Businesses paralysed by capital controls', 10.7.2015 (http://www.kathimerini.gr/822990/article/oikonomia/epixeirhseis/oi-kefalaiakoi--elegxoi-parelysan-tis-epixeirhseis, in Greek); *Kathimerini*, 'Turnover in free-fall at commercial shops, except for food and fuel', 9.7.2015 (http://www.kathimerini.gr/822788/article/oikonomia/epixeirhseis/

se-eley8erh-ptwsh-o-tziros-sta-emporika-katasthmata-plhn-trofimwn-kai-kaysimwn, in Greek); *Kathimerini*, 'No one wants to keep their money in a bank anymore' 9.7.2015 (http://www.kathimerini.gr/822809/article/oikonomia/ellhnikh-oikonomia/kaneis-den-8elei-pleon-na-exei-lefta-sthn-trapeza, in Greek).

11. See the *Guardian*, 'Greek Economy Close to Collapse as Food and Medicine Run Short', 3.7.2015 (http://www.theguardian.com/world/2015/jul/03/greece-economy-collapse-close-food-medicine-shortage).

12. See my 'Start-up concerns over capital controls' in the Greek edition of *Kathimerini* on 18.7.2015 (http://www.kathimerini.gr/824135/article/epikairothta/ellada/neofyeis-anhsyxies-logw-capital-controls).

13. Yannis Varoufakis, 'Why Europe should fear Fine Gael-like "reasonableness" much, much more that it fears SYRIZA', blog post, 3.6.2012 (http://yanisvaroufakis.eu/2012/06/03/why-europe-should-fear-fina-gail-like-reasonableness-much-much-more-than-it-fears-syriza/#more-2320).

14. This is Varoufakis's own account, as given in a number of interviews and profiles – e.g. the extended 'Greek Warrior' piece in the August 3 edition of *The New Yorker* (http://www.newyorker.com/magazine/2015/08/03/the-greek-warrior).

15. 'Finance Ministry slows blogging down but ends it not', 27.1.2015 (http://yanisvaroufakis.eu/2012/06/03/why-europe-should-fear-fina-gail-like-reasonableness-much-much-more-than-it-fears-syriza/#more-2320).

16. See *Spiegel Online International*, 'Varoufakis: "Austerity Has Done Nothing to Solve Greece's Problems"', 16.2.2015 (http://www.spiegel.de/international/europe/interview-with-greek-finance-minister-giannis-varoufakis-a-1018443.html).

17. See *Kathimerini English Edition*, 'Greece warned against reversing bailout deals', 30.1.2015 (http://www.ekathimerini.com/166762/article/ekathimerini/news/greece-warned-against-reversing-bailout-deals).

18. See *New York Times*, 'Greece's Feisty Finance Minister Tries a More Moderate Message', 29.1.2015 (http://www.nytimes.com/2015/01/30/business/international/greeces-feisty-finance-minister-tries-a-more-moderate-message.html?_r=0).

19. 'Eligibility of Greek bonds used as collateral in Eurosystem

monetary operations', ECB statement, 4.2.2015 (https://www.ecb. europa.eu/press/pr/date/2015/html/pr150204.en.html).

20. Reza Moghadam, 'Halve Greek Debt and Keep the Eurozone Together', *Financial Times*, 26.1.2015 (http://www.ft.com/intl/cms/s/0/4cdc1898-9c1c-11e4-a6b6-00144feabdc0. html#axzz42boXn8K2); *Wall Street Journal*, 'The Lazard Banker Shaping Greece's and Ukraine's Financial Fate', 4.2.2015 (http://www.wsj.com/articles/the-lazard-banker-shaping-greece-and-ukraines-financial-fate-1423067028); Pigasse, a noted Germanophobe, a proponent of an aggressive renegotiating approach and a critic of French president François Hollande, was a close adviser to Varoufakis in the early weeks of the negotiation.

21. See his interview on SKAI television (in Greek): http://www.skai.gr/player/tv/?mmid=269274

22. The term 'creative ambiguity' was first used by Varoufakis in a television interview with Antenna TV on February 27 (https://www.youtube.com/watch?v=guAzIfXqTos, in Greek).

23. See the aforementioned interview on SKAI TV (note 21).

24. The full Eurogroup statement can be found here: http://www.consilium.europa.eu/en/press/press-releases/2015/02/150220-eurogroup-statement-greece/

25. Among the many international stories about the remarks at the time, this is how the London *Independent* reported on it, on March 10: http://www.independent.co.uk/news/world/europe/greece-threatens-to-unleash-wave-of-migrants-on-the-rest-of-europe-including-isis-jihadists-10097432.html

26. See *Ethnos,* 'Konstantopoulou revives the committee on German war reparations', 9.3.2015 (http://www.ethnos.gr/politiki/arthro/h_zoi_konstantopoulou_anasystinei_tin_epitropi_gia_tis_germanikes_apozimioseis-64152760/, in Greek); *Guardian*, 'Athens Insists "Open Wound" of German War Reparations Must be Closed', 8.4.2015 (http://www.theguardian.com/world/2015/apr/08/greece-germany-war-reparations-demands).

27. See *Bloomberg,* 'ECB Said to Limit Greek Lenders' Treasury Bill Holdings' (http://www.bloomberg.com/news/articles/2015-03-24/ecb-said-to-limit-greek-lenders-treasury-bill-holdings).

28. For the next paragraph, see my 'Two missions to issue a new currency', 24.6.2016 (http://www.kathimerini.gr/846938/article/epikairothta/politikh/dyo-apostoles-gia-ekdosh-nomismatos, in

Greek). A shortened version is available in the English edition, entitled 'Grexit choice was explored last year, but Tsipras was not convinced' (see: http://www.ekathimerini.com/205359/article/ekathimerini/news/grexit-choice-explored-last-year-but-tsipras-was-not-convinced).

29. On the background to this harebrained scheme, see *Kathimerini*, 'The secret meeting in May on a Plan B', 11.10.2015 (http://www.kathimerini.gr/834417/article/epikairothta/politikh/h-mystikh-syskeyh-ton-maio-gia-to-plan-v, in Greek).

30. See the *Financial Times*, 'Christine Lagarde Dashes Greek Hopes of a Loan Respite', 16.4.2015 (http://www.ft.com/intl/cms/s/0/7032744e-e452-11e4-a4de-00144feab7de. html#axzz42boXn8K2); *Financial Times*, 'Lew urges Greece to speed up reforms', 18.4.2015 (http://www.ft.com/intl/cms/s/0/679c2956-e556-11e4-bb4b-00144feab7de. html#axzz42boXn8K2). After his meeting with Varoufakis, Lew said that Athens had to take a lead by coming forward with detailed proposals after going through budget measures line by line, adding that the situation would not be resolved by 'speeches and rhetoric'.

31. See, for example, his SKAI television interview referenced above (note 21).

32. This was revealed by EU Economic and Financial Affairs Commissioner Pierre Moscovici to the Brussels correspondent of *Liberation*, Jean Quatremer (see, for example, this blog post from August 2015: http://bruxelles.blogs.liberation.fr/2015/08/27/yanis-varoufakis-bien-failli-en-venir-aux-mains-avec-jeroen-dijsselbloem-droit-de-suite/).

33. See the *Financial Times*, 'Tsipras Reshuffles Negotiating Team to Sideline Varoufakis', 27.4.2015 (http://www.ft.com/intl/cms/s/0/ac356b9e-ece1-11e4-a81a-00144feab7de. html#axzz42mRP8YNt).

34. This was revealed by Thanos Katsambas, who at the time was still Greece's representative in the IMF, in an interview with *Real News* published on 8 February 2016 (available here, in Greek: http://www.real.gr/DefaultArthro.aspx?page=arthro&id =483631&catID=1). Katsambas had tendered his resignation after Varoufakis's visit to Lagarde in early April because he was shut out of the meeting, but had stayed on for a few more weeks. In the above mentioned interview, he said that the prime minister had

fallen victim to 'ημμαθείς' advisers and that the negotiations had collapsed because of his insistence on keeping Varoufakis in his post, even though it was clear already from March that he was not taken seriously either by the IMF or by the US government.

35. See *Kathimerini*, 'The dramatic background of the May repayment to the IMF', 12.9.2015 (http://www.kathimerini.gr/830620/article/ epikairothta/politikh/to-dramatiko-paraskhnio-ths-apoplhrwmhs-toy-dnt-ton-maio).

36. Varoufakis has spoken or written of this on a number of occasions. Sachs confirmed his participation to me in an interview with *Kathimerini* in August 2015 (available here: http://www.kathimerini. gr/828180/article/epikairothta/politikh/tzefri-saks-parallhlo-nomisma-8a-odhgoyse-se-grexit, in Greek).

37. See the *Wall Street Journal*, 'Greece's Creditors Make Some Concessions as Showdown Approaches', 3.6.2015 (http://www. wsj.com/articles/greek-prime-minister-alexis-tsipras-heads-to-brussels-for-bailout-negotiations-1433329492).

38. See the *Wall Street Journal*, 'Greece to Bundle its June IMF Payments', 4.6.2015 (http://www.wsj.com/articles/greece-to-bundle-its-june-imf-payments-1433439795).

39. See the *Guardian*, 'Jean-Claude Juncker Accuses Alexis Tsipras of Lying over Bailout Talks', 7.6.2015 (http://www.theguardian.com/ world/2015/jun/07/jean-claude-juncker-angrily-accuses-greek-alexis-tsipras-lying-bailout-talks).

40. See *Bloomberg*, 'Europe Struggles Towards Solution as Tsipras Rips Creditors', 16.6.2015 (http://www.bloomberg.com/news/ articles/2015-06-16/tsipras-goads-creditors-for-greek-woes-as-merkel-sees-little-new).

41. It should be noted that 93% of the Greek proposal consisted of increases in taxes and social insurance contributions. It also included some revenue projections that were wildly optimistic. See *Kathimerini*, 'The Bill of the Measures Proposed by the Greek Government Runs Up to 7.9 Billion', 23.6.2015 (http://www.kathimerini. gr/820456/article/oikonomia/ellhnikh-oikonomia/79-dis-o-logariasmos-metrwn-poy-proteine-h-ellhnikh-kyvernhsh,   in Greek).

42. For the run-up to the referendum decision, see *Kathimerini*, 'The path from "No" to the new harsh set of measures' (referenced above, note 1).

43. See my 'Two missions to issue a new currency' (referenced above, note 28).

44. For the paragraphs that follow, see my 'The concerns, the agitation and the machinations' in *Kathimerini*, 24.1.2016 (http://www.kathimerini.gr/846939/article/epikairothta/politikh/oi-anhsyxies-o-ekneyrismos-oi-diergasies, in Greek).

45. This was revealed in my 'When Angela Merkel proposed Grexit', published in *Kathimerini* on February 21, 2016 (http://www.kathimerini.gr/850340/article/epikairothta/politikh/otan-h-agkela-merkel-proteine-grexit); the shortened English version can be found here: http://www.ekathimerini.com/206193/article/ekathimerini/news/merkel-proposed-grexit-to-hollande-before-key-eurogroup-in-july-2015

46. See *Kathimerini*, 'Tsipras: The state is at risk of destruction', 11.7.2015 (http://www.kathimerini.gr/823063/article/epikairothta/politikh/tsipras-yparxei-kindynos--anatina3hs-toy-kratoys, in Greek). Konstantopoulou, who was at that time Speaker of the House, revealed later that on the previous night – 9 July – Tsipras had told her that the situation was such that only a government of national unity or a dictatorship could handle it.

47. For this meeting, and the background to the crucial final negotiation, see my 'When Angela Merkel proposed Grexit' (referenced above, note 45).

Index

Academy of Athens, 228
African chameleon, 132
aftherata (homes built without permits), 124–5
Aggelopoulos, Dimitris, 96, 109
Agios Panteleimonas, 193, 209
Akrini village, 165
Albanians, 19, 196
Alexandria, Greek colony in, 74
Alexandroupoli, 220
Aluminium of Greece, 154
Amygdaleza detention centre, 216
Ano Liosia landfill, 6, 10
ANTARSYA group, 110
antibiotics, over-prescription of, 64
anti-competitive practices, 116–17
Apollon Athinon football team, 54, 61
Apostolidis, Nikos, 165–7
Apostolopoulos, George, 71
Aravossis, Konstantinos, 4–5
Arsenis, Kriton, 131, 135, 138
arson, 124–5, 239
Arvanites, 9–10, 17
ASEP (state recruitment council), 166
Asia Minor, eviction of Greek population, 126
Aspropyrgos steel plant
    pier project, 117–18
    strike, 94–112, 155
Asylum Service, 206–7, 215
ATE Bank, 238
Athanasopoulos, Takis, 145–8, 151–2, 161–2
Athens
    assassination of CIA station chief, 225
    detention of foreign nationals, 214–15
    downtown lawlessness, 193, 208–14, 259–60
    earthquake, 96
    illegal development in, 124

    public transport, 13
    registration of asylum claims, 204–6, 215
    smog, 41
    urban development projects, 189
Athens Bar Association, 160
Athens Olympics, 63, 142, 211–12
Athens Review of Books, 91
Attica
    heavy industry, 10, 118
    illegal development in, 124–6
    waste management plan, 4–6, 10–11, 17, 22–3, 26
Avgi newspaper, 84, 183

ballaki euthinon ('little ball of blame'), x, 213
Baltic Dry Index, 177, 180
Baltsis, Triantafyllos, 166–7
bank deposits, 241–2
bank employees, 88–9, 113
Bild magazine, 282
bond markets, 51, 81
bribery, 30, 48, 62, 64, 173
Buiter, Willem, 241
Bulgaria, 3–4
'business compensation', 35

Caccia, Guglielmo, ix
cancer patients, 54–8, 64, 68
'Can't Pay Won't Pay' movement, 12–14, 20, 159
Capodistrias, Ioannis, xi
Chania, 220
charatsi (property tax), 159–60
childhood poverty, 72
CO2 emissions, 164–5, 170
coastline, length of, 131
Common European Asylum System, 208
'Conspiracy of the Cells of Fire', 239

Constantakopoulos, Achilles, 122, 141
Constantakopoulos, Konstantinos, 121
Constantakopoulos, Vasilis, 120–2, 128–30, 132–4, 141
Constantine I, King, xii
Corpus Christi, blasphemy charges, 216
corruption, reporting of, 48
Costa Navarino development, 119–20, 123, 128–35, 139–41
crime rate, increasing, 210
Croatia, 129
Cyprus, xiii, 28, 185

De Lillo, Don, 3
Dekemvriana riots, 219–21
and extremist movement, 238–40
Dekleris, Michael, 127–8
DEKOs (state-owned enterprises), 143–5, 147, 149, 156, 162
Delphi oracle, 9
democracy, 'managed', xii–xiii
Democratic Left, 85, 226
demography, and ageing population, 78–80, 82
Dendias, Nikos, 210, 214, 216, 218
Denmark, 131
Der Spiegel, 30
detention facilities, 199–200, 215–16
Diamantopoulou, Anna, 222, 230, 261
diaploki (business–government collusion), 20
doctors, 64, 88, 233, 228
and bribery, 48, 64
and tax evasion, 28–30, 34
drachma, devaluation of, 93, 163
Drassi party, 88
Drymiotis, Andreas, 38

Economou, George, 177–80
EEC, Greek accession, xiii–xiv, 96
Eleutherotypia, 81–2, 84
emigration, 221, 233–4
Emporiki Bank, 142
energy market, 152–6, 160–1, 163, 168
engineers, 29, 53, 79, 88, 234, 228
environmental protection, 119–20, 126–8, 130–2, 135, 138
EOPYY health insurance fund, 66–9

Epilektos textiles company, 155
EU carbon trading scheme, 156, 164–5
EU Task Force for Greece, 44
euro
introduction of, 76–7, 86, 211
possible Greek exit, 162–3, 241–46
support for membership of, 243–5
European Court of Human Rights, 136, 205, 215
Evros, 197–8, 203–4, 206–7, 214, 216
Exarcheia, 19, 98, 219, 227, 239

fakelakia, 64
family networks, 53, 235
family-owned businesses, 28
fasolada (bean soup), 100
Featherstone, Kevin, 77
First Reception Service, 206
football, 60–2
foreign direct investment (FDI), 137–8
Fotopoulos, Nikos, 146–8, 150–5, 157–61, 168
Frontex, 198, 202–4, 207
fuel market, restrictions on competition in, 116
fuel taxes, 36–41, 52, 117
Fyli landfill, 6, 10–11, 23–6
Fyssas, Pavlos, 194–5, 218, 287

GDP, falling, 52, 65
Geneva Convention on Refugees, 203
GENOP union, 146–50, 152, 156–9, 283
Georgia, 233
Gerakas, 236
Gerasimidou, Eleni, 100
Germany, 4, 197
response to euro crisis, 244–5
shipping industry, 180–1
working hours, 254–5
Giannakou, Marieta, 229
Giannitsis, Tasos, 75, 83, 86, 88, 90
Glavinis, Thodoris, 104–7, 109
Golden Dawn, 110, 190–5, 208–9, 211, 216–18, 240, 254, 281, 285–87
'founding myth' of, 259
links with police, 214–15
members of parliament, 216–17
and Orthodox Christianity, 216
Perama attack, 190–1, 194, 285

government bonds, 68, 89, 163
government employees, appointment of, 31, 44
government spending
    budget deficit, 51–2, 158
    cuts in, 51–3, 89
Grammatiko landfill, 6–7, 11
Greek civil war, xii, 75, 120, 221
Greek Communist Party, xii–xiii, 14
    Golden Dawn attack on, 190–1
    KNE youth wing, 8, 101
    resistance to Nazi occupation, xii, 75
    and steel strike, 94–5, 98, 101, 109, 111, 115
Greek Constitution, 119, 123, 138, 140, 223
Greek Orthodox Church, 10, 14, 16
    Golden Dawn and, 216
Greek shipping register, 174–6, 186
Grigoropoulos, Alexis, 219–20, 230, 239
GSEE union confederation, 80, 86
Guevara, Che, 147
Gulf of Eleusina, 117–18, 176
Guru Bar, 211–12

Halyvourgia Volou/Halyvourgia Thessalias, 95–6
health and safety, 48, 79
health care, 54–60
    spending on, 64–5, 68–70
health insurance
    integrated, 65–6
    national scheme for, 70
Hellenic Coast Guard, 202–3
Hellenic Halyvourgia
    pier project, 117–18
    and steel exports, 99, 155
    strike, 94–112, 115
Hellenic Marine Environment Protection Agency, 122
Hellenic Ornithological Society, 139
Hellenic Rescue Team, 200
Hellenikon social health centre, 55, 58–60
Hephaestus, 36
Heraklion, 220
higher education, 222–33, 261
    and asylum clause, 223–7, 230
    and 'democratic five', 228
    hostility to private enterprise, 231–3

reforms of 1982, 223–6
reforms of 2011, 47, 220, 222–4
tolerance of corruption, 228–9
highway tolls, 13
Hitler, Adolf, xii, 194
home ownership, high levels of, 56
Hot Doc, 27
HRADF (Hellenic Republic Asset Development Fund), 161, 163

Iatrou, Stavros, 1–2, 8–15, 19, 23
IKA pension and health insurance fund, 58, 67, 77, 92
immigration, 195–204
    and Dublin II regulation, 196–7, 205, 208
    and lawlessness in Athens, 208–14
    and rise of Golden Dawn, 192–3, 195, 208–9, 211, 218
income tax, 29, 52
indigent status, 56–7
inequality, rising, 72
inflation rate, 117
internal devaluation, 115–17, 244
Italy, 129, 197
ITDAs (Integrated Tourist Development Areas), 119, 123, 128, 130–1, 135, 139–40

Jeannet, Anne-Marie, 210
journalists, 53, 79, 88
Julius Caesar, 192

Kalyvia, 16–17, 19
Kaminis, George, 210–11, 213
Kammenos, Panos, 251
Kantaris, Manolis, 208–9, 211
Kapeleris, Yannis, 39–40
Karamanlis, Constantinos, xiii, 142
Karamanlis, Costas, xv, 142
Kasidiaris, Ilias, 110
Katavati, Eleni, 107–12
Kato Patissia, 209
Keratea, 1–3, 6–23, 27
    illegal development in, 18–19, 21
Keynes, John Maynard, 74
Kifisia, 71, 101, 109
Kloutsinioti, Rania, 124, 131
Kolonaki, 30, 34, 71

Komotini detention centre, 216
Korkoneas, Epaminondas, 219–20, 239
Koufodinas, Dimitris, 14
Kougias, Alexis, 239
Koutroumanis, George, 102
Koutsoukos, Yannis, 102
KYADA (homeless shelter), 71
Kynigos, 129

labour markets, 113–15
Lafzanis, Panayotis, 150
'Lagarde List', 27, 49
Lambrinidis, Spyros, 231–2, 234, 237
land and forest registries, 18, 50, 123–5, 154
LAOS party, 222
Latvia, 4
Lavreotiki, 11, 15, 23
Lavrio, 8, 12, 19
Lavriou Avenue, 17, 21
lawyers, 29, 53, 79, 88, 228
legal system, 135–8
Lekkas, Nikos, 42
Lenin, V. I., 147
Lesvos, 198–203, 206
Levantis, Kostas, 11–12, 15, 19, 21–3
Liaropoulos, Lykourgos, 69–70
'Liberty' ships, 174
lignite, Greek dependence on, 164–5
Linear B script, 122
Lithuania, 4
Livaditou, Zoe, 200
Lloyd's List, 181
Lloyd's of London, 120, 123
LNG transportation, 169–71, 181
loggerhead turtles, 132
Los, Mattheos D., 175–6

Magiatis, Spyros, 236
malaria eradication, 139
Mallios, Evangelos, 192, 225
Malta, 4, 185
Mandra, 10
Manesis, Nikos, 96–9, 101–11
Manesis, Yannis, 95
Manos, Stefanos, 88
manufacturing, and energy costs, 155–6
Martinos, Andreas, 189, 257
Martinos, Dinos, 257

Martinos, Thanassis, 179–80, 182, 188
Martinou, Athena, 178–9
Matsaganis, Manos, 84–5, 91, 113
Médecins du Monde, 200
media industry, 137–8
Mega channel, 216
Messinia, 119–22, 129, 131–5, 140
Messinis, Stavros, 234–5, 237
Metadrasi, 204
Metapoliteusi, 225–6
Metaxas dictatorship, 77
methadone, 212
Michaloliakos, Nikos, 191–3, 195, 209, 217
military junta, xiii, 225
military service, 231
milk market, 116–17
minimum wage, cuts in, 91, 114–15
Mitsopoulos, Michael, 53, 73
Mitsotakis government, 77
mobile marketing, 235–6
Molyvos, 201
Mondrian, Piet, ix
Moraitakis, Nikos, 236–8
Mount Hymettus, 56, 124
Mount Penteli, 124
multinationals, and transfer pricing, 28
Mussolini, Benito, xii
Mytilene, 199, 201

National Division, xii
National Gallery heist, ix–xi
Natura 2000 network, 131–2, 135
Nazi occupation, xii, 75, 212
neoliberalism, 221–2
nepotism, 182, 224
Nestor, King, 122
Netherlands, 4, 185
New Democracy, xiii, xv, 20, 37, 191, 218, 221, 225, 246, 247, 249, 252, 269, 271
    and DEKOs, 147, 149
    and election of 2009, 20
    and elections of 2012, 112
    and higher education reform, 222
    and pensions reform, 75, 82–3
    and shipping industry, 186
New York Times, 244
newspapers, 137
Niarchos, Stavros, 174, 189

Nikaia, 194
Nikolakopoulos, Babis, 42–3
Nikolaos, Bishop of Mesogaia and
    Lavreotiki, 14–16, 21
Northern Sea Route, 169–71
November 17 terrorist group, 14, 96, 110,
    192, 225

Ob River, 169, 171
Odysseus, 167
OECD System of Health Accounts, 69–70
oil crises, 174, 176
oil prices, falling, 93
oil-refining industry, 116
old people, poverty among, 90–1
olive trees, 134
Onassis, Aristotle, 174, 189
opengov platform, 31–3
Operation Xenios Zeus, 214–15, 217
organized crime, 240
OTE telecoms company, 89, 142
Ovriokastro archaeological site, 7, 21

Pagani detention centre, 199–200
Pakistani ragmen, 24–5
PAME union federation, 98, 100–1,
    106–12, 190
Panagopoulos, Perikles, 189
Pangalos, Theodoros, 10, 16–21, 227
Panhellenic Seamen's Union, 175, 186
Panousis, Yannis, 226, 228, 230
Papaconstantinou, George, 27, 30, 34, 92,
    172, 186
Papademos, Loukas, 89, 102, 186, 243
Papandreou, Andreas, xiii–xiv, 76, 85, 96,
    147, 151, 226, 245, 256
    and higher education reforms, 223–4
    and shipping industry, 176, 188
Papandreou, George, 7, 25, 37, 101, 159,
    223, 246, 257
    and bailout referendum, 162–3
    and e-government, 30–1
    and privatization, 150–1
    and shipping industry, 172, 186
Papantoniou, Evangelia, 77
Papantoniou, Yannos, 77
Papaspyrou, Nicholas, 123
Papila shipyard, 190
Papoutsis, Christos, ix, 21–2

Pappas, Christos, 216, 260
Parthenon, 127
PASOK, xiii–xv, 10, 31, 37, 66, 125, 191
    and DEKOs, 147, 149
    electoral collapse, 20
    and energy sector, 150–1, 157
    and higher education, 222–3, 226–7
    and Keratea troubles, 16–17
    'Old PASOK', 147
    and pensions reform, 75, 85–6, 92
    and shipping industry, 176, 186
Paulson, John, 242
Pelagidis, Theodore, 53, 73
Pelegrinis, Theodosis, 223, 288
pensions, 52, 57, 74–93, 184
    and arduous professions, 79, 87
    Chilean model, 81–2, 84
    data on, 91–2
    and disability, 80, 87–8
    and poverty, 90–1
    reform of, 74–93, 151
    three-pillared model, 80, 82, 84, 86–7,
        90
    two-tiered insurance model, 87
Perama, 190–1, 194, 218
Perikles, 127
Petrou Ralli aliens directorate, 204–6
pharmaceutical products, shortages of, 68
Philalithis, Anastasios, 66, 68
Picasso, Pablo, ix
Pinochet, General Augusto, 81, 84, 92
Piraeus Metal Union, 190
planning
    ektos schediou domisi ('building outside
        the plan'), 126, 129
    and illegal development, 18–19, 21,
        124–6
    and legal system, 136–7
    regional and urban, 123–4, 128–35
    see also environmental protection;
        ITDAs
planning offices, 48
police brutality, 214–15, 217, 238–9
Police Officers' Union of Attica, 3, 22
political prisoners, xiii
Polytechneio generation, 90, 222
Polytechneio uprising, 225, 227, 280
Polyzogopoulos, Christos, 80
Portugal, 65, 114

Poulikogiannis, Sotiris, 190–1
PPC power company, 61–2, 145–68, 282–83
    Agios Dimitrios power plant, 163–6
    burning of lignite, 153, 155–6, 164
    pension arrangements, 89, 149–50, 156
    privatization, 156–8
    and property tax, 159–60
    recruitment, 165–6, 168
    reduction in wage costs, 156
    and RWE deal, 148, 150–1
    and unpaid bills, 160
prices, rising, 116–17
private tutors, 28–9
privatization, 161–3
Prokopiou, George, 169–70, 172–3, 181–2,
    186, 188–9
property sales, and taxes, 28
property taxes, 13, 52, 184
    linked to power grid, 16, 159–60
Psyrri, 211–12, 214
public administration, 38–9, 93
public hospitals, 13, 48, 68, 216
    see also 'Sotiria' public hospital
public procurement, procedures for, 33
public transport, 13
Pylos, 122, 129–32, 140–1

racially motivated attacks, rise in, 217
Rakintzis, Leandros, 157–8
receipts, issuing of, 28, 34, 48
renewable energy sources, 155, 159
restaurant bills, 28
retirement age, xvii, 80, 86–7, 90, 149
Rizomyloi, 129, 140
Rizospastis, 75
road tax, 34
road freight transport market, 261
Roma, 24–5
Romania, 3–4
Romanos, Nikos, 239–40
Romanos resort, 129–31, 135, 141

Sachinides, Philippos, 150
Samaras, Antonis, 40, 45, 112, 262, 281,
    290
    and elections of 2012, 242–49
    and immigration, 216–17
Sappho, 198
Saraliotis, Vasilis, 219, 239

Saronikos, 23
Sarris, Dr Vangelis, 57–8
Schengen zone, 195–6, 205, 207–8
self-employment, 29, 56, 62
Sgouros, Yannis, 24
shipowners
    abductions of, 189
    and tax avoidance, 28
    and tech start-ups, 238
shipping fuel, tax-free, 41, 184
shipping industry, 169–89, 267, 283, 284
    charter rates, 177–8, 180
    company structures, 172, 181–2
    employment in, 188
    and favourable tax treatment, 173, 183–8
    and 'flagging out', 176, 186
    Greek merchant fleet, 171–4
    post-war renaissance of, 174
    and rise of China, 177–8, 180–1, 284
    tonnage tax systems, 184–5, 187–8
    and trade surplus, 188
Sifonios, George, 98–103, 105, 107–12
Simitis, Costas, 74–7, 83, 85–6, 93, 228
Sofiadelis, Antonis, 203
'Sotiria' public hospital, 54–8
Souliotis, Kyriakos, 67
Sounio archaeological site, 21
South Field lignite mine, 164, 166–7
Spain, 65, 113–14, 122, 197
Spinellis, Dr Diomedes, 30–43, 47–8
Spraos, John, 74–8, 80–7, 92
Stamati, Vicky, 167
Stathakis, George, 183, 185, 187
Stathopoulos, Michael, 226–8, 230
Stavropoulou, Maria, 206–7
steel industry, 95–7, 99
Stournaras, Yannis, 83, 92
Sweden, 84, 197
swimming pools, 30
Swiss bank deposits, 27, 30
Synaspismos party, 84–5
Syntagma Square protests, 158
Syrian civil war, 201–2
Syrigos, Dr Konstantinos, 56–8
SYRIZA, 8, 84, 94, 115
    and elections of 2012, 242–3
    rise in support for, 19–20, 191
    and shipping industry, 173, 183–4,
        186–8

Ta Nea newspaper, 165
Tatsos, Nikos, 33–4, 42–5
tax administration, 33–6, 41–4
    and appointment of permanent
        secretary, 45–7
    digitization of, 49–50
    recommendation for independent
        agency, 41–2
'tax conscience', 49
tax evasion, 27–30, 45, 49–51, 53, 70, 184
tax offices, 35–6, 46
tax officials' union, 42–4
tax police, 30, 42, 46–7
Taxi Beat, 235–6
taxi drivers, and issuing of receipts, 28
tech start-ups, 234–8
TEIs (institutes of technological
    education), 233
television and radio, 137, 159
Themistocles, 8
Theocharis, Haris, 36, 38–40, 43, 46,
    49–50
Tinios, Platon, 74–7, 80, 82–5, 90–2
Tombazis, Alexandros, 133
tourism policy, 128–9
Trichet, Jean-Claude, 115
Tsipras, Alexis, 15, 19–20, 159, 187,
    241–74
Tsochatzopoulos, Akis, 167
Turkey, 188, 233
    and immigration, 192, 197–8, 200–1,
        203, 207
    tourist industry, 129, 132–3

Ukworji, Christian, 215
unemployment, 52, 67, 72–3, 78, 95, 104,
    115, 244
    and anti-immigrant sentiment, 210
    European, 113
    graduate, 233
    youth, 221, 233, 244
unemployment benefits, 72–3
Union of Greek Shipowners, 171, 175–6,
    186–7, 189
unit labour costs, 114–15
Upstream, 235–7
US health-care system, 70
US State Department, 215
utility bills, 156, 160

VAT, 28, 34, 52, 117
Vaxevanis, Kostas, 27–8
Velouchiotis, Aris, 8, 147
Velvedo, 238
Venizelos, Eleutherios, xii
Venizelos, Evangelos, 27, 92, 150, 158–9
venture capital, 235–6
Vichas, Dr George, 58–60
'Vikings', 53, 65, 73
Voedokilia beach, 131
Volos steel plant, 95, 97, 103–7, 109
Vourloumis, Panagis, 142, 145
Vroutsis, Yannis, 112
Vyronas, 56, 60, 63

wages, falling, 114–15, 117
Wall Street Journal, 116
War of Independence, xi–xii, 216
waste management
    EU policies, 3–4
    and 'garbage crises', 5
    policy in Attica, 4–6, 10–11, 17, 22–3,
        26
woodstoves, and particle pollution, 41
Workable, 236–8, 288
working hours, 254–5

Xafa, Miranda, 163
xenophobia, 211

Yalova wetlands, 131–2, 138–9
Yannibas, George, 54–5, 63
Yannibas, Polydoros, 54–5, 58, 60–4

Zouganelis, Konstantinos, 211–14